LOOT!

RUSSELL CHAMBERLIN

with 120 illustrations, 10 in colour

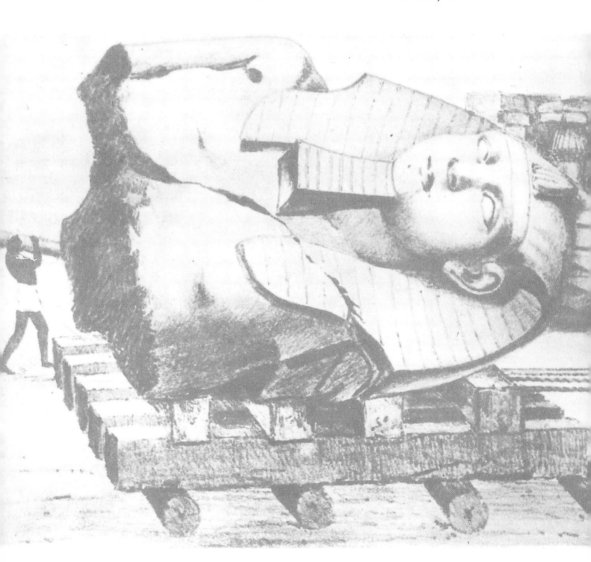

LOOT!

The Heritage of Plunder

THAMES AND HUDSON

Titlepage: Transportation of the statue of Ramesses II (see p. 53 ff.)

Printed and bound in Japan by Dai Nippon

Contents

IV

THE THIRD WORLD

Introduction

During the 1970s, when the debate about the propriety of one nation holding the cultural treasures of another moved out of museums into parliaments and became ever more heated as a result, a new word – *elginisme* – began to make the rounds. Coined by the French (no mean practitioners in the art themselves) the word is, of course, derived from the British Lord Elgin and could be defined as 'the retention by richer nations of the cultural treasures of poorer nations – usually obtained under duress'.

Loot! is an attempt to give shape to a still-emerging pattern. *Elginisme* has been with us, in one form or another, since the beginning of history – ever since Tribe A conquered Tribe B and carried off their tribal gods. But, since the late eighteenth century – starting point of the present study – *elginisme* has not only become epidemic, but has also become the object of legal and moral scrutiny, forcing us to juggle with problems of almost metaphysical subtlety regarding ownership of objects. Jurists who debated the return of objects looted by Napoleon would, one supposes, be totally flabbergasted to learn that their successors, 150 years later, would be debating the 'ownership' of folk dances and folklore. Such debates are a commonplace in the chambers of the huge UN organization known inelegantly as WIPO – World Intellectual Property Organization.

Some of the subjects discussed in this book were first investigated long ago, their essential details enshrined in formal studies: a major source of information on the restitution of Napoleonic loot, for example, is a thesis published in the *American Historical Review* nearly forty years ago. But other stories are still surfacing: the identity of the person who acquired the Codrington Papers in December 1980 is still a secret; and scarcely a month passes without a report about some object looted by the Nazis turning up in some part of the world. Viewed separately, the stories appear simply as a colourful series of anecdotes whose only underlying theme, perhaps, is the simple greed of human nature. Grouped by their components, they tell an odd tale – the continuing influence, even in late twentieth-century technological societies, of fetishes. *The Oxford English Dictionary* defines a fetish as 'something irrationally reverenced', a definition which fits all the objects to be discussed. They may be made of precious metals and gems, or of common stone or wood: they may conform to conventional canons of beauty, or be ugly or totally shapeless – the shape or substance of the object is quite irrelevant to the value vested in it. And that value has now achieved a political significance as newly emergent countries, each seeking an identity, demand that which was taken by their conquerors.

The book opens with the story of the Elgin Marbles because that story contains within itself every element of the controversy, surfacing every few years to plague museum curators and fill the arts columns of newspapers. Central to the controversy is the Sultan's right – or otherwise – to dispose of the property of the Greeks, whom the Turks happened to have conquered. If he had such a right, then no national heritage is safe and Germany is entitled to the loot collected by Hitler and Goering. If he did not have such a right, then the contents of a number of museums in Europe – Germany, Britain and France in particular – are being held illicitly.

But Elgin's action is usually considered without reference to its background and, to provide that background, use is made here of an excellent but little-known account by a young contemporary of Elgin's – Charles Cockerell's *Travels in Southern Europe* – which places the much maligned action in a rather different light.

This first section ends with what is perhaps the oddest story of all – the unrebuked plundering of Egypt. For nearly 200 years, passionate partisans of Greece have been reviling Lord Elgin's removal of a number of battered pieces of marble: for nearly 200 years Egypt has been plundered of a fantastic collection of objects, ranging from human remains to priceless artifacts, with scarcely a voice raised in protest. Even the late President Sadat's noble plea – that the mummies starkly exposed in countless museums should be given decent burial – has been totally ignored.

The second section of the book, *The Sacring of the King*, pinpoints the idea of the fetish. The Ashanti regalia, the Stone of Scone and the Crown of St Stephen come from three utterly different traditions: they consist of, variously, almost priceless golden objects, a valueless lump of sandstone and a rather ugly, mis-shapen headpiece. One is in an alien museum, one continues to have potent significance in a coronation ceremony, and one is a potential source of embarrassment to the anti-monarchical, a-religious state which claims it. Yet each continues to act as a catalyst, embodying the totally intangible idea of racial unity.

The third section is devoted to Napoleon and Hitler because they are, in this context, the alpha and omega of looters. Napoleon was the first to identify the State with his proclivities, looting not to gain personal trophies, or to decorate a personal triumph, but for the greater glory of France. Hitler, one may fairly confidently predict, is the last who will attempt such a plan. *The Warlords* is therefore in part a record of an extinct species. But in the controversies over the restoration of many of the looted objects, the voice of the lawyer blurs what, to the layman, is the clear voice of justice. This is particularly true of the French savants who passionately maintained that a treaty – even one executed at gunpoint – legalized the act of loot. And of the postwar German scholars who as passionately argued that purchase – even compulsory purchase – equally granted legality.

And finally the fourth section, *The Third World*, touches on that aspect of the controversy which is so very characteristic of our day – the awareness of emergent countries of their own identities and the demands for the return of those objects that enhance these identities. So-called Third World countries are a remarkably mixed bag. They include, even in this brief selection, oil-rich Nigeria, with a population of 56 million, and the tiny island of Antigua, heavily dependent upon overseas aid and with a population of 77,000. In between, there are Peru – still lost in the Middle Ages – and New Zealand, a white man's country becoming aware of its brown origins. But all share the awareness vigorously expressed by Nigeria: 'These antiquities are vital to us as a people as they enable us to establish our identity, and hence restore our dignity in the community of nations.'

I
CLASSICAL
LANDSCAPE
WITHOUT FIGURES

1

The Marbles of Greece

Daughter of Jove! In Britain's injur'd name
A true-born Briton may the deed disclaim.
Frown not on England – England owns him not;
Athena! No – the plunderer was a Scot.

BYRON: 'The Curse of Minerva'

'If the infidels are attracted by these blasphemous
figures, the temptation shall soon cease for when that
dog has gone I will destroy them.'

Turkish headman, quoted by Charles Cockerell
in *Travels in Southern Europe*

There is a nice irony in the fact that it was the French who coined that useful word *elginisme*, for the person from whose name they derived it was not only one of their victims, but they also made a spirited attempt to relieve him of his prize. Thomas Bruce, seventh earl of Elgin, was a hostage in France while the marble sculptures, with which his name was to be so infamously associated, were scattered between the Eastern Mediterranean and England, arousing the envy of his captors. And there is an irony behind the irony in that the true, if innocent, originator of this most celebrated act of cultural plunder was not Elgin himself, but a rising young architect in his employ: Thomas Harrison.

In 1795 Elgin, a career diplomat then aged 29, decided to marry, and promised his wealthy young bride a handsome new mansion as a wedding present. He engaged Harrison to build Broom Hall and the architect, who had studied in Rome, persuaded his client that the 'classical' style was the only fitting one for a gentleman's residence.

Elgin agreed. Four years later he was offered the plum posting of ambassador to Constantinople at the court of the Sublime Porte, as the

13

sultanate was known. Harrison was overjoyed. This was an unrivalled opportunity, he told Elgin, to 'transport Greece to Scotland'. What Harrison meant, and what Elgin understood him to mean, was simply that Elgin's influential position with the sultanate would allow him to make detailed drawings of ancient Greek architecture and sculpture. Fashionable society in Britain, influenced by such bodies as the Society of Dilettanti, was turning to Greek culture, so long overshadowed by Roman. If Lord Elgin would but supply his architect with copious and faithful copies of Greek art and architecture, then Harrison would build for him a perfect Classical Greek building. Elgin would be the envy of fashionable society. Again, Elgin agreed.

He left England in the summer of 1799 with his bride and his personal secretary, an energetic young man called William Richard Hamilton. In Naples, he and Hamilton engaged a Neapolitan painter, Giovanni Lusieri. Elgin and his wife then went on to Constantinople, leaving Hamilton and Lusieri to assemble a team of craftsmen who, according to a detailed brief, were to go to Athens and 'carefully and minutely measure every ancient monument', making plaster casts of the more interesting. Nothing at all was said about removing any of the sculptures.

Hamilton and his team arrived in Athens to find that its greatest glory, the Acropolis, was a squalid mess. A little over a century before, on 26 September 1687, Venetian gunners had lobbed a mortar shell on the Parthenon, then being used as an ammunition store by the Turks. The resultant explosion had totally destroyed the building, but the Turks continued to use the Acropolis as a fortress. Houses and hovels appeared to fill in the gaps between some of the world's noblest buildings – the depressing new structures being composed either of material cannibalized from the ruins or, far worse, whitewashed from their remains. Marble, when burnt, yields lime – a fact which has done far more to destroy the classic cities of antiquity than any amount of activity by barbarians. The English party had specific experience of this. On being asked what had happened to a number of statues that were obviously missing,

The Turkish owner pointed with a sardonic smile to the lime in the wall which had been made from the sculpture that once stood there. . . It was impossible to ignore the fact that the ruin of the noblest works of art in the world was progressing with giant steps.

Such is the balanced opinion of Adolf Michaelis, the German archaeologist whose account of the Elgin controversy does not err in favour of Elgin.

The English party were operating under very considerable difficulties. The Disdar, or governor of the fortress, at first refused to allow them access, partly from a sense of religious affront – the Moslem Turks viewed the Christian desire to obtain pagan images with a mixture of outrage and bewilderment – but mostly, it would seem, from cupidity. Hamilton eventually arranged for his team's access to the Acropolis on payment of a swingeing £5 a day to the Disdar, but even then found that they were obliged to work under humiliating restrictions. The Disdar forbade them, for example, to erect scaffolding to copy the higher sculptures, for this would enable the infidels to peer down into the domestic courtyards of good Moslems. After a year's work the team had drawn, and made copies of, only the lesser works that could be tackled at ground level.

It was at this dispiriting stage that they had a visitor of an unusual kind.

Dr Philip Hunt, Chaplain to the British Embassy at Constantinople, was the kind of clergyman which the Anglican Church frequently produces to the benefit of scholarship if not of religion. He shared to the full the prevailing British passion for antiquities, but where his compatriots still tended to satisfy themselves with elegant drawings and descriptions, Dr Hunt wanted the real thing. And he thought on the grand scale. At one stage he even proposed to move the Palace of Mycenae to Britain. Defeated by its size, he turned his speculative gaze upon the Erechtheum: it would fit nicely upon a British man-of-war, he later assured a slightly dazed Lord Elgin.

Hunt arrived in Athens in early 1801 to watch incredulously as Elgin's agents went about their uninspiring task. Unerringly, he divined the source of their problems – the local Disdar. Go over his head, he urged: approach Constantinople. In a lively letter to Elgin, he urged him to use his influence as an ambassador to obtain a firman that would free his agents in Athens from pettifogging local restrictions. And it was not sufficient simply to get permission to erect scaffolding and make plaster copies. Elgin should also request 'the liberty to take away any sculptures which do not interfere with the works or walls of the citadel'.

Hunt's letter arrived in Constantinople at an ideal moment. Nelson had just fought and won the Battle of the Nile, British influence was in the ascendancy in the Eastern Mediterranean. Britain's ambassador, the seventh Earl of Elgin, was showered with honours. It seemed a little matter to accede to his slightly eccentric request to take away some of the battered stones from the Turkish fortress on the Athenian Acropolis. Elgin received his firman.

The original Turkish firman has long since been lost, the copy transmitted to posterity being in Italian. The crucial clause gave Elgin permission to take away 'qualche pezzi di pietra con iscrizione e figure'. The whole controversy of the Elgin Marbles turns on that word 'qualche'. Usually, it is translated as 'some' and the translation should therefore read 'some pieces of stone with inscriptions and figures'. But it can also be translated as 'any'. Whether or not the original firman gave Elgin this sweeping permission, his agents so interpreted it, immediately beginning with the dismantling of the Parthenon frieze.

The size of the operation can be gauged from the fact that it occupied more than 300 workmen for over a year. Edward Dodwell, an English visitor to Athens at the time, was appalled by what he saw. 'Everything relative to this catastrophe was conducted with an eager spirit of insensate outrage, and an ardour of insensate rapacity, in opposition not only to every feeling of taste but to every sentiment of justice and humanity.' In defence of Lord Elgin it should perhaps be remarked that he was not present during the operation, apart from one brief visit in the spring of 1802. But far from deploring his agents' action he urged them to greater speed, anxious to get the marbles away from Greece before the tide turned in favour of the French. By 1803 some hundreds of pieces of sculptured marble, including a column from the Erechtheum, seventeen figures from the Parthenon pediments and fifteen metopes, were boxed in 200 chests waiting to be shipped to Scotland to adorn Broom Hall. Elgin, as a high-ranking diplomat, obtained permission to ship the treasures by HM warships. It would cost him nothing, but he had already paid out £28,000 for the work of dismantling and boxing the marbles.

His treasures safely packed, he set off home. Unwisely, he took advantage of the fact that there was a brief peace between Napoleon's France and England and returned home overland. While he was en route, war broke out again, he was taken prisoner and held as hostage until 1806. Released on parole, he at last reached England to find that his comfortable world was collapsing around his ears. His wife left him for another man, his diplomatic career was in ruins, he lost his seat in the House of Lords – and his marbles, his precious Grecian antiquities, were the subject of a vicious controversy.

The attack on Elgin was led by a certain Richard Payne Knight. It is difficult now to understand the reason for the sheer venom, the personal hatred which Payne Knight displayed towards a man who had done him no harm, either professional or personal. In his brilliant book on the collecting mania, *The Taste of Angels*, Francis Henry Taylor summed up Payne

Looters or conservationists? Charles Townley, the eighteenth-century British collector, entertains his friends in the Park Street Gallery, Westminster (now 14 Queen Anne's Gate). His antiquities were later acquired by the British Museum.

COLLECTING MANIA

Sir William Hamilton, like Richard Payne Knight (who was later to engage in a vigorous attack on Elgin and his 'over-rated' marbles), was a member of the Society of Dilettanti, which survives to this day. Its fashionable members acted as self-appointed arbiters of taste in late eighteenth-century England. Hamilton himself – not to be confused with his namesake, Elgin's secretary – was one of the first Englishmen to champion the collection of Greek vases: the hydra to his left in the portrait (*right*) is now in the British Museum and is seen again *below right*. Gillray even caricatured him in the shape of a vase (*below*). The specimens he obtained in expeditions to southern Italy in 1789 and 1790 (*left*, Hamilton and his wife at the opening of a tomb) were first offered to the King of Prussia and eventually sold for 45,000 guineas.

THE ELGIN MARBLES

The luckless Lord Elgin (*below left*) in a confident and sprightly pose before he was overwhelmed by his troubles. His acquisition of a group of fifth-century BC Greek sculptures from the Parthenon in Athens created the literally classical case of *elginisme*.

The Marbles were first stored in a large shed which Elgin built on the corner of Park Lane and Piccadilly in London. The government bought the collection from him in 1816 for £35,000 – much less than his expenses.

(*below*) The exquisite sculpture known as 'the tired horse of Selene' and (*below right*) Dionysos or Heracles, from the Parthenon and depicted in the painting of 1819 (*right*), which shows the temporary gallery in the British Museum where the treasures were first put on display.

FROM ATHENS TO LONDON

The controversy over the Elgin Marbles was the first of the modern debates over 'loot' and is still perhaps the most emotive. Byron was one of the many who demanded the return of the Marbles to Greece, the most recent such demand being made in the Westminster Parliament in 1982. But today the British Museum still holds among its collections the sculptures (including those *left* and *below*) from the Parthenon – itself seen *opposite* photographed from the east.

In April 1811 C. R. Cockerell and his companions said goodbye to Lord Byron over a glass of port, and sailed for Aegina – where the most momentous discovery of their lives awaited them. In the ruins of the great honey-coloured temple of Aphaea they unearthed a remarkable freize. Soon the sculptures became the object of keen bidding and, after a comedy of errors and confusion, at last fell to Ludwig of Bavaria. A distressed Cockerell, convinced that Ludwig had used bribery, tried and failed to reverse the sale. (*above*) The temple in Cockerell's time and (*below*) a dying warrior from its east pediment – today to be found in a Munich museum.

Knight as one who 'bore all the complexities and difficulties inherent in the true archaeologist – jealousy, infallibility coupled with a sense of perse-cution and a madness for his own subject . . . the very essence of the archaeological character and temper'. Knight was a leading member of the Society of Dilettanti, elegant young men who possessed both taste and money all well wrapped up in an arrogant self-confidence. Knight was their self-appointed arbiter of taste, their touchstone of all that was fashionable in the world of art. It may well be that Knight, as Francis Taylor suggests, was the very model of the intransigent academic, 'for not even a statesman at a peace conference is more unable to repudiate a previously held opinion than the academic potentate who passes as authority in his particular field'. But it may also be that he was simply loyal – over-loyal, perhaps – to his friends in the Dilettanti and could not bear to think that their pretty antiquities were about to be shadowed by those collected, at one swoop, by a Scottish laird – antiquities believed by many to be from the hands of Phidias himself. Whatever the cause, Knight adopted the manners of a gutter-snipe to attack the wretched Elgin on his belated return to England. At a dinner party where a careless – or malicious – host had brought the two together, he shouted across the crowded room, 'You have lost your labour, my lord. Your marbles are over-rated. They are not Greek: they are Roman of the time of Hadrian.'

The majority of the cases containing the marbles had arrived in England by 1805, the year before Elgin was released. War had broken out between England and Turkey, the French had re-established themselves in Athens and, smarting over the affair of the Rosetta Stone (see page 50), had tried to turn the tables by seizing eighty of the chests. English supremacy at sea prevented them from getting their booty away and, in due course, the chests turned up in England. Twelve more chests sank with their freighter off the island of Cerigo, but were raised, two years later, at a cost to Elgin of £5,000. Altogether, it was not before 1812 that all the marbles were assembled in England.

Elgin had long since abandoned the idea of taking them to Scotland. Already he was turning over in his mind the possibility of selling them to the government and so recouping his increasingly heavy financial investment in them. Despite the jibes of Payne Knight and his friends the tide of opinion was gradually turning in his favour. Had not the French government actually offered him his freedom if he would but pass the marbles over to France? And had not Ludwig of Bavaria, that prince among collectors, made a special journey to London to try and buy them?

Far more important was the opinion of the artists who came to inspect the marbles stored in a large shed which Elgin had had built on the corner of Park Lane and Piccadilly to act as gallery. Undoubtedly the most influential artist to see the marbles was Canova. Posterity owes him a particular debt. When, on his ill-fated journey through Europe, Elgin had visited Canova in Rome, he had asked him to 'restore' the sculptures. The Italian resolutely refused. 'They were the work of the ablest artist the world has ever seen,' he declared. 'It would be a sacrilege for me, or any man, to touch them with a chisel.' After Canova had seen the sculptures in London, Elgin obtained from this impeccable source what amounted to a written certificate of merit:

Oh, that I had but to begin again, to unlearn all that I had learned. I now at last see what ought to form the real school of sculpture. I am persuaded that all artists and amateurs must gratefully acknowledge their high obligation to Your Lordship for having brought these memorable and stupendous sculptures into our neighbourhood.

And if Elgin's fellow Britons found such Italianate sentiments somewhat sugary and flowery, there was the scarcely less enthusiastic reaction of such a solidly English painter as Benjamin Robert Haydon. In his memoirs Haydon describes how he was so bowled over by the sculptures that he rushed out to find his friend, the painter Henry Fuseli, and insisted on him immediately accompanying him to the shed where the sculptures were stored. 'At last we came to Park Lane. Never shall I forget his uncompromising enthusiasm. He strode about saying "De Greeks were godes! de Greeks were godes!"' And in a latter to Elgin, he finished, 'You have immortalized yourself, my lord, by bringing them.'

Elgin had indeed immortalized himself – but not in the way he expected or would have relished. The attacks by such as Payne Knight and his cronies can be put down to spiteful envy. The attacks from such as Byron cannot be so dismissed. Although wealthy English dilettantes had been picking up Greek marbles for at least a century, there was, from the very beginning, a general feeling that Elgin had gone too far, that the rape of the most beautiful building in the world – even one so heavily damaged as the Parthenon – just could not be countenanced. Such sentiments were in the beginning confined to those who visited Athens and actually saw the ugly gaps, like gaping wounds freshly made in the marble's warm ivory. A British traveller lamented:

It is painful to reflect that these trophies of human genius, which had resisted the silent decay of time during a period of more than twenty-two centuries, which had escaped the destructive fury of the iconoclasts, the considerable rapacity of the Venetians and the barbarous violence of the Mohammadans, should at last have been doomed to experience the devastating outrage which will never cease to be deplored.

Byron, with a poet's skill, turned that sense of indignation into a literally lapidary phrase, carving into the rock of the Acropolis: 'Quod non fecerunt Gothi, fecerunt Scoti' (What the Goths spared, the Scots destroyed). He followed up that opening shot with a fierce salvo of satire, directed not only against Elgin but also his supporters, embodying it not only in such pieces of temporary polemic as 'The Curse of Minerva' but also in the immortal verse of 'Childe Harold', hurling yet more wounding phrases at 'the modern Pict':

> Cold as the crags upon his native coast
> His mind as barren and his heart as hard.

By now, Elgin had had enough. The wife, for whom he had planned to bring Greece to Scotland, had abandoned him; the marbles which should have earned him fame as a connoisseur were being used to condemn him as a philistine. He was in need of money. In 1816, therefore, he offered the marbles to the British Government for the sum of £74,240.

On Elgin's calculation, it was by no means an outrageous price. The total cost of dismantling, packaging and, later, salvaging at sea, ran to some £33,000. Giovanni Lusieri's salary came to £12,000 – a sum Elgin must have bitterly regretted paying, for it was Lusieri, for some devious reason, who had taken Byron round the Acropolis pointing out the damage that had been wrought. The expense of building the gallery in Park Lane, together with all the incidentals of transporting and guarding the marbles, took care of another £6,000. Elgin claimed, reasonably enough, that if he had invested the whole sum it would have earned him £23,240. He added this to the initial outlay and came up with that grand total of £74,240.

The British Government offered him £35,000.

Meanness is expected of governments. But the British Government did have a certain justification in offering Elgin less than half what he had spent. The marbles had not only been transported by warship – that is, at the public expense – but, it was claimed, Elgin acquired them in his capacity of a public servant, as Ambassador.

There is little doubt that it had indeed been Elgin's position which had influenced the Sublime Porte to give him those wide-ranging powers in Athens. But there is also little doubt that Elgin was very considerably out of pocket over the affair. Recourse was had to the universal British panacea – a committee. In June 1816 a Parliamentary Committee was convened to consider 'Whether it be expedient that the collection mentioned in the Earl of Elgin's petition should be purchased on behalf of the public and, if so, what price it may be reasonable to allow for same.'

It is not often that the ethics of art acquisition are solemnly debated by Parliament. The Committee not only took evidence from a string of leading artists that the marbles were 'in the very first class of ancient art' but also heard from others – including Elgin's old secretary William Hamilton and the ebullient Dr Hunt – that the Acropolis was in very bad condition and that it was an act of virtue to acquire and preserve such treasures of the past. After sitting for eight days, the Committee recommended that the marbles should indeed be purchased for the nation – at a price of £35,000. In vain, Elgin protested that such a sum would not cover even his original outlay, much less the interest he had lost upon it. Take it or leave it, was the attitude of the Committee behind their courteous phrases. Elgin took it, bitterly, and stepped out of history, leaving it to the marbles to carry his name down to posterity and obloquy.

It is inevitable that the Elgin Marbles should have become the classic case of *elginisme*. The bitter controversy received an even sharper edge when, in 1832, the Greeks shook off the Turkish yoke and, almost as their first national act, began restoring the Acropolis. What had been a casual – perhaps even praiseworthy – act, in connection with an unregarded building, became an unforgiveable act of vandalism when that building became a symbol of a gallant little nation's fight for freedom. Small wonder that the searchlight of public opinion should have been, and should continue to be, trained upon this cause célèbre.

But searchlights dazzle as well as illuminate, and the notoriety attending the removal of the Parthenon sculptures obscured the fate of Greek antiquities throughout the Turkish empire. The marbles were still being ferried between Greece and England when a young architect began to explore that dying empire at risk of his life and health, throwing light upon the tragic fate of most of those antiquities – and almost casually digging up a treasure that was only relatively inferior to that of the Parthenon.

On 14 April, 1810 young Charles Cockerell, then just twenty-two years of age, boarded the curiously named despatch boat *Black Joke*, 'with ten guns, 35 men, one sheep, two pigs and fowls', bound for Constantinople. As an architectural student Charles Cockerell would much rather have been bound for Rome to carry out his studies in Italy. But Napoleon had closed all Italy to Englishmen and Cockerell considered himself fortunate to have been given the opportunity of studying Greek architecture in situ. Lord Elgin's old secretary, William Hamilton, now Under-Secretary of State for Foreign Affairs, was a friend of Cockerell's father and had used his influence to obtain for Charles the unpaid appointment of courier carrying despatches to Malta and Constantinople.

Such an appointment at least assured him free passage, plus the security of a warship and, on arrival at Constantinople, an introduction to the influential people who could steer him through the thorny jungle of Turkish bureaucracy. All the remains of ancient Greece lay under the iron fist of the Sublime Porte and, even if they were deemed to be far less important than the ruins of Rome, their study could quite profitably fill young Mr Cockerell's year or so abroad until such time as Napoleon was defeated and he could enter Italy, the true nursery of architecture. In the event, he was to spend seven years travelling backwards and forwards over the coasts and islands of the Turkish Empire – those coasts and islands that had once been part of Greece – recording superb architectural remains lost in a squalor of indifference.

The journey from Plymouth to Constantinople took nearly six weeks, with brief stop-overs in Gibraltar and Malta. His first encounter with Turks was picturesque enough. It took place in a small village on the northern shore of what was still known as the Hellespont:

It was evening, and under the shade of a fine plane tree by a pool lined and edged with marble, before a fountain of elegant architecture, sat on variegated carpets some majestic Turks. They were armed and richly dressed. Their composed, placid countenance seemed unmoved at our approach.

It was forbidden for foreign warships to approach Constantinople, and the civilian party therefore disembarked and entered a rowing boat. That small craft was to be their uncomfortable home for five days as they moved slowly up the Dardanelles. The great city that had changed its name three times in its history struck the impressed young man with the force of a revelation.

We approached Constantinople as the sun rose, and as it shone on its glorious piles of mosques and minarets, golden points and crescents, painted kiosks and gardens. Our Turks pulled harder at their oars, shouting 'Stamboul, guzel azem Stamboul!'. . . Nothing but my despatches under my arm recalled me from a sense of being in a dream. In forty days I had jumped from sombre London to this Paradise.

Over the next seven years Cockerell was to modify very substantially his first opinion of Turks and became ever more contemptuous of Turkish architecture: 'The mosques are always copies of Santa Sophia and have no claim to originality.' But to the end, Constantinople retained its fascination for him.

Cockerell recorded his impressions in a series of letters home to his parents, together with a running journal. Many years later, his son edited these passing impressions with the apologetic remark that 'the letters and memoranda of a youth of twenty-two, who disliked and had no talent for writing, naturally required a great deal of editing'. But in fact Charles Cockerell had a fresh, lively style that exactly conveys the excitement of a young man abroad in a strange, dangerous, fascinating world. His picture of the extraordinary city, part European, part Asiatic, peopled by swaggering, arrogant Turks lording it over cringing Greeks and Jews and Armenians, is a priceless vignette of a society on the brink of change.

Cockerell paid his respects to the ambassador, Robert (later Sir Robert) Adair, and the Secretary, Stratford Canning, who obtained for him a firman that allowed him to explore the city and sketch. He was pleased, but not overawed, to find himself dining in company with Byron, not then at the height of his fame and notoriety, and made a number of friends among the young English expatriates, including a fellow architect, Foster, who was to become his constant companion for several years. In contrast to the dedicated Charles Cockerell, most of these young men were frankly idling their time away. 'We all met at dinner very often but they are all, even architect Foster, too idle to be companions any further than that.'

After five months of high and low life in Constantinople Cockerell left for Athens and there he made the acquaintance of a group of young men, quite different from the golden idlers of Constantinople, who were to influence him for the rest of his life. Foremost among them was Baron Haller von Hallerstein, a gifted artist some fourteen years older than Cockerell. Five years later, he was to owe his life to Hallerstein. In the grip of yellow fever, abandoned by his doctor, he had literally been given up for dead – the English vice-consul actually placed his seal upon the 'deceased's' effects. At risk of his own life, Hallerstein nursed him, forcing the doctor to attend to him until the danger had passed.

Hallerstein was travelling on a tiny allowance from his patron, Ludwig of Bavaria, and Cockerell was able to put several useful little commissions from his compatriots in Hallerstein's way. The party included Otto von Stackelberg, a German antiquarian, the Danish archaeologist Peter Oluf Bronstedt, a painter called Linkh and a number of German and Danish antiquarians all devoted to bringing the neglected antiquities of Greece before the European public. Cockerell also met Giovanni Lusieri, Elgin's agent, and struck up a warm friendship with Fauvel, the same French consul who had tried to spirit Elgin's marbles away. Curiously, neither in his letters nor his journal did Cockerell make any comment upon Elgin's depredations, although they were fresh to see, and Byron, who was still firing off his salvos, was in Athens at the time.

For the next eight months the young man spent a highly enjoyable time as part of that group, well-to-do but also dedicated, whose centre was Byron. He worked hard, sketching, studying, formulating an idea for a major work on the antiquities of Greece. He developed the most profound contempt for the descendants of Homer and Phidias and Leonidas. 'The Greek men in their slavery have become utterly contemptible, bigoted, narrow-minded, lying, and treacherous.' He retained a certain grudging admiration for the martial qualities of the Turks, though disgusted by their barbarity and appalled by their ferocity and cruelty towards the abject people in their power.

In April 1811 Byron prepared to leave for England – actually taking ship on the same transport that was carrying some of Elgin's marbles – and Cockerell entrusted his most recent letter to his parents to the poet. Byron's departure broke up the circle and four of them – Hallerstein, Cockerell, Linkh and Foster – decided to tour the Morea. Before leaving, they agreed to sail across to Aegina, some three hours from Athens. 'As we were sailing out of the port in our open boat we overtook the ship with Lord Byron on board. Passing under her stern we sang a favourite song of his, on which he looked out of the windows and invited us in.' After a glass of port, the four young men continued on to Aegina – and to the most momentous discovery of their lives.

Their initial intention was simply to analyse and reconstruct the superb ruined temple on Aegina (Cockerell believed it to be dedicated to Zeus Panhellenius but subsequent investigation shows that it was the temple of Aphaea, goddess of woods, the moon and the underworld). Even the waves of mass tourism that today wash around every major Greek site are unable to erode the haunting enchantment of the great honey-coloured temple. From its platform high above the ancient port, high above the vineyards and pine trees, the visitor looks back into history: in the purple distance lie Salamis and Attica and Athens, the beautiful, deadly enemy of this island republic. The ruins, as Cockerell and his friends found them, were well preserved. There was a layer of earth on the temple floor deep enough to nourish a good crop of barley, 'but on the actual ruins and fallen fragments of the temple itself no great amount of vegetable earth had collected, so that without very much labour we were able to find and examine all the stones necessary for a complete architectural analysis and restoration'.

They obtained provisions and labourers from the town, and set to work. And here Cockerell's unstudied prose conveys a marvellously fresh impression of a group of young men enjoying excellent health, working hard in idyllic surroundings at a task which utterly absorbed them – but also entering with zest into unsophisticated pleasures. 'Our fuel was the wild thyme. There were abundance of partridges to eat and we bought kids of the shepherds. And when work was over there was a grand roasting of them over a blazing fire with an accompaniment of native music, singing and dancing.'

The friends had planned to spend some three weeks working on the temple in order to record it. But on the second day, in an astonishingly casual manner, they made one of the great art discoveries of the world. Working in the barley-field,

one of the excavators struck on a piece of Parian marble which, as the building itself is of stone, arrested his attention. It turned out to be the head of a helmeted warrior, perfect in every detail. It lay with the face turned upwards and as the features came out by degrees, you can imagine nothing like the state of excitement to which we were wrought. Soon another head was turned up, then a leg and a foot and finally, to make a long story short, we found no less than sixteen statues and thirteen legs, heads, arms etc all in the highest preservation.

As Cockerell remarked, considering the fact that the treasure was scarcely three feet deep in soft earth, and that Aegina was on the tourist circuit – hundreds visited it annually – it was astonishing that it should have remained undiscovered.

What they had found was the frieze of the temple. What they also found very rapidly was that, 'However much people may neglect their own possessions, as soon as they see them coveted by others they begin to value them'. The labourers quickly spread the news that the rich foreigners had found a treasure and the local dignitaries lost no time in trying to get their share of whatever was going. They turned up in a body, claiming that the excavations would bring bad luck to the island. Correctly divining the motives behind the protest, the young men took energetic steps to protect their find. Foster and Linkh immediately left for Piraeus with the sculptures in their care while the other two bargained with the islanders, eventually assuaging their religious susceptibilities with the equivalent of £40.

For money had now entered the story. Back on the mainland the four young men rented a large house and, with the enthusiastic aid of other expatriates, set to work restoring the frieze. And as, gradually, head was added to torso and torso to limb and the stupendous figures again took shape, it became obvious that they had made a find of very great importance. 'Our council of artists here considers them as not inferior to the remains of the Parthenon, and certainly only in the second rank after the torso of the Vatican and other chefs d'oeuvre.' They had to conduct their work in secrecy lest the Turks, ever hungry for cash, should intervene. Giovanni Lusieri, according to Cockerell, 'was dying with jealousy'. He had, it would seem, some idea of the potential of Aegina and had planned to obtain digging rights from the governor. The fact that an Italian intended to farm the search for Greek antiquities from a Turk with no reference whatsoever to the opinions of the Greeks was so commonplace a matter that Cockerell did not even comment upon it. All concerned seem to have regarded the marbles buried in Greek soil as a species of wild crop, to be harvested by whoever had the money.

The two young Englishmen in the party, Foster and Cockerell, were well-heeled enough to afford the luxury of altruism. But the two Germans, living on a hand-to-mouth basis, had a lively awareness of the capital asset they had obtained. Basing their calculations on the price of marble statuary in Rome, they estimated the value of the frieze at between £6,000 and £8,000.

News of the find had sped through Europe and offers were already coming in for it. The four agreed that the collection should not be broken up, and that they should be sold to the highest bidder. Foster and Cockerell patriotically offered to waive their share if the marbles were sold to England and, in due course, two British emissaries did arrive with an offer to buy out Linkh's and Hallerstein's share for £2,000. But Hallerstein's patron, Ludwig of Bavaria, had already let it be known that he was prepared to go up to their maximum and the deal fell through. Undaunted, Cockerell contacted his father in England, urging him to find some influential figure who would match Ludwig's offer. It was a letter which was to have farcical results.

By the middle of July, work on assembling the frieze was completed. The group were anxious to continue their exploration of Greece and came to a decision that was to have embarrassing results for Cockerell. They would put the marbles to a public auction. In order to do this, it was necessary to get them out of the country, away from the acquisitive Turks; and they were smuggled out to Zante, at that time under British control. The auction was scheduled for eighteen months time on 1 November, 1812, notices were sent off to all English and Continental papers and, with what was evidently a sigh of relief, young Cockerell abandoned the wheeling and dealing of merchants for his favourite occupation, exploring the remoter areas of Greece. A month later he returned to Athens – to find a letter waiting from his father. He had persuaded the Prince Regent to offer £6,000 for the collection and a man-o'-war was even at that moment en route to Athens to pick it up. 'Here was a bitter disappointment to be unable to accept so splendid an offer, and a painful embarrassment as well for I had led the government quite unintentionally to believe that they had only to send for the marbles to secure them.'

Contrary winds delayed the warship and a month passed before, on 29 November 1811, the brig-of-war *Pauline*, under Captain Percival, sailed into the Piraeus to collect the marbles. It was a dismal day of torrential rain when Cockerell, loyally accompanied by Hallerstein and Linkh, went aboard to explain to Captain Percival that not only were the marbles no longer in Athens but in Zante, 'and even if they had still been here he could not have taken them, as they were now to be sold by auction'. And, to give a final twist, they were obliged to beg his assistance in moving them to Malta, for it was feared that the French were planning an attack upon Zante. Percival, on learning that he had made the two-month-long journey from England to no avail, was not unnaturally highly indignant. But eventually he accepted the situation, lavished ale and porter upon the young exiles, and very generously agreed to transport the marbles to Malta.

The comedy of errors was not yet finished. In October 1812 buyers and agents began to arrive for the auction in Zante, though the sculptures were now in Malta. Two representatives of the British Museum were even in Malta, admiring the sculptures, fully prepared to pay the maximum for them, placidly awaiting the arrival of the auctioneer – while bidding was actually taking place in Zante. The sculptures fell to Ludwig of Bavaria for £6,000, precisely the figure that the Prince Regent in England had offered eighteen months earlier.

Cockerell was convinced that their agent had been bribed by Ludwig and, deeply distressed, sought means of invalidating the sale. National honour was at stake: that was made very clear by British periodicals deploring the 'mistakes' that had been made. Failing to prove the sale illegal, Cockerell attempted *force majeure*. Malta was under the direct control of Britain and through his old and influential patron William Hamilton he tried to get the British government to intervene direct and physically prevent the removal of the marbles from Malta. But even the British Foreign Office jibbed at quite so unabashed a display of jingoism and, two years after he had paid for his marbles, Ludwig of Bavaria received them.

The affair of the Aegina frieze had obliged Cockerell to extend his stay in the Eastern Mediterranean beyond the original tour of a year or so. But, very vividly, the reader receives the impression from his letters and journals that he would, in any case, have stayed on. Asia Minor had entered his blood. He despised the Greeks, viewed the Turks with a mixture of suspicion and contempt; but the lovely, austere coasts and islands, with their poignant evidences of a vanished civilization that had been the cradle of the western world, moved him most deeply. Though never foolhardy, he seems to have been quite devoid of fear, penetrating remote, bandit-infested lands where the only law was that of survival. He discovered that, in one such place, he was the first stranger to arrive since 1766 – more than forty years before. He would go anywhere, endure any deprivations in quest of his beloved antiquities – digging where necessary, occasionally carrying away sculptured remains but, in the main, perfectly content simply to measure and draw and reconstruct on paper.

That tough seaman Captain Beaufort (whose name was to be immortalized in the Beaufort scale of storm intensity) records how he encountered the young man at sea off the Turkish coast.

We had the pleasure of meeting Mr Cockerell, who had been induced by our reports to explore the antiquities of these desolate regions. He had hired a small Greek vessel, and had already coasted part of Lycia. Those who have experienced the filth and other miseries of such a mode of conveyance, and who know the dangers that await an unprotected European among these tribes of uncivilised Mohammedans, can alone appreciate the ardour which could lead to such an exercise. I succeeded in persuading him to remove to His Majesty's ship, in which he might pursue his researches with less hazard and with some degree of comfort.

As it happened, that particular voyage ended in tragedy, for an ensign was murdered and Beaufort himself badly wounded by Turks in a village they were exploring; Cockerell himself only just escaped injury.

Remarkably, the four explorers of Aegina repeated their feat at Bassae. In investigating a foxhole, Cockerell found a bas-relief which led them to the discovery of what were to be known as the Phigaleian Marbles. These, too, were auctioned, Cockerell on this occasion ensuring that the bidding was straightforward; and the marbles went to the British Museum. The original group of four broke up: Foster, a susceptible young man, continually falling in and out of love, marrying a lady from Smyrna (to his parents' disgust), and the loyal Hallerstein dying of the disease from which he had saved his friend. Cockerell joined other groups, made other friends, but followed his own instincts and inclinations and in his unobtrusive manner became a foremost expert on Asia Minor and its Greek remains.

And most clearly from his pen there emerges the picture of how these superb remains were regarded both by the Turks, who had suzerainty over them, and the Greeks, whose heritage they were. Near the ancient city of Sardis, the beautiful Ionic temple which three years earlier had possessed five columns, now had only three: 'The other two were blown up by a Greek who thought he might find gold in them.' On Samos, he found only one column of the temple of Juno remaining – Turkish warships had used the remainder as targets for gunnery practice. The Turks were deeply puzzled and suspicious of his motives. At Salonica a group watched with disapproval while he went about taking measurements of the theatre. 'While examining some statues I heard one of them exclaim, "If the infidels are attracted by these blasphemous figures the temptation shall soon cease for when that dog has gone I will destroy them".' But even urban sophisticates were as puzzled. Cockerell describes how, in the Morea, he visited the waiwode on business: 'After enquiring after his great friend Elfi Bey (Lord Elgin) the man asked what on earth we came here for, so far and at so much trouble. Did it give us preference in obtaining public office, or were we paid.' In vain Cockerell tried to get across to him that his sole motivation was love of antiquity, Greek antiquity in particular: 'He only thought the more that our object must be one we wished to conceal.'

But one man, at least, eventually appreciated the fact that this Frank really did have a passion for nothing other than old battered stones. The Disdar of the Athenian acropolis, with whom he was particularly friendly, offered him a parting gift when he finally left Greece:

He asked me if I would like to bring a cart to the base of the Acropolis at a certain hour of the night. I accordingly arranged this. As I drew near the Acropolis there was a shout from above to look out, and without further warning the block which formed one of the few remaining pieces of the southern freize of the Parthenon was bowled down the cliff. My men successfully caught it and put it in the cart and it was taken to Piraeus and loaded that same night onto my ship.

In 1882, sixty-five years after young Mr Cockerell sailed off with one of the bits of the Parthenon overlooked by Lord Elgin's agents, the German archaeologist Adolf Michaelis summed up the affair of the Elgin Marbles as it appeared to an informed, temperate European scholar. He criticized the brutal manner in which the marbles had been prized out of their surrounds. 'The removal of the statue of the Erechtheion, in particular, had severely injured the surrounding architecture.' He conceded that Elgin had probably abused his position: 'It may be doubted whether Lord Elgin was quite discreet in thus using his official position to further his private undertaking, or whether the interpretation of that firman was in accordance with the views of the Turkish government.' But taking everything into account – the indifference of the Greeks, the active hostility of the Moslem Turks towards sculpture – Michaelis concluded: 'Only blind passion could doubt that Lord Elgin's act was an act of preservation.'

Charles Cockerell's artless eyewitness account amply justifies Michaelis's conclusion. But Cockerell's record was not published until 1903 and then enjoyed only a brief life, whereas the tide of 'anti-*elginisme*' that had set in with Byron was running ever stronger. The Greek struggle for independence gave it added force for it had all the elements that would appeal to romantic northerners: David against Goliath, Christian against Moslem, familiar European against alien Asiatic. And Byron's death at Missolonghi gave sanctity to sentiment.

The Greeks were not slow to exploit that sentiment. In 1832, shortly after gaining their freedom from the Turks, they began restoration work upon the Acropolis. There was something deeply moving about a tiny, desperately poor nation setting aside funds to restore its patrimony, to bind up the wounds of the beautiful buildings that were part also of the heritage of all mankind. As well as restoration, a bold, long-term project of excavation was also initiated. In 1886, fifty years after the project began, untouched earth was reached and there, in a trench, were discovered nine perfectly preserved Korai. The Athenians themselves had buried them, just before the Persians sacked the Acropolis in 480 BC, to protect them from vandalism. Now, almost miraculously, they had returned to a new-born nation to add volume to the swelling cry: 'Return the Elgin Marbles.'

That cry was to be repeated again and again over the next half century or so. In 1924, on the centenary of Byron's death, the philhellenic diplomat Harold Nicolson went personally to the then Prime Minister, Ramsay Macdonald, and made an impassioned plea for the marbles to be returned as a fitting gesture to mark the centenary. Macdonald was a man who, it might have been supposed, would have responded warmly to such a plea on behalf of a small, poor nation. But the politician had killed the romantic. Such a return would establish a precedent, he told Nicolson: then were would they all be?

So the marbles remain in the British Museum, the very epitome of that bitter definition of museums as 'cemeteries for murdered evidence'. But Time, which has a disconcerting trick of turning truth into paradox, is still at work on the story of the Elgin Marbles. The sculptures on the Acropolis are today in greater danger than they have ever been before in their long life – not from mines or bombs or vandals but from the Athenians themselves. Or, rather, the pollution caused by them. The same topographical factors which led to the domination of Athens in the classic period contribute now to its industrial growth. It is, for all practical purposes, an industrial city – certainly far more so than any other comparable historic city. Nearly 90 per cent of all Greek industry lies within ten miles of the Acropolis. The famous violet light is now, as often as not, a dirty grey from the dust of the quarries that have gouged great scars in the immortal hills, or the only too familiar smog colour of an industrial landscape.

And of what pollution has spared, Time itself has taken a heavy toll. The fissures in the stone, created by the original Venetian explosion, fill with moisture which freezes in winter, flaking off more marble. The metal cramps which the original builders themselves inserted in the blocks are proving a threat, for they expand as they corrode, splitting the stone they are meant to support. The more important sculptures have followed the Elgin Marbles into the safety – and sterility – of a museum. The great figures on the pediment of the Parthenon have been lowered, the Maidens have gone from the Erechtheum, their place taken by fibre-glass and cement replicas. Time seems to have resolved the Elgin Marbles controversy partially, at least, in favour of Lord Elgin. To quote Michaelis again: 'Only blind passion could doubt that Lord Elgin's act was an act of preservation.'

2

The Plundering of Egypt

'My purpose was to rob the Egyptians of their papyri.'

GIOVANNI BELZONI

Housed in a glass case in Norwich Castle Museum, flanked by a suit of Samurai armour and a collection of Polynesian weapons, are two Egyptian mummies. One was given by King George V in 1931, the other by a certain 'J. Morrison, London' in 1827. A medical examination of the latter shows that it is the corpse of a woman, although the coffin itself belonged to a man. No further information is available on either mummy, nor does the museum have any record of how it acquired them. It is reasonable to assume that the one given by George V came from the royal country house at nearby Sandringham. He was very fond of this mansion and frequently stayed there. The mummy is the kind of gift that royalty only too often receives, to its embarrassment, and it would have been natural for the king to think of Norwich Museum when wondering how to get rid of the thing.

But who was J. Morrison and why was he wandering round Norfolk, in the early nineteenth century, with the 3,000-year-old corpse of an Egyptian woman? History is silent on this point. History is also silent on the identity of Mummy 1770, which was unwrapped under the blaze of television lights in Manchester University Medical School in June 1975. All that is known for certain is that it was given to Manchester Museum in 1896 – possibly by Sir Flinders Petrie as a quid pro quo for assistance. Manchester could afford to sacrifice a mummy for dissection: it has twenty-six other human mummies plus six heads and assorted limbs, and a quantity of animal mummies. In Bristol, in 1981, yet another mummy was unwrapped before the camera. This, too, was one of several presented by an archaeologist – Edouard Naville – in return for help in financing an expedition. Both mummies were in an advanced state of disintegration, completing their millennial-long journey in the island of Britain and not, as they had hoped, in the other world.

The sheer quantity of Egyptian artifacts that found their way into the museums of Europe and North America is staggering. From the great national galleries, with their colossal stone statues, their rows of mummies, their ranks of figurines and tools, their acres of frescoes and papyri, to the little country museum, housed in some antique merchant's home, devoted to local exhibits but proudly boasting a scarab or mis-shapen chunk of stone – all bear testimony to an obsession. Egyptology was the sacred cow of scholarship, the great museums being fully prepared to starve their other collections so long as they could lay hands on yet another statue, more papyri, another mummy. And returning tourists would proudly present to the museum in their home town some artifact – frequently faked – they had bought on impulse, had found fitted ill into their neat homes and had gladly parted with in exchange for a cardboard accolade, 'Presented by. . .'.

The plundering of Egypt has been going on for 2,000 years and more. Rome was particularly fascinated by this beautiful, mysterious country which, though so incredibly wealthy, was wholly within their power. After the Caesarian conquests, Egyptomania was as strong in Rome as it was to be in London nineteen centuries later. There are probably more Egyptian obelisks in the capital of Italy than there are in the capital of Egypt.

From the time of Herodotus onward tourists have been travelling down that narrow stretch of cultivated land on either side of the Nile marvelling at the titanic monuments, seeking their own pale immortality by carving their alien names in the hard stone, occasionally filching a piece of souvenir. But after Rome, there was little interest or profit in plundering enormous masses of carved stone which possessed no intrinsic value. The hereditary castes of grave-robber who made a profession of looting the rich tombs of their predecessors can perhaps be seen as a species of self-appointed economists engaged in redistributing Egypt's wealth among the lower classes. 'We are going to take plunder for bread to eat', one of them is recorded as saying during a celebrated legal trial of the reign of Rameses IX – a trial which incidentally showed that high-ranking court officials in Thebes were engaged in the re-distribution.

The major international trade in loot was, bizarrely, that of mummies. Or, to be exact, mummy flesh. 'Mummy is become merchandise. Mizraim cures wounds and pharaoh is sold for balsam', said Thomas Browne in the fashionable Jacobean exercise of romanticizing death. Thomas Browne was

Giovanni Battista Belzoni and his 'discoveries', among them 'A Colossal Head called the Young Memnon (in the British Museum)' and 'An Obelisk, removed from the Isle of Philio with much difficulty and danger in passing down the first Cataract of the Nile (now in England)'.

THE PROGRESS OF
SIGNOR BELZONI

The energetic Paduan graduated from the stage of Sadler's Wells Theatre in 1803 (*above left*) to a medal commemorating the opening of the pyramid of Chephren at Giza in 1818 (*above*). Belzoni's exploits at Giza (*below*) and elsewhere (*below right*) bore great fruit: from Thebes came Ramesses II, the Younger Memnon – ready to be moved in 1834 (*above right*), and in the British Museum today (*far right*).

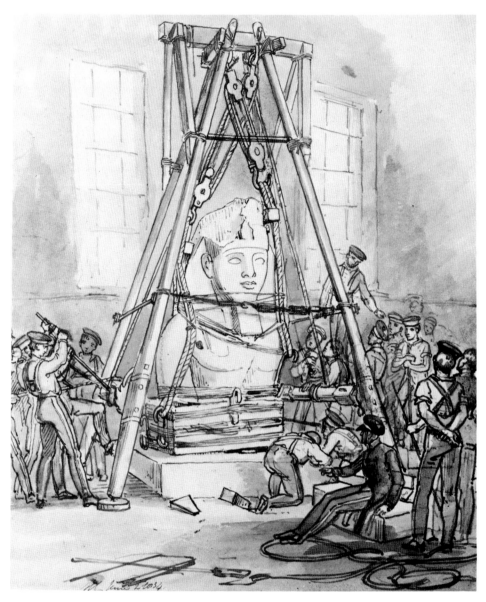

HOW THE SUN-GOD'S MONUMENTS WENT ON THEIR TRAVELS

The two obelisks known as Cleopatra's Needle were given their name several thousand years after their first erection in *c.* 1486 BC. One is now in Central Park, New York; the journey of the other is seen here. The launch from Alexandria in a specially constructed metal vessel named *Cleopatra* in 1877 (*below left*) was followed by a stormy passage. Twice shipwrecked, the obelisk was finally re-erected on the Embankment beside London's River Thames, where it stands today.

MIXED MOTIVES

Mummies examined by curious rather than mercenary Western travellers in the seventeenth century (*left*) and (*below*) a nineteenth-century view of 'An Interior of a mummy pit or sepulchral chamber at Thebes, with a Fellahs [peasant] woman searching for papyri and ornaments'.

The results of such expeditions as those by Amelia B. Edwards (*far right*), who disapproved of random looting (*right*), provided much material for the great Western collections. Fascinated by Egypt from childhood, she first visited the country in 1877 and became an important force in encouraging both popular and academic interest in its antiquities.

(*opposite below*) The mummy of an adult man finds his home in the British Museum.

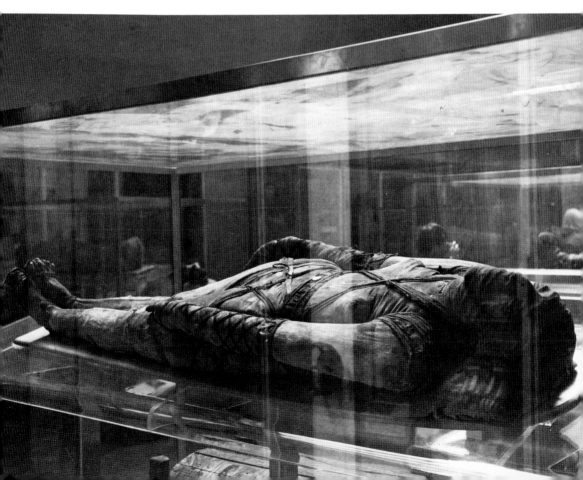

(*above*) Members of the French Scientific and Artistic Commission, part of Napoleon's expeditionary force, measure the giant fist of a statue of Ramesses II at Memphis in 1798 – today the piece is in the British Museum. (*below*) Bernardino Drovetti and his men. Drovetti, French soldier and arch-rival of Belzoni, made his fortune out of the European passion for antiquities of every description.

The making of a mummy: sketches based on descriptions by the man who has been called 'the founding father of Egyptology' – Jean-François Champollion.

also a doctor and meant exactly what he said when describing, if in poetic terms, the use of mummy-flesh as drugs. The bituminous substance known, in Persian, as *mummia* – used for the mummification of bodies – bore a very close resemblance to the pissasphalt that had long been used in the Middle East for the treatment of certain ailments. Nothing more clearly demonstrates the vast scale of Egyptian mummification than the fact that it became commercially viable to extract the mummia from the corpses as substitute for the naturally occurring substance. Another trial, this time in 1424, throws light on the process and the reason for it. The accused confessed 'that they were removing the corpses from tombs and were boiling the dead bodies in water over a very hot fire until the flesh fell off: that they then collected the oil which rose to the surface of the liquid to sell it to the Franks, who paid 25 pieces of gold a hundredweight for it'.

But though there might be a lively trade in precious artifacts from tombs and the actual corpses of their occupants, the tombs themselves, together with the temples and colossi, dreamed on undisturbed. Their very origins were forgotten as successive waves of alien foreigners dominated the country, placing their own transient impress upon it. The real plunder of Egypt began with the dawning knowledge of its past – and both were directly linked to the expedition of Napoleon Bonaparte. With that eye of his to his position in history, Napoleon ensured that the Expeditionary Force which left France in May 1798 should also include savants specifically charged with recording, and deciphering as far as possible, the enigma that was Egypt. This body of scientists, artists, draughtsmen, surveyors, historians was known contemptuously as 'The Donkeys' by the fighting soldiers. But by one of those neat quirks of history it was the despised Donkeys who were to leave the mark of France upon Egypt long after the defeated Expeditionary Force had trailed ingloriously away. Their influence was to survive even the long period of British dominance – certainly long enough and strong enough to plague Howard Carter and Lord Carnarvon over the controversy of Tutankhamun's tomb in the 1920s.

Napoleon's Scientific and Artistic Commission was housed in a splendid Cairene palace, headquarters of the newly established Egyptian Institute. For three years the Commission laboured devotedly in the wake of Napoleon's army, investigating, recording, speculating. It was they who, combining a wide range of disciplines from archaeology to zoology via hydraulics and astronomy, laid the foundations of that quasi-science called Egyptology which was to have such immense influence in Europe and America in the nineteenth and early twentieth centuries. Steadily, the Institute peeled off the deep layers of myth and legend that obscured the ancient history of Egypt, their most dramatic breakthrough coming in July 1799 when, at one of the regular meetings at the Institute, one of their number announced the discovery of a large block of basalt, covered with finely carved writing, which had been uncovered during the digging of fortifications near the town of Rosetta. And it was the Institute who, realizing the significance of the find, translated the Greek portion of the text on the Rosetta Stone and so turned the first key that was to open up the long history of Ancient Egypt.

A month after the finding of the Stone, Napoleon fled Egypt, leaving his hapless army to fend for itself. In Alexandria, General Menon surrendered to General Hutchinson – and immediately an undignified bickering over the possession of antiquities broke out. The British claimed all antiquities discovered by the Commission as part of the spoils of war. The French refused. One of the savants, Geoffroy Saint-Hilaire, couched that refusal in elegant Gallic invective: 'Sooner than permit this iniquitous and vandal spoliation we will destroy our property, we will scatter it among the Libyan sands or throw it into the sea. It is celebrity you are aiming for? Very well, you can count on the long memory of history. You also will have burnt a library in Alexandria.' Those words are frequently cited as a noble example of the intellectual and artist defying the brutish soldier, but attention is less often drawn to Saint-Hilaire's concept of ownership. The treasures created by Egyptians, which had reposed for thousands of years in the sands of Egypt, were now 'our property'. It did not occur to the English commander to query the concept of 'finders keepers' because he himself shared it to the full. Disconcerted by the vigour of the protest, Hutchinson allowed the French to retain 'their' property – with the exception of the Rosetta Stone. Word of it had already reached England, coming to the august ears of King George III himself. It was too prestigious an object to be allowed to escape, and it ultimately joined the Elgin Marbles in the chilly splendour of the British Museum.

Britain's abstraction of the Rosetta Stone marks the beginning of an open season for the plunder of Egypt that was to last for nearly 150 years, virtually until the country at last gained independence. Savants and tourists, plain thieves and solemn scientific expeditions all took their toll, feeding the hungry museums first of Europe then of America. Like Greece, Egypt was ruled by an alien power; unlike Greece, which threw off that alien rule at a crucial period, Egypt continued under the rule of a foreign dynasty whose only interest in the heritage of Egypt was the value it might command in the open market, either as booty or as gift to important foreigners, with their inexplicable lust for old bones and stones. In 1806 Mohammed Ali, a Macedonian Turk who had risen to high position in the Turkish army, proclaimed himself pasha: he and his descendants were to rule Egypt, if under the shadow of Britain. Mohammed Ali was an energetic, forward-looking man, fascinated with Western technology, impressed by the military power of the British and very happy indeed to make generous gestures to them, using the heritage of a subject people to do so.

Nothing better illustrates the vulnerability of Egypt than the long-drawn saga of the great obelisk, now in London, known as Cleopatra's Needle. In 1802 the Earl of Cavan obtained permission from Mohammed Ali to raise the fallen obelisk, and set it up as a memorial to the British victory over the French. It speaks much for Cavan's awareness of just what the ordinary Egyptian felt towards these foreigners trampling over Egyptian soil that he turned down a proposal to erect the monument in Alexandria, the obvious and appropriate place for it, because (he thought) the natives would simply knock the monument down the moment the British had left. Instead, the British soldiers in Egypt were invited to contribute a day's pay to move the obelisk to England. The 'gallant troops' did so – but nothing happened: the obelisk continued to lie half buried in Alexandria.

Nothing happened for nearly a century: there seems, indeed, to have been a feeling of unease among official circles in London regarding the true ownership of the obelisk. In 1821 the Turkish Viceroy asked the British consul Samuel Briggs what gift would make an appropriate present to King George IV and Briggs took the opportunity of having the gift ratified. The Viceroy agreed. There was some difficulty with the Greek landlord of the land upon which the obelisk lay, who demanded compensation for its encumbrance. The fact that the obelisk had been encumbering that patch of sand for 2,000 years before the Greek was born was not deemed worthy of comment. But an agreement was patched up with him and Briggs was able to write triumphantly to *The Times*: 'The English nation may now feel quite sure of its property as both the Khedive, owner of the country and of all hidden treasure, and Mr Dimitri, owner of the land where the treasure lies, have each in the most formal manner abandoned all their rights in the favour of England.' A Turk and a Greek had generously agreed to give a piece of Egypt to Britain.

But still nothing happened. In January 1847, 45 years after the first proposal was made to shift the obelisk to England, Prince Albert (in a letter to Lord John Russell) neatly demonstrated that national passion to acquire Egyptian artifacts which was becoming a European obsession: national honour hung upon it. 'I hear that the French government is trying to get hold of it (the obelisk) and move it to Paris. This would be a real disgrace to our government.' Albert tried to get official action but was politely brushed aside. In 1851 the company building the Egyptian Court for the Crystal Palace offered to bring it over at a cost of £7,000. The British government airily gave permission, but declined to underwrite the cost.

By now 'national honour' really was at stake. The French swooped in, picked up a magnificent obelisk at Luxor and erected it in the Place de la Concorde while the British were still debating costs. In 1859, a writer in the magazine *All the Year Round* recorded:

The last time the writer saw it, not very long ago, a Briton was sitting upon it, knocking off enough of the inscribed stone for himself and fellow travellers with a hammer. The writer expostulated with his brother Briton and reminded him that the wonderful relic of bygone days did not belong to him, but had been handsomely presented to the British Nation, and therefore belonged to it. 'Well, I know it does,' he answered, 'and as one of the British Nation I mean to have my share.'

It was not until 1877 that, through the generosity of a private citizen, funds were raised to transport the great obelisk and at last set it up in London.

Shortly afterwards, the newest of Western States, the USA, acquired its obelisk. James Evarts, the Secretary of State, in formally presenting this obelisk to the city of New York, emphasized that it was the first of all obelisks to be given voluntarily by the Egyptians, and then went on to give an admirably succinct reason why foreign nations wanted to possess these enormous but uninspiring lumps of stone:

These obelisks mark a culmination of the power and glory of Egypt, and every conqueror has seemed to think that the final trophy of Egypt's subjection and the proud pre-eminence of his own nation could be shown only by taking an obelisk – the chief mark of Egyptian pomp and pride – to grace the capital of the conquering nation.

The decades following the Napoleonic campaign in Egypt bear a curious resemblance to the Chicago of the 1930s, where rival gangs battled for their rich fiefs. Looking back on the period Howard Carter, the discoverer of the tomb of Tutankhamun, remarked: 'Those were the great days of collecting. Anything for which a fancy was taken, from a scarab to an obelisk, was just appropriated and if there was a difference of opinion with a brother excavator one laid for him with a gun.' The note of admiration – of, indeed, envy – is very clear, the voice of a man irritated by what he regarded as the smothering red tape of a corrupt bureaucracy.

Egypt, once a military battleground between British and French, now became a cultural battleground and remained so up to World War II. In a sense, the French brought their problems on themselves. After its expulsion from Egypt, Napoleon's Scientific Commission produced, between the years 1809 and 1813, one of the great works of Egyptology. Its *Description de l'Egypte* was published in twenty-four folio volumes, superbly illustrated, authoritatively written, bringing for the first time to the cognoscenti of Europe a full, detailed, vibrant picture of the world's oldest civilization. The Rosetta Stone had yet to be translated so that much of the *Description* was speculative, much of it enigmatic. But that, if anything, increased its appeal. The impact upon the fashionable world was immense. A swarm of northerners descended upon the Nile: most were the advance guard of the later tourist invasion, sensation-seekers somewhere between the elegant Grand Tour of the previous century and the mass tourism of the following century. But among these sheep were a number of wolves. Two of them, both Italian-born but working for different northern nations, became bitter rivals and stand out in this early period.

Bernardino Drovetti was born in Piedmont in 1776 and came to Egypt initially as a colonel in the French army. He became the consul-general for France, made himself indispensable to that other alien Mohammed Ali, pasha of Egypt, and devoted himself to making his own fortune. A tough, no-nonsense soldier with a glowering, formidable expression, he was nevertheless flexible and imaginative enough to detect a new trend while it was still in its embryonic stage. And the trend which was to make his fortune was the European passion for Egyptian antiquities.

The splendidly named Giovanni Battista Belzoni was two years younger than his arch rival. Born in Padua in 1778, he was possessed by wanderlust. He began his wandering at the age of 13 by going to Rome. Subsequently, he surfaced in the Netherlands where he seems to have picked up a living as a pedlar, and by 1803 he was in England. A giant of a man – over six foot six inches tall and broad in proportion – he first came to public notice performing a strong man act at Sadler's Wells where he would present such turns as carrying twenty people at once.

Strong man acts were two a penny in nineteenth-century England, but Belzoni was an original in every way. He was extremely handsome, with a dashing, devil-may-care manner that gave verve to his otherwise unexceptional theatre performances, so that he was able to build up a highly successful act. But with the defeat of Napoleon, the world had opened out and the ever-restless Belzoni, accompanied by the newly-acquired English wife who was to be his most loyal supporter, left England for Constantinople and then for Egypt. His debut there was, improbably enough, as a hydraulic engineer. Aware of Mohammed Ali's single-minded intention to modernize Egypt, Belzoni developed a waterwheel which, by all accounts, would have been infinitely more efficient at raising water than the slow, wasteful traditional method of the shadoof. During the trial, however, his young assistant unfortunately broke his leg, and the experiment was abandoned.

Belzoni had sunk everything into the venture and was now in the unenviable position of being discredited and penniless in an alien land. But he was also a survivor. Among the many acquaintants this immensely clubbable man had made in Cairo was the remarkable Swiss traveller John Burckhardt, who called himself Sheik Ibrahim ibn Abdullah. Burckhardt gave him a vivid description of the marvels of the upper Nile, in particular of the great temple of Abu Simbel – and of an extraordinary head, known as the Young Memnon, which lay in a temple complex near Thebes. This colossal head, weighing some seven tons, was a thing of great beauty and Burckhardt himself had toyed with the idea of getting it to England. The task of moving it had defeated him: it had defeated even the French army, but it would not defeat Belzoni, spurred on by the necessity of hunger.

It so happened that the new English consul Henry Salt was not only himself a passionate Egyptophile but had also been specifically charged by the Under Secretary for Foreign Affairs to keep an eye open for important antiquities – 'another Rosetta Stone' or its equivalent. It will come as no surprise to the reader to discover that the Under Secretary of State for Foreign Affairs was the ubiquitous William Hamilton, for Elgin's erstwhile personal secretary weaves his way in and out of all such enterprises and would, in due course, earn the cordial hatred of the French. Now he urged Salt to spare no expense to uphold English honour against Gallic acquisitiveness. 'Whatever the expense of the undertaking, it would be most cheerfully supported by an enlightened nation, eager to anticipate its rivals

Some of Giovanni Belzoni's adventures in his energetic and single-minded hunt for the treasures of ancient Egypt.

in the prosecution of the best interests of science and literature.' Assured by Burckhardt that the Young Memnon would indeed be a valuable acquisition within the generous terms of his brief, Salt advanced Belzoni £25 to collect the statue and anything else of value he could lay his hands on. In June 1816 Giovanni Belzoni embarked upon his career of collector – or plunderer – of antiquities.

The impression conveyed by Belzoni himself is that of charlatan or, at best, of showman. It is virtually impossible to take seriously as an 'archaeologist' a man who was prepared to open up a tomb with a battering ram, as Belzoni did. His expeditions up and down the Nile valley were almost entirely devoted to acquiring saleable antiquities. Almost – but not entirely so. An index to the man's complex character is provided by the exquisite watercolours with which he illustrated his book describing his activities in Egypt and Nubia. They show a remarkable combination of precision and sensitivity that is almost impossible to associate with the ex-strong man of Sadler's Wells. He possessed, too, that instinct for an archaeological site – the ability to home in on this, rather than that, apparently equally barren piece of land – which even the most scientific modern archaeologist needs to possess if he is not to spread his investigations over an impossibly large area. Again and again some almost invisible variation in the terrain would lead him to poke a stick in a crack, or uncover the few inches of sand that hid a vital clue. It was this instinct that led him to the concealed small entrance in the Pyramid of Kephren that eventually opened its interior to exploration.

Belzoni displayed on his first expedition in search of the Young Memnon all the characteristics that would make him the most successful archaeological buccaneer of all time: the incredible physical stamina; the ability to wheedle and persuade; the ability to improvise; and above all, the insatiable curiosity that led him on and on. Almost immediately he found that he was in direct competition with Drovetti – and Drovetti had had time and money to establish himself. Belzoni had to assemble, in remote areas, all the basic essentials of an archaeological expedition: labourers to dig and haul, carpenters to design transport, together with all the necessary equipment. Again and again he found the local headman unable or unwilling to help: it was the wrong time of the season; there was no wood available; potential labourers were busy in their own fields. It was not difficult to establish that Drovetti was behind the refusals, even though Drovetti, in a spirit of what seemed to be mockery, had generously 'given' Belzoni an immense sarcophagus in Karnak – if he could get it away.

Belzoni triumphed over all difficulties. He had no bottomless supply of funds with which to outbribe Drovetti, simply his own overwhelming character and the ability to think quickly on his feet. Like the occasion when he encountered a local headman smarting over what the man considered an insult – a present of anchovies and olives which Drovetti had incautiously made him instead of a more handsome present. 'The effects of a few little salted fish contributed the greatest share towards the removal of the colossus', Belzoni noted; and promptly made the most of it.

He found the enormous bust of the Young Memnon in the sand at Luxor where it had lain for centuries. His equipment to move those seven solid tons could not have been cruder: some stout planks and rollers and ropes. It is difficult to establish from his own description just how he got the mass on to the crude sledge he had designed, though he noted complacently that the labourers who accomplished it thought he had done it through a charm. His watercolour shows that he employed the same transport system that the pharaohs themselves had used – vast numbers of labourers tugging a sledge on rollers. The sculpture was brought to the banks of the Nile and, while waiting for the water to rise high enough to float it off, Belzoni continued his exploration in the Upper Nile. He followed Burckhardt's footsteps to the great temple of Abu Simbel and, undeterred by the size of the task before him, arranged to excavate the vast mound of sand that all but concealed the temple front. Like young Charles Cockerell in Greece, he met the bewilderment and suspicion of the local Turks, who just could not believe that a Frank had made this long and arduous journey simply in quest of carved stones. On his way back to Luxor he stopped in the exquisite little island of Philae and here, in the name of 'His Britannic Majesty's Consul General', took possession of an obelisk. At Karnak, whose great temple overwhelmed him with its magnificence, he found that the French had staked out all the potentially worthwhile sites and were busily digging. With that unerring instinct of his he uncovered a temple with a rich cache of black granite statues.

Back at Kurneh, the river had risen high enough for the expedition to tackle the task of moving the Young Memnon. It was a massive operation, entailing the building of a causeway out into the river whence the immense block of granite was loaded onto a specially adapted barge. On 24 November, nearly five months after he had left Cairo with little more than determination and imagination, he returned in triumph, bearing the great head as his journeyman's piece in his newly adopted trade. And Consul Henry Salt gave him £50 for his trouble.

Belzoni's means of financing his activities are never very clear. Over the next ten years, this extraordinary man was to conduct a vast one-man raiding operation on the Nile antiquities, organizing an army of workmen, arranging a complex system of transport to move scores of valuable objects, some of immense size, between Luxor and London. But one is never quite certain who, exactly, paid for it all. Initially, he was working to Henry Salt's brief and, in that sense, could almost be described as an employee of – or a contractor employed by – the British government. But Salt later branched out as an entrepreneur and collector in his own right and the sale of at least one of Belzoni's major discoveries, the great alabaster sarcophagus of Sethi, went to line Salt's pocket. Even allowing for the incredible cheapness of labour in early nineteenth-century Egypt, the total of £75 which Belzoni received for bringing in the Young Memnon seems a ridiculously small sum.

But Belzoni was apparently satisfied and almost immediately set off again to the Upper Nile. It was on this occasion that he made contact with the Kurnese, the remarkable dynasty of tomb robbers who made their home among the tombs of Kurneh, across the river from Luxor. They were, in Belzoni's view, the most devious, cunning and dangerous of all the Arab tribes scattered along the Nile. Behind Kurneh was a vast necropolis, an intricate maze of tombs and burial caves that housed a literally uncounted number of mummified corpses. Belzoni's purpose in visiting the necropolis was quite simple, quite unequivocal. 'My purpose was to rob the Egyptians of their papyri, of which I found a few hidden in their breasts, under their arms, in the space above the knees, or on the legs or covered by the numerous layers of cloth.'

He had as guides the Kurnese with whom, master of bonhomie as he was, he rapidly established amiable relations. And his description of this great city of the dead has a macabre fascination rendered exotic by his stilted English. He seems to have been a man without the slightest sense of fear, indifferent to the phobias which beset ordinary men. Some of the passages in the necropolis were little more than a foot wide, an almost impassable hazard for a man of his size. Almost – but not quite: wherever his lithe, agile guides managed to go, somehow the massive Belzoni was just behind. Every footfall brought a fine cloud of dust into the already oppressive air, 'a dust so fine that it enters the nose and mouth to such a degree that it requires a great power of lungs to resist it'. To get at the valuable papyri, it was necessary to break up the bodies, thereby filling the air with mummy dust, 'rather unpleasant to swallow'. In a celebrated passage that has an authentic touch of nightmare, he describes how he was all but overwhelmed by a shower of disintegrating corpses. Fatigued, he had seated himself upon a mummy: 'It crushed like a band box. I naturally had recourse to my hands to sustain my weight but they found no better support so that I sank altogether among the broken mummies with a crash of bones, rags and wooden cases which raised such a dust as kept me motionless for a quarter of an hour, waiting till it subsided again.'

Belzoni's cordial relationship with the Kurnese enabled him to present a clear picture of these people who pursued the oddest of all possible trades. In theory, they were peasants: in practice, they found that rifling the dead gave a far higher return than trying to wrest a living from the land. Originally, they ransacked the corpses in search of conventional treasure – ornaments made out of precious metals and gems. But under the tutelage of Belzoni, they extended their activities, seeking not only the papyri for which the scholars of Europe would give high prices, but also the little sentimental objects – the dried wreaths of flowers, children's toys and the like – in which tourists would delight. A born entrepreneur, Belzoni gave some pattern to their haphazard searching, paying a number of trusties a regular wage in return for their assurance that they would deliver everything up to him.

As well as earning a living from the dead, the Kurnese lived upon the dead in a more literal sense. Their homes were not only carved out of the same stone as the tombs: frequently, indeed, they consisted precisely of tombs from which the earlier inhabitants had been ejected. They used mummies, and bits of non-saleable mummy-cases, as fuel, and even the hardened

Giovanni Battista Belzoni confessed himself shocked by the way in which these families lived among fragments of human beings.

Belzoni's success at Kurneh aroused the anger of Drovetti's agents, one of whom threatened to cut his throat. It was a threat he took seriously enough to transfer his activities elsewhere. Throughout his ten years in Egypt, his relationship with the French Consul General was ambiguous: in their personal contacts civilized niceties were observed, but in the field something near open war prevailed. When Belzoni was moving the obelisk from Philae, Drovetti's agent, Rosignano, tried to prevent him by force, mustering a party of desperados and himself threatening Belzoni with a rifle: 'I have no doubt if I had attempted to dismount [from his donkey] the cowards would have despatched me on the ground and said that they did it in defence of their lives as I had been the aggressor.' He rode on and, in the face of that massive contempt, Rosignano exploded with rage. Somebody fired a pistol: 'I thought it high time to sell my life as dear as I could.' And the incident would undoubtedly have ended in bloodshed had not Drovetti, who was present, ordered his men to back off.

But a new arrangement with Henry Salt had put Belzoni in competition not only with the French Consul General, but also the British, his erstwhile patrons. As he put it sardonically, wherever he decided to dig, the agents of both parties would hasten to claim the site for their principals. 'I verily believe that if I had pointed out one of the sandbanks or the solid rock, they would have said they just intended to have broken into it the next day.' But the soil of Egypt was rich enough to support even three such treasure-hunters – particularly one with so well-developed an instinct as Belzoni. And, to be fair, it must be recorded that, although his primary motivation remained plunder, the secondary motivation – that of archaeological discovery – was becoming ever stronger. The tomb of Sethi I yielded him, as prize, that splendid sarcophagus. But he also went to immense trouble to record, both in painting and by wax impression, the superb series of murals that decorated the tombs. And it was this tomb which, again, gives posterity a yardstick to measure the mores of the day regarding the wholesale plundering that was in progress. News of the splendid murals rapidly spread, but became distorted. The local aga arrived post haste at the tomb, demanding his share of the treasure: rumour had turned the intrinsically valueless murals into a fantastic treasure consisting of a golden bird stuffed with rare gems.

Giovanni Belzoni returned to England, with his faithful wife Sarah, in 1820. He found that he was a celebrity, a role in which he delighted and played for all that it was worth. In an incredibly short space of time, he had written his book *Narrative of operations and recent discoveries . . . in Egypt and Nubia*, arranged a magnificent display in the newly built Egyptian Hall in London, and entered into negotiations with the British Museum for the sale of the tomb of Sethi I. But, as Elgin found before him, the British Museum regarded it as a public duty to pay little or nothing for its treasures. The Trustees seemed, too, to have had their suspicions regarding the ownership of the sarcophagus. Certainly Henry Salt claimed it and, after negotiations with the British Museum broke down, sold it for £2,000 to the wealthy architect Sir John Soane, who placed it on exhibition in his private house.

The sarcophagus is still there, a massive testimony to the power of an idea. Over the past century and a half since its discovery, the collecting and housing of major antiquities has shifted, probably irrevocably, from the private to the public field. It is not often that posterity has the opportunity to get the feeling of one of the great private collections, to experience fully the magpie syndrome which led wealthy men to cram their homes with masses of stone, valued for their age alone. It is possible to get that feeling in the Soane Museum. Although it is today a public museum it is still, in essence, a private house filled with bibelots and objects d'art. The great alabaster sarcophagus is almost grotesquely out of keeping, a massive survival from a remote past, whose brooding presence reduces to triviality much that surrounds it.

Belzoni never returned to Egypt: he went, instead, to Africa and died there of a fever. But his flamboyant showmanship in London – including the first public dissection of a mummy – brought the glamour of Egypt into the homes of the British. And across the Channel, in France, a similar wave of Egyptomania began building up. Never before, or since, has there been such massive and sustained plundering of a country's heritage as took place in Egypt throughout the nineteenth and early twentieth centuries. Prodded by the remonstrances of the great scholar Champollion, the decipherer of Egyptian hieroglyphics, in 1835 the Egyptian government established an Antiquities Service which was supposed to control the activities of foreign archaeologists. A rule of thumb system was worked out whereby, in theory at least, the Egyptian government and the archaeologist divided the discoveries between them.

But with the advent of mass tourism in the late nineteenth century, the task of protecting Egypt's heritage became almost impossible. Scores of sellers of 'antikas' – real or forged, priceless or common – lay in wait for the

The Sarcophagus of Sethi I – 'This marvellous effort of human industry and perseverance',
according to Sir John Soane, who became its delighted purchaser in 1824.

tourist hordes. The plunderers ranged from dealers, via tourists, to such
respectable scholars as Wallace Budge, who in the 1880s supplied the British
Museum with some of its most valuable pieces of Egyptiana, including the
Papyrus of Ani.

It was Budge who put forward that defence which unscrupulous
archaeologists were to use again and again: archaeological treasures were
safer in the keeping of a great museum than in the hands of ignorant
'natives'. 'Every unprejudiced person must admit that, once a mummy has
passed into the care of the Trustees and is lodged in the British Museum, it
has a far better chance of being preserved than it could possibly have in any
tomb, royal or otherwise, in Egypt.'

Supplementing the Budge thesis was the thesis of 'Who pays?' advanced
by Sir Frederick Kenyon, Director of the British Museum, during the
argument regarding the division of the spoils of the Tutankhamun
discovery: 'If a country owning ancient sites adopts a policy of rigid
exclusion or refuses to permit ancient objects to leave the country, it means

that the hunting of old sites will be done largely by natives and art dealers.' Despite the characteristically arrogant tone of this statement, in which descendants of the creators of the treasure become 'natives', Kenyon made a valid point in the context of his day.

The Tutankhamun discovery coincided with the birth of Egyptian nationalism. It should perhaps be noted that the first reaction of the Wafdist, or nationalist, party to the news of the incredible find was that the treasures should immediately be sold and the money used to reduce the national debt. But this greatest of all archaeological discoveries became a potent symbol of nationalism. It was exacerbated by some remarkably clumsy actions on the part of the discoverers Carter and Carnarvon – of thirty-four celebrities invited to visit the tomb on an open day in 1923 only six were Egyptian – and by their granting exclusive reporting rights to the London *Times*. That particular arrangement irritated everybody. 'By handing over what may be called journalistic rights in the Valley of the Tombs they treated the find in advance as their own private property. The Egyptian government with its newly awaked sense of nationality has forwarded the contrary view that King Tutankhamun and his belongings are the national treasure of Egypt', thundered the *Times*'s downmarket rival, the London *Daily Express*. A Coptic Christian, a certain Athanasius Bokter, injected a note of comedy by claiming the treasure as a member of the only existing race which could, by any stretching of the imagination, be called the descendant of the original owners. No clearer evidence of Egyptian helplessness, of their inability to claim their own, can be provided than that extraordinary court case where an American judge arbitrated between the claims of the Englishman Howard Carter and the French Director of the Egyptian Antiquities Service, Pierre Lacau, over right of access to the tomb.

The sheer glamour and scale of Belzoni's and Howard Carter's activities in Egypt serve to keep their names before the public. Almost unknown outside the ranks of Egyptologists is the name of Ludwig Borchhardt, Director of the German Institute in Cairo, who, in or about 1912, perpetrated a bare-faced swindle upon an ignorant government that has bedevilled Egyptian-German relations ever since.

In 1912 Borchhardt was digging in the 'library' of Tell el Armarna, a site which had produced some of the most vital clues to ancient Egyptian history. Following established practice, he showed the results of the dig, 'many chests full', to an official of the Antiquities Service. The material, also according to now-established practice, was divided 50/50 between the Egyptian and German governments. In due course, the German share was

Napoleon's Expeditionary Force included a Commission on the Sciences and Arts – led by Baron Denon, on whose drawing this depiction of the Sphinx was based.

taken to Berlin and put on display. There it aroused interest, if no particular excitement.

In 1923 there suddenly appeared in the Museum what is arguably the most beautiful piece of sculpture on the planet, the limestone bust of Queen Nefertiti, wife of the heretical pharaoh Akhenaten. It is an extraordinary piece of work, not least because it bears little resemblance to other, known, portrait busts of the queen. These show a woman with pleasant, but not otherwise outstanding features, whereas the limestone bust is of a woman of almost eerie beauty, a beauty so timeless that, unretouched, the bust has been used in modern cosmetic advertisements. Its appearance not unnaturally caused a sensation in Berlin – and an explosion of anger in Cairo. How had so unique a piece of work ever left Egypt?

When tackled, Ludwig Borchhardt's response was, in effect, a shrug. He insisted that the bust had been displayed, along with other finds, to the official of the Antiquities Service in Tell el Armarna. The official had 'passed' the bust, and he had taken it out of Egypt as he had a right to do.

The answer begged many questions. How could any official possibly make such a mistake? And if such a mistake had been made, why had the bust been hidden from the public for nearly a decade before being put on display? The official who approved the division of finds was tracked down – and proved to be neither an Egyptian nor an expert in that field. He was a Frenchman, Lefebvre, and his specialization was the interpretation of papyri. He was asked how on earth it was that he gave permission for the removal of so priceless an object as the Nefertiti bust. He 'could not remember'. Pressed further, it appeared that he had given a blanket permission – in other words, he had approved the transmission of a large number of boxes containing a number of objects, but not specifically a limestone, coloured portrait bust of the wife of Akhenaten. There was, inevitably, a suspicion of bribery but no proof.

So the matter remained for over twenty years. Periodically the Egyptian government protested, periodically the German government evaded the issue. The bust became one of the prize showpieces of Berlin, featuring prominently in tourist publicity. On Sunday 8 April 1945, Josef Goebbels, recording the utter collapse of the Third Reich in his diary, singled out the fate of the bust for special reference. 'Our entire gold reserves amounting to hundreds of tons and vast art treasures, including the bust of Nefertiti, have fallen into American hands. The criminal derelictions of duty have allowed the German people's most treasured possession to fall into enemy hands.' The bust disappeared briefly, but re-emerged after the war and was re-housed in the Prussian State Museum. But in the interim, Germany had become divided into two separate states and a brisk argument broke out regarding the ownership of the bust. The Federal Republic produced an official pamphlet entitled *Wem Gehort Nofretete* (To whom does Nefertiti belong) rehearsing in minute detail the claims of West Germany – without once referring to the possible claims of its original owners, the Egyptians themselves.

But meanwhile, in Europe generally, the climate of opinion regarding colonial plunder was changing. In the 1970s the historian Philip Vandenberg began assembling material for what he called an 'archaeological biography' of Nefertiti and promptly met a block: Borchhardt's descendants did all they could to prevent him arriving at the truth about the transaction.

In 1978 the German newspaper *Die Zeit* commissioned Gert von Paczensky to unravel the story.

Paczensky's researches show that there is no doubt whatsoever that Ludwig Borchhardt was perfectly aware that the Egyptians would not allow the bust to leave Egypt, and took steps to avoid producing it to an informed investigation. Regarding Lefebvre, he took the view that it was no part of his, Borchhardt's, duty to teach another man his job. He had informed the Berlin Museum that a special consignment was on its way and should be treated with special consideration. There is no indication of how the bust was actually got out of the country. (For what it is worth, the present writer was told by an archaeologist in Iran that Borchhardt made a number of plaster copies of the bust, left a copy in Tell el Armarna and smuggled the original out with the rest.) The museum authorities were warned that under no circumstances was it to go on display. In accordance with academic convention, Borchhardt had recorded the bust's existence in the transactions of a learned society, but in such bald terms, and with such deliberately bad photography, that the value of the piece could not be recognized. In May 1918 the Museum Director Schafer was recorded as saying privately: 'My colleagues and I were obliged to say that we had no space to display the bust. We were very embarrassed to have to give such a feeble reason.' And in May 1924 Borchhardt himself is recorded as saying, 'I hid our most precious find in Berlin as long as I could.' In Egypt, the officials of the Antiquities Service tried to evolve a face-saving formula: would Borchhardt simply admit to having made a 'mistake'? He refused. As a result of the Nefertiti incident, his freedom to excavate was severely limited and though this must have been a grievous burden to an Egyptologist, it was accepted as the price. Seventy years after it was taken out of the sands of Egypt the bust of Queen Nefertiti, 'the most beautiful woman who ever lived', remains in Germany. In the words of the American scholar John Wilson, 'it represents to Egyptian nationalists the powerful exploitation of their assets by Western scholars'.

II
THE SACRING OF
THE KING

De generatiõe ꝛ regno ſcĩ regis Stephani primi regis hũgaroꝛ

emeric⁹

3

The Gold of Ashanti

'Are Her Majesty's Government aware of the very deep
feelings of the Ashanti people about the return of these
sacrosanct objects – which are supposed to contain the
soul of the whole people?'

LORD MONTAGU OF BEAULIEU

Outside: the grey, cold skies and bitter wind of a London February. Inside:
Africa – a stunning recreation with a blaze of gold, a brilliance of robes, soft
breezes stirring the plantain thatch of a native hut, babble of African voices.
The crowd of fifty or so moves slowly through the dense rain-forest of the
Gold Coast, passing a tribal burial ground, and comes to a halt in the town
square of Kumasi. Before us is what appears to be part of a large wattle and
daub building with a cool verandah, on the steps of which are a number of
large drums. My neighbour, a brilliantly robed Ghanaian, looks at it with a
touch of awe. 'The Palace of the Asantehene: I've often heard about it but
never seen it.' But nor has any other living person, for it was burnt down by
the British punitive expedition in 1874. This, like all the other buildings in
the square, is a re-creation made from photographs. We are in the Museum
of Mankind's exhibition, entitled 'Asante Kingdom of Gold' and the
Asantehene himself, Otumfuo Opuku Ware II, has journeyed with his
entourage from Ghana especially to open it.

In the reconstructed town square we halt for a short ceremony. The
Director of the Museum presents a replica of the great bowl of the
Mildenhall treasure to the Asantehene who, in return, presents one of the
stools for which Ashanti is famous. We move on, coming into the centre-
piece of the exhibition. It looks like an up-market jeweller's shop with its
blaze of gold objects resting on velvet behind immensely strong bullet-proof

glass. The Asantehene pauses long before it, his face impassive. It is impossible to guess what his thoughts are, but they must be, at the very least, wry, for it is as though Queen Elizabeth II, having been invited to open an exhibition celebrating British history in Accra, should find herself contemplating the British Crown Jewels. For these golden objects form part of the regalia of Ashanti, taken during that sack of the city in 1874 which resulted in its destruction by fire.

Ever since the early sixteenth century Europeans had been cautiously establishing their bases on the fever-ridden West African coast. They endured its terrible climate for two reasons: gold and slaves. There was so much gold, of the finest quality, that this whole stretch of country would become known as the Gold Coast: as early as 1502 the Portuguese were taking out fifteen shiploads a year.

Over the following centuries the Europeans scrambled for the riches supplied to them by the coastal tribes. None penetrated inland, through the forbidding 'bush' which formed a solid wall a few miles from the coast. From that 'bush' came the slaves and much of the gold for which Europeans had an insatiable hunger, gold in the form of exquisite ornaments as well as dust or nuggets. Their appearance meant nothing to the traders who hastened to melt them down into humdrum, but measurable, bullion.

Meanwhile, behind that jungle barrier, a powerful nation was coming into being, the Kingdom of the Ashanti. They were quite different from the coastal tribes, on whom they looked with contempt, and they formed a complex society centred on the king or Asantehene, whose power was vested in a mysterious Golden Stool that had descended from heaven into the hands of the first Asantehene. They were a martial people, something like the Zulus in their organization, and, like the Zulus, addicted to militarism. These people, expanding towards the coast, eventually came into contact with the coastal tribes and, through them, with the Europeans. But it was not until 1817 that a European made his way along the endless forest paths to the Ashanti capital of Kumasi.

The European was T. E. Bowdich, the 26-year-old agent of the British West Africa Company, charged by his masters to make contact with this developing nation and see what, if any, trading prospects there were. It took Bowdich and his five European companions three weeks to travel the 150 miles from the coast to Kumasi.

They found a city of some 15,000 people – a square built, solidly handsome people, somewhat shorter than the average European. And

On the route to Kumasi, 1841: 'a messenger appeared on the opposite bank, with a letter from the King of Ashanti'.

Bowdich's lyrical description of them and their city was doomed to be mocked and rejected by his readers in England, so totally did it conflict with the accepted European view of Africans as naked, miserable savages.

Our observations had taught us to conceive a spectacle exceeding our original expectations, but they had not prepared us for the extent and display of the scene which burst upon us. The sun reflected with a glare scarcely more supportable than the heat from the massy gold ornaments which glistened in every direction. The Cabooceers [chiefs], as did their superior captains and attendants, wore Ashantee cloths of extravagant price. They were of incredible size and weight, and thrown over the shoulder exactly like a Roman toga. A small silk fillet encircled their temples, and massy gold necklaces, intricately wrought, suspended Moorish charms: a band of gold and beads circled the knees; small circles of gold, like guinea rings and casts of animals, were strung round their ankles; rude lumps of rock gold hung from their left wrists which were so heavily laden [with golden ornaments] as to be supported on the heads of their handsomest boys. Gold and silver pipes and canes dazzled the eye in every direction. Wolves and rams heads, as large as life, cast in gold, were suspended from their gold-handled swords . . . .

Over the half century following Bowdich's visit, a scenario familiar in these days of empire was unfolding itself. Increasing contact between an expanding, vigorous black nation and a probing, inventive European people resulted in increasing friction. It was long before 'the British lion roared'. Even the murder of a governor whose skull, gold-chased, served as the Asantehene's drinking vessel failed to force action from a distant government who looked with no particular enthusiasm on its duties to protect the coastal natives.

But in 1867 a new Asantehene ascended the throne. His name was Kofi Karikari, promptly anglicized into King Koffee or Coffee giving a music-hall touch to a grim and efficient young man whose ambitions were anything but music hall. 'My business shall be war', he announced. The actual point of conflict was humdrum enough: the British bought the coastal fort Elmina from the Dutch, ignoring Kofi's claim that it was tributary to him. Incensed – or, perhaps, forced into it by his military-minded generals who were undoubtedly spoiling for a fight – King Koffee solemnly filled the skull of the unfortunate governor and drank a toast, then marched down to the coast at the head of a sizeable army. Thus began what the British were to call the Ashanti Wars but to which the Ashanti and their successors gave the name of the Sargrenti War. For Sargrenti was the Ashanti version of the name of the remarkable and singular leader of the punitive expedition, Sir Garnet Wolseley.

Wolseley was a young general, and a decidedly unorthodox one. Unorthodox in that he had gained his position by merit, and not by purchase; unorthodox in his attitude to his men, treating them not as dumb cannon fodder but as intelligent human beings who would fight the better for being informed. His pamphlet, 'Advice to Soldiers', in which he outlined the problems and solutions peculiar to fighting in the tropics, would not have been out of place in the egalitarian atmosphere of World War II. Small of stature, quick-minded and popular, he was surrounded by men of a similar turn of mind, contemptuously known as The Wolseley Ring but all destined for high rank and brilliant careers.

The Sargrenti War is one of the most richly documented of all the colonial wars. Ever since the Crimea, the war correspondent had come into his own. Every newspaper which could afford to do so ensured that it had a representative wherever The Flag was being carried against the enemy. Wolseley, for all his enlightened approach to his men, regarded the press corps as an unmitigated nuisance and did all he could to forestall the reporters, on one occasion even despatching an empty vessel to England in order to beat the correspondents. And the correspondents took their revenge by subjecting his conduct of the war to a barrage of criticism.

I   The Erechtheum, 1751. While James Stuart and Nicholas Revett busied themselves in measuring and recording the antiquities of Athens, the Greeks – under Turkish rule – were in a poor position to revere their heritage.

The doyen of the press corps – certainly in his own eyes – was Henry Morton Stanley, then enjoying world-wide fame after his encounter with Livingstone. He was on the Gold Coast as special correspondent for the *New York Herald* with an apparently bottomless expense account: it enabled him to make one of those gestures in which he excelled, the commissioning and provisioning of his own, personal steam launch with which he explored the rivers and the coast. His account of the campaign *Coomassie and Magdala*, based on his newspaper reports, is a gem of its kind – fast moving, fresh, as readable now as when it poured pell mell from his pen. And though he was writing for an American paper, his attitude to England is well summed up in his preface. His book is about 'the story of two expeditions which England undertook in Africa, in behalf of her honour, her dignity, humanity, and justice'.

With Stanley was that spinner of good stories G. A. Henty, representing the London *Standard*, eagerly collecting material either for his editor or for the rattling good yarns that came so easily off his pen. There was a special correspondent of *The Times*, Winwood Read, and F. Boyle of the *Telegraph*. And the essential war artist was present in the person of Melton Prior of the *Illustrated London News*. Stanley made use of Prior's illustrations for his book and they marvellously complement the text: the soldiers with their beards and pith helmets, moving with enormous dignity and confidence among exotic blacks, breathe the very spirit of Victorian England as she set out to take over a world.

And in addition to the professional writers were the amateurs, ready to cater to the Victorian passion for news from exotic places: Brackenbury, Wolseley's own Military Secretary, copiously keeping notes for his two-volume book on the war; the missionary who fell into King Koffee's hands but survived to leave an account from the inside; and Wolseley himself in his memoirs – all combine to build up a picture of the march to Kumasi.

The first enemy was the climate, that awful Gold Coast penance which was to gain for the place the name of White Man's Grave – the ferocious, vertical sun which drove the victim into shade, where promptly he would feel clammy and cold. Stanley described the military base at Cape Castle as:

A town like a smoking volcano, blazing and burning in the hollows between the seven hills, domed by a sky of brass seven times heated by fire. In these smoking hollows, subjected to the heat of the sky of brass, are young English officers, fresh from the cool shades of the willows, the elms, and the oaks of England.

And in that humid furnace was generated the ubiquitous 'fever'. Europeans heard about it with dread long before they arrived on the coast. 'I

V   The Crown of St Stephen – argued and fought over by soldiers, statesmen and art historians for centuries, seen by many as a symbol of Hungarian national identity for ever.

suggest every man take a coffin with him', was the sardonic advice given by an old Gold Coast hand to Wolseley. The 'fever' affected Africans as well as Europeans: out of ninety-two labourers despatched from Sierra Leone, forty-two fell ill.

And after the horrors of the Coast were the torments of the 'bush'. The bluejackets and marines were better off than most soldiers of their day under Wolseley's sensible regime. Instead of being forced to march and fight and die in red tunics buttoned up to the neck, they wore sensible loose uniforms, more closely related to the battledress of modern wars than the toy-soldier finery of their own day. But even this mitigated, not eliminated, the difficulties and horrors that confronted them. 'Bush', Stanley remarked, was a misnomer. It should be called jungle. 'It is so dense in places that one wonders at first sight how naked people can have the temerity to risk their bodies in what must necessarily punish their unprotected cuticles most painfully.' That awful jungle, covering thousands of square miles, was not only a physical but a psychological barrier. Europeans are accustomed to horizons, the ability to rest the eye on long distances. Here, vision ended with the sweating shoulders of the men ahead and, on each side, the solid green wall only rarely broken by, perhaps, a patch of lilies gleaming in the underwater gloom or a clearing of plantains. Wolseley's 'Advice to Soldiers' had, to a certain extent, prepared the green troops for this. 'Fighting in the bush is very like fighting in the twilight: no one can see further than a few files to right or left. Great steadiness and self-confidence are therefore required from every person engaged.' To meet these conditions, Wolseley broke with hallowed army tradition, making his units as small as possible and so emphasizing the need for independence for each man. But the soldiers were to have good heart. 'It must never be forgotten that Providence has implanted in the heart of every native of Africa a superstitious awe of the white man and dread that prevents the negro from daring to meet us face to face in combat.' And if that were not enough, then the soldier should remember that with his breech-loader he was equal to at least twenty Ashantis 'wretchedly armed as they are with old flint muskets firing slugs or pieces of stone that do not hurt badly at more than 40 or 50 yards'.

Stanley, for one, was convinced that this was an unnecessary war: 'Having acquired such rich territory from the Dutch, the British should not have been so greedy as to take it all. They should have been aware of the Ashantee anxiety to have some strip of the coast.' Certainly King Koffee seemed to have no liking for war. Over the next few weeks there was a constant stream of envoys from Kumasi, each wearing the solid gold plate on his chest that signified his role as herald. Their king was astonished at Sargrenti's advance: had he not ordered his own troops to withdraw? A century later, Kofi Karikari's political successor, the present government of Ghana, was quite certain of his relatively pacific intentions:

It is palpably clear from the records, as well as from Asante oral traditions, that the Asante did not want to fight the British and did not believe that the British troops would actually go to Kumasi. Indeed, not only did the Asantehene withdraw [his] army from the coast in November 1873, but actually disbanded it on his return home.

But whatever Kofi did, or did not, intend there is no doubting the British intention, for Wolseley summed up his war aims in a letter to the Secretary of State. 'There is, sir, but one method of freeing these settlements from the continued menace of Ashanti invasion and this is to defeat the Ashantee army in the field and, if necessary, to pursue it into its own land and march victorious on the Ashantee capital.' With that in mind, Wolseley could afford to treat Kofi's advances with disdain. In reply, he simply gave the king an ultimatum: the release of all prisoners, in particular three European missionaries whom he held; the handing over of hostages, including the Queen Mother – an almost sacrosanct person in Ashanti eyes – and an indemnity of 50,000 ounces of gold to recompense the Great White Queen for the heavy expenses of this war.

Gold gleams throughout the Ashanti story: one wonders in retrospect whether the punitive expedition would have been quite so dedicated if the major product of Ashanti had been anything else but this potent lure. At a current price of £3 12s an ounce, the indemnity demanded by Wolseley represented a sum of around £200,000 – a respectable total, certainly, but one that would certainly not show a profit when the final costs of the campaign were calculated. In the event, he contented himself – or was obliged to content himself – with much less.

But the mystic lure of gold was quite out of proportion to its humdrum value on the market. Men remembered Bowdich's account of the gleam and glint of gold that was everywhere in Kumasi – of the chief's hands so weighed down with gold ornaments that they had to be supported on the heads of young boys; of how the very executioner was accoutred in gold; of gold in dust form, in boxes or, as nuggets, tied up in carefully calculated bundles of cloth. The very market women took the price of their yams and *akki* and salt fish in gold dust.

Bowdich did not exaggerate: Ashanti society was underpinned by gold. The metal came into circulation either directly from mines worked by slave labour, or through taxes of one sort or another. Tax collectors circulated through the kingdom, equipped with satchels, weights and scales, collecting taxes usually in the form of gold dust. By custom they were allowed to retain a generous 15 per cent. Gold dust was the established form of currency; the scales used for weighing it became an art form. Periodically, the soil in the great market place of Kumasi was washed to obtain that which had been spilt and this went to the Asantehene. All nuggets, too, were supposed to be surrendered to the Asantehene, who returned a proportion of their value to the finder in the form of dust. It has been estimated that the Great Chest – which was, in effect, the reserve treasury of the kingdom – contained an estimated £1,500,000 at contemporary values. Although adulteration of gold dust was punishable by death, it was not unknown for brass filings to be used to pad out the weights. The story is told of a senior chief whose treasury, after his death, was found to contain a large proportion of brass filings. His body was dug up and decapitated.

Like a will-o-the-wisp the gleam of Ashanti gold drew the British expeditionary force deeper into the bush. For the green soldiers from England it might have seemed an outpost of hell (Wolseley had not thought fit to follow up Stanley's suggestion of importing elephants to make a path through the terrible jungle). But the soldiers of Kofi Karikari were also victims. The entire campaign was to cost the British sixty-eight dead and 394 wounded (apart from the thousand-odd who fell victim to 'fever'): the Ashanti lost over 3,000 in dead alone. Their antiquated firearms, in which odds and ends of scrap metal and small stones were dropped on to loose powder, proved no match at all for the army's modern breech-loaders, as Wolseley had prophesied: even in the claustrophobic environs of the bush, the British Sniders proved devastating. As his army fell back, the messages from Kofi Karikari became almost pleading. The missionaries were released – and hastily began scribbling their memoirs – and the king, communicating with the inexorable British commander through a native missionary called Joseph Dawson, begged His Excellency to halt the advance.

Stanley was dubious about the long-term advantage of occupying Kumasi, though realizing that national 'honour' demanded it.

A score of valuable lives may be lost on the journey: half a million pounds sterling will be added to the expenditure but England's honour demands that the army shall enter Coomassie and go through the farce of taking possession. Hostages will be demanded, and probably a much larger number of ounces of gold than the king can ever pay will be imposed as a fine and the army will return to re-embark for home, having accomplished absolutely nothing for, in ten years or so, the Ashantees will

re-invade the Protectorate and the same anger and impotent wrath will be roused
just as fruitlessly as before.

It proved a remarkably exact forecast.

The British expedition – consisting of 118 officers and 1,044 men
supported by 449 African troops – entered Kumasi at 5.30 p.m. on 4
February 1874. It was an anti-climax, disconcerting in its unexpectedness.
The king himself had retired from the city, taking with him the mystical
Golden Stool that was the symbol of the Ashanti nation, though the city
itself was full of armed men. But these same warriors, who had so bitterly
disputed the British advance, bravely enduring the enemy's infinitely
superior firepower, now calmly accepted their arrival in the tribal capital as
though they were so many tourists. Wolseley was in a dilemma: to have
attempted to disarm some 5,000 men would almost certainly have led to an
explosion. But to leave matters as they were, with Kofi Karikari lurking in
the bush, would be simply to postpone the problem. In an uncharacteristic
show of indecision, he temporized, sending a reproachful envoy to the king,
urging him to come to Kumasi and discuss the matter, then settling down
for the night as though he was in his own headquarters. And when the army
awoke in the morning it was to find the city virtually deserted, the thousands
of armed men having quietly melted into the night.

It was his biggest mistake, in Stanley's opinion:

Had Sir Garnet taken the precaution to set a cordon of guards around the city at
each end of the street with strict orders to allow the entry of every Ashantee who
desired to come in, but on no account to permit one man to depart with his weapons,
Sir Garnet would have enhanced his success without a doubt. . . . Not one weapon
should have left Coomassie, nor even one sword or sheath knife, nor anything of the
value of a farthing or half a farthing, until the king had submitted himself wholly to
the mercy of the conqueror.

But though the king might have escaped, his capital and his palace were
alike in the hands of the conqueror. Stanley, like most of the expeditionary
force, was much impressed with Kumasi: the size of the city, some three and
a half miles in circumference, its cleanliness and order. There was one
jarring note, the awful execution site upon which Bowdich had remarked
over sixty years before:

A narrow footpath led into this grove, and now the foul smells became so suffocating
that we were glad to produce our handkerchiefs to prevent the intolerable and
almost palpable odour from mounting into the brain and overpowering us. It was
almost impossible to stop longer than to take a general view of the great Golgotha.

We saw some thirty or forty decapitated bodies in the last stages of corruption, and countless skulls which lay piled in heaps and scattered over a wide extent.

This evidence of human sacrifice, later substantiated by Kofi's executioner who said simply that he had lost count of the number of people he had killed over the previous weeks of crisis, became a useful propaganda weapon.

The following day, 5 February, Wolseley waited in vain for the return of the king. A violent rainstorm burst over the city in the late afternoon and the situation of the 'conquerors' was distinctly unenviable. Kumasi was obviously untenable and Wolseley prepared to evacuate it. But before the British left, he intended that there should be some financial compensation: he therefore gave orders that the palace should be ransacked of every object of value.

The palace was an immense building. Brackenbury, the Military Secretary, estimated that 1,000 men could easily have been quartered within it. Stanley had already taken an inventory of the extraordinary collection of objects that were piled in disorder in the domestic quarters, a collection which gave the impression that the contents of a suburban house in Croydon had been mixed with the trappings of a sultan's palace. There was a copy of the London *Times* of 17 October 1843 – thirty-one years old – and, for some extraordinary reason, a copy of the provincial *Bristol Courier* of the same date. There was a 'portrait of a gentleman', numerous English engravings, Kidderminster carpets and porcelain and chinaware, as well as what might reasonably be expected to be found in the palace of a savage potentate.

Brackenbury, as Military Secretary, had the responsibility of supervising the work of the prize agents and he leaves a vivid account in his memoirs. The storm that had broken that afternoon still rumbled and crashed overhead, with tremendous gusts of rain beating on the thatched roof. They had only four candles and it was by this flickering, uncertain light that the plunder of the Ashanti regalia was undertaken. The men worked in haste, ripping open boxes, taking only the most obviously valuable such as:

those gold masks whose object it is so difficult to divine, made of pure gold hammered into shape. One of these, weighing more than forty-one ounces, represented a ram's head and the others the face of savage men, about half the size of life. Box after box was opened and its contents hastily examined, the more valuable ones being kept and the others left. Aggrey beads and coral ornaments of various descriptions were heaped together in boxes and calabashes. Silver plate was carried off, and doubtless much left behind. Swords, gorgeous ammunition belts, caps mounted in solid gold, knives set in gold and silver, bags of gold dust and nuggets; carved stools mounted in silver, calabashes worked in silver and gold, silks embroidered and woven, were all passed in review. The sword presented by her Majesty to the king was found and carried off: and thousands of things were left behind that would be worth fabulous sums in cabinets at home.

The prize agents were working to a deadline, for even while they were ransacking the treasure chambers, sappers were laying mines around the palace. Wolseley had determined to destroy both city and palace before retreating, and this was accomplished. The army left shortly after daybreak at 6 a.m.: two hours later the sappers went to work. Brackenbury witnessed the destruction of Kumasi:

The town burnt furiously, all these three days of rain failing in any way to impede the progress of the devouring element. The thick thatched roofs of the houses, dry as tinder except just on the outside, blazed as though they had been ready prepared for the bonfire, and the flames ran down the framework that supported the mud walls. Slowly, huge dense columns of smoke curled up to the sky, and the lighted fragments of thatch drifting far and wide upon the wind showed the King of Ashantee, and all his subjects, that the white man never failed to keep his word.

The army made its way with extreme difficulty to the coast. In his letter to the Secretary of State for the Colonies, Wolseley claimed that his difficulties had been caused by the freakish storms, but in a caustic note Stanley remarked: 'The real cause of our panic-like departure from Coomassie was want of food, which the General's inattention to the Transport and Control Department caused.'

And back in what passed for civilization, the Expeditionary Force turned to the liquidation of its assets – changing into cash the treasures taken from the palace. The sum raised was just £5,000. Even allowing for nineteenth-century money values, this cannot possibly represent either the loot taken from the palace, or that which is at present in the Museum of Mankind. Stanley was of the opinion that the failure to police Coomassie on that critical first night cost the expedition dear:

It is certain that much valuable plunder was taken from Coomassie during the night. Assistant-Commissary Ravenscroft, while looking for gin to supply the troops with 'grog', stumbled upon a house whose courtyard was crowded with objects of value. In the morning, when he visited the house again, he found the whole had been carried away.

This may well have been so. But it is just as likely that the looters were members of the Expedition, following the soldier's time-honoured right of 'liberating' property, to use the sardonic World War II term. Indirect confirmation of this is provided by a newspaper report in 1976. A gold headband of Ashanti workmanship came on the market: 'It had been stolen by a Lieutenant Frederick Cowan of the Royal Welch Fusiliers. He found it in the king's dressing room in the palace.' Put up for auction by Cowan's descendants, it fetched $6,000. Wolseley acted completely honourably, bidding for items that he wanted in open auction. 'I had set my heart upon a bronze group of about fifty little figures representing the King of Ashanti being carried in state and had asked one of my staff to bid £6 for it. It went for £100.'

In 1971 Lord Montagu of Beaulieu raised, in the House of Lords, the question of the return of the Ashanti regalia which he described as having been removed as 'war booty'. The Under Secretary of State for Foreign Affairs took exception to the harsh term: 'My lords, perhaps the term "booty" is not appropriate. This is part of an indemnity which was agreed by the former King of Ashanti.' Technically, he was correct. In making his report on the campaign, and describing the terms he finally agreed with Kofi Karikari, Wolseley had said:

I thought it very doubtful whether the whole of the money [the 50,000 ounces of gold originally demanded] will ever be obtained by Her Majesty's government but as the payment of a few thousand pounds cannot be a matter of relatively so great importance, I have caused the wording of this clause to be carefully so framed as to be clear that the money is only to be paid in such instalments, and at such times as Her Majesty may direct. The whole question of the money will thus be open for solution in any way HMG may think fit.

The solution was ultimately found by simply ignoring the problem. The king actually paid over 1,000 ounces of gold – worth around £4,000 – and this, together with the £5,000 raised by auction, appears to have been the entire sum extracted from the Ashanti – a sum which has to be set against the campaign's estimated cost of £1 million. Wolseley appears to have been uneasily aware that, had he put pressure upon the king, he might have increased the amount paid: 'I thought it exceedingly probable that additional pressure might have induced them to pay the larger sum, but I consider the main point was to obtain the treaty of peace and that the money being important chiefly as a proof of complete submission, the quantity actually now paid was of comparatively secondary importance.' The British government was therefore owed the difference between the £9,000 raised and the £200,000 originally demanded: in this sense, therefore, the Under Secretary of State's definition of the regalia as 'indemnity' is legally correct.

But the regalia is more than a collection of objects of precious metal. As Lord Montagu put it, 'Are Her Majesty's Government aware of the very deep feelings of the Ashanti people about the return of these sacrosanct

Golden head from the Ashanti regalia, taken by the British during the 1874 punitive expedition and today in the Wallace Collection in London.

THE VIOLENT ROAD TO THE GOLD OF ASHANTI

The young T. E. Bowdich gave news of extravagant Ashanti ceremonies (*bottom*). Henry Morton Stanley – enjoying worldwide fame after his encounter with Livingstone – reported on the Kumasi campaign (*left*, the burning of Kumasi). *The Graphic* bluntly described the auctioning of the treasures as 'The sale of loot' (*below left*), while a late nineteenth-century photograph (*below*) reveals a casually dominant British officer in the presence of the Ashanti ruler.

ASHANTI HERITAGE

In February 1982 the Museum of Mankind in London staged a spectacular exhibition in which the British relationship with Ashanti – now a part of Ghana – was traced from the beginning. Gold was much in evidence – here a sword with gold handle (*left*), a hat with gold decorations (*opposite below*), and the gold finial of a royal Ashanti umbrella (*above*). The sheer mass of gold ornaments worn on formal occasions is well displayed in the procession (*opposite above*).

WHO 'STOLE' THE STONE OF SCONE?

For nearly 700 years after the English king, Edward I, removed it from Scotland the Stone of Scone lay in Westminster Abbey – set into the coronation chair (*below left*) on which Queen Elizabeth II sits at her own coronation (*below right*). After its disappearance at Christmas 1950, it was eventually found wrapped in the flag of Scotland at Arbroath Abbey (*opposite*) and returned to London after its 'holiday' – just too late to be seen by Scots football supporters outside Westminster Abbey (*right*). Some say that the 'real' Stone remains in Scotland.

(*left*) Charles IV, the last Habsburg Emperor, wearing the Crown of St Stephen with its distinctive bent cross. The Emperor abdicated on 12 November 1918. The Empress Zita (shown with him) refused to renounce her imperial claims and went into exile. More than sixty years were to pass before she returned to Austria (in 1982) to visit the grave of her daughter. The travels of the Crown itself finally came to an end when it was returned to Hungary by the USA in 1978 (*below*).

objects – which are supposed to contain the soul of the whole people?' And it is at this point that the European observer enters very deep and disturbed waters indeed. William Fagg, doyen of African art historians, in an article in *The Connoisseur*, warns against any facile attempt to make value judgments on African religions, the Ashanti in particular: 'The Ashanti soul is a highly complicated thing.' Malcolm McLeod, Director of the Museum of Mankind, in his book *The Asante*, enters a further caveat: 'The Asante freely acknowledge that many parts of their culture are understood only by particular groups within that culture.' Even more than their fellow Africans, the Ashanti think in terms of symbols. It was commonly assumed that the axes carried by Wolseley's sappers 'were to show that Ashanti would be cut down, and the spades indicated that Ashanti would be dug up'. The symbolism goes far beyond that currently used in Western lay society, more closely resembling the charged potency of, for example, the wafer in Catholic religion. The gold ornaments of the Ashanti regalia range from witty conversation pieces, based on local proverbs, to the massive breast-plates – commonly called 'soul-bearer's badges' – whose exact significance defies western interpretation.

It is probable that only a small proportion of the regalia now held by the Museum of Mankind came directly to the Museum as 'booty', most of it being obtained as gifts or on the open market as purchase. In *The Connoisseur* article, William Fagg traces the movements of one of these items. It is a soul-bearer's badge, 'one of the two largest and finest known'. Fagg believes that so fine a piece as this would have been brought home by Wolseley himself, but the first documentation referring to it is a commission given to the goldsmith and jeweller Robert Garrard by the third Marquess of Exeter in 1874 to design a suitable setting for the badge. Garrard came up with a magnificent silver-gilt dish, with the badge set in the centre, the Marquess's coat of arms and an unequivocal legend engraved on the base. 'The gold ornament in the centre of this dish is a portion of the indemnity paid by the Ashanti King Coffee Calcalli to Her Majesty's Forces under the command of Major-General Sir Garnet Wolseley, January 1874.' Sub-sequently the dish and badge passed to the family of Major-General Lord Cheylsmore, whose descendants sold it to the British Museum. The most spectacular piece of the regalia, a $7\frac{3}{4}$-inch-high golden head, described by Fagg as 'the largest gold work known from Ashanti or indeed from anywhere in Africa outside Egypt', came into the possession of the wealthy collector Sir Richard Wallace and is now in the publicly owned museum known as the Wallace Collection.

The psychological or spiritual significance of the regalia makes any possible question of its return a very special and thorny problem. The case for the return of the Elgin Marbles rests on a simple 'Yea or Nay'. If it is decided ever to return them, then only one people on earth have a legal and moral right to them – the Greeks. And there is only one place where they should be housed – on or near the Acropolis of the city of Athens.

But Ashanti today is part of a larger state, the Republic of Ghana, and Ghana consists of a number of distinct tribal entities. If the regalia is returned to the Asantehene's political successor, the Government of Ghana, then, reasonably, the Ashanti people would have a substantial grievance. But the return of the regalia, with its enormously powerful associations, to one tribal unit could very well cause a dangerous imbalance in a not particularly stable country. When I put the question to the non-Ashanti but Ghanaian editor of an African magazine, his reply was succinct: 'It would be fatal to give it to the Ashanti – it would simply bolster feudalism.'

The inescapable impression one receives is that, despite lip service to the idea of return, the Government of Ghana would be considerably embarrassed. During an early stage of investigation into the possibility or desirability of return I was fortunate enough to make contact with European friends of the Ashanti royal family and arrangements were begun for me to meet the Asantehene on his visit to London. Then, in London, I was told, 'You are treading on very dangerous ground'. It seemed a melodramatic assessment of what seemed to me, a European, a matter of purely historical interest, but whatever the significance of the remark, shortly afterwards my hopeful contact withered and died. When the Asantehene came to London to open the Museum of Mankind's exhibition, it was as a guest of the British Government and not of the Ghanaian. The office of the Ghanaian High Commission, indeed, denied any knowledge of his movements, although the High Commissioner attended the official opening.

But the office of the High Commission does not seem to be too well-informed about other Ashanti facts of life. In 1975 the deputy High Commissioner told the American journalist Michael Cope that the British Museum held the most sacred of all Ashanti pieces, the Golden Stool, which really does represent the soul of the nation and on whose behalf the Ashanti nearly went to war against Britain. During my own researches I, too, was told that the Museum held this sacrosanct object.

I asked the Museum of Mankind's Director, Malcolm McLeod, if this was the case. 'The Golden Stool has never been more than twenty miles from Kumasi', he said emphatically. Documentation substantiated his

The Ashanti king questions a missionary on his motives in wishing to visit Kumasi and receives an account of the power of the Gospel in answer.

remark, providing incidentally a corollary to the story which G. A. Henty would have loved.

Exactly as Stanley had prophesied, it proved necessary to send another expedition into Ashanti. This one took place in 1900 and was led by Sir Frederic Hodgson, KCMG, Governor of the Gold Coast, a blimpish character wholly different from the subtle, flexible Wolseley. Hodgson arrived in Kumasi after the reigning Asantehene had been deposed and exiled. He treated the assembled chiefs to a stern lecture, upbraiding them for the trouble they had given, reminding them that the 50,000 ounces of gold levied twenty-six years before still had not been paid. Then he turned to the question of the Golden Stool:

What must I do to the man, whoever he is, who has failed to give to the Queen, who is the paramount power in this country, the stool to which she is entitled? Where is the Golden Stool? Why am I not sitting on the Golden Stool at this moment? I am the representative of the paramount power: why have you relegated me this chair? Why did you not take the opportunity of my coming to Kumasi to bring the Golden Stool and give it to me to sit upon?

It is an indication of Sir Frederic Hodgson's ignorance of the customs of the country over which he now ruled that he was totally unaware that no human being had ever sat upon the Golden Stool. To have done so would have been a sacrilege as great as for a group of people to eat breakfast on the high altar at St Paul's. The chiefs, ignorant of his ignorance, took his demands as provocation and out of them arose the humiliating siege so vividly described by his wife.

The British had been seeking the Stool for over four years, ever since exiling the last Asantehene, correctly divining that it represented a core of resistance, but ignorant of the fact that it represented not simply a throne, but a bond between the living, the dead and those yet unborn. Hodgson's private secretary, a certain Captain John Armitage, had been given the task of following up local rumours and finding the Stool. In yet another of the many memoirs that originated from the Ashanti Wars, Armitage tells the story in detail. A local youth, Esumi by name, claimed to know the whereabouts of the Stool and Armitage, with a company of Hausas, set off with the youth as guide:

The track along which we wound was scarcely discernible, and led us through the deepest recesses of the forest. Even the Hausas and the usually noisy carriers were overawed by the silence. Not a leaf stirred, and our party seemed to walk as noiselessly as possible, as if afraid of disturbing an unseen foe. When the coughing bark of some large ape broke the stillness, everyone started involuntarily. For over three hours, we marched silently in single file until we suddenly entered a large clearing planted with banana and plantain and cocoa, while nestling in the centre were three small huts which had evidently not been occupied for some time. Here, according to our guide, under the flooring of the huts, lay the Golden Stool.

They found nothing: involuntarily or otherwise, their guide had led them into an ambush from which they barely escaped with their lives. For over four months – from March until their break-out in July – Hodgson and his company, including the sprightly Lady Hodgson, were besieged in Kumasi. The Ashanti Wars ended, inevitably, with the country being formally annexed. Nothing further was heard of the Golden Stool until 1920, when pieces of it began to appear for sale. The perpetrators were a group of villagers who had discovered the whereabouts of the Stool and, persuading themselves that it was the black, wooden Stool that was sacred, not its golden ornaments, decided to make their fortune. The entire nation went into mourning when the sacrilege was discovered and there is little doubt that the villagers would have been executed had it not been for the colonial government. They were, instead, exiled and the remains of the Stool placed in the Royal Mausoleum, later to be incorporated into a new Stool.

The Golden Stool of Ashanti, supreme symbol of a people's identity, has therefore never left Ashanti. But the power of the regalia, and the reality of a monarchy within a modern republic, was most vividly demonstrated during that official opening of the Ashanti Exhibition at the Museum of Mankind in February 1981. The Asantehene attended in full ceremonial, preceded by an advance party which included his gun-bearers and the 'linguists' – officials bearing ceremonial staffs who are at once the mouthpiece and interpreter of the king. That the King of Ashanti should be welcomed by a member of the British Royal Family – in this instance, the Duke of Gloucester – and high-ranking officials from the Commonwealth Office, was a matter of protocol – although also indicating the British acceptance of Ashanti self-valuation. But the spontaneous welcome by the British community of Ashanti Ghanaians had nothing to do with protocol. For an evening, the rather bleak rooms of the Museum of Mankind became an outpost of Africa, a brilliant swirling of coloured robes in complex dances, a tremendous cacophony of drums, a glitter of gold on dark skins that T. E. Bowdich, the first European to venture into its heartland, would have recognized more than a century and a half later.

4

The Stone of Scone

'Oh, they got away with the – – –
And took it away up North'

Radio comedy programme *Take It
From Here*, 1951

Traditionally, the deadest, dullest period for newspapers in England is the
day immediately following the Christmas holidays. For two days the nation
has retreated behind its front doors, turning in on itself to celebrate the
family festival that excludes every one and everything outside the circle of
immediate friends and neighbours. 'Christmas Day is the day I would chose
to invade Britain', a newspaper sub-editor caustically remarked. 'We
wouldn't know anything about it until December 27.'

In 1950, the Scots still maintained a separate pattern of public holidays
from the English, taking off New Year's Day as a public holiday, but enjoying
only Christmas Day as a holiday, going to work on that Boxing Day which
had become sacrosanct to their Saxon neighbours. On 26 December 1950,
therefore, the later editions of Scottish newspapers were able to scoop, by a
full twenty-four hours, their mighty southern rivals in what was the biggest
domestic news story since the ending of the War. The Stone of Scone, that
had lain in Westminster Abbey for 665 years, had been stolen in the early
hours of Christmas morning. Stolen? 'Recovered, not *stolen*', insisted the
Glasgow Bulletin, and this was to be the leitmotif of the controversy over the
next four months.

As England came out of its surfeit of food and drink, so its newspapers
made up for lost time. *The Times*, still the authentic voice of the English
upper classes, thundered in its traditional manner: 'Sacrilege at Westminster: a coarse and vulgar crime.' 'Is nothing sacred?', whimpered the *Daily
Mail*. 'The King Greatly Distressed', announced the *Manchester Guardian*

and published a plea from the Dean of Westminster, Dr Don – himself a Scot – denouncing 'this squalid deed . . . a senseless crime carefully planned and carried out with great cunning'.

The BBC, which under the direction of John Reith was to the ear what *The Times* was to the eye, handed down an edict to its staff from Sinai: no reference was to be made to the matter save through the authorized news channels. Frank Muir and Denis Norden, scriptwriters of the brilliant comedy programme *Take It From Here*, regarded the edict as a challenge. There was currently circulating a popular song whose theme was never disclosed but was signified by three thumps of a drum, thus:

> Get out of here with the (boom, boom, boom)
> Before I call the cops

Muir and Norden, determined to get in a topical reference to the story that was shaking the British Empire, juggled with the song and came up with the version heading this chapter. It brought the house down: their audience loved it. The two young scriptwriters far better expressed the mood of the English to the audacious act than all the sub-editors in Fleet Street. The English did indeed think it was a lark, no more. Hindsight gives a rather different picture. Looking back it is possible to see that, though the motives of the four young people who moved the Stone were idealistic and their actions were not only harmless but brought much-needed relief into gloom-filled public affairs, the removal of the Stone marks a moment of change in the domestic affairs of Britain. Hereafter, increasingly, minorities realized that the best way to draw their case to public attention was by acting in a bizarre – or, if necessary, violent – manner. The removal of the Stone of Scone in 1950, and the setting off of firebombs in Wales in the 1970s are separated by time, not by logic.

The object known variously as the Coronation Stone, the Stone of Scone or, for the more romantic, the Stone of Destiny, possesses no financial value whatsoever. It is a roughly rectangular block of coarse-grained, reddish sandstone, geologically similar to that which occurs in the district of Perthshire in Scotland. It weighs about 450 lbs and on each end of it are iron rings which are evidently located to enable a pole to be passed through and so make it easier to carry. King Edward I inserted a plate in it which bore the following legend:

> Ni fallat fatum, Scoti hunc quoqunque locatum
> Inveniunt lapidem regnare tenentur ibidem

99

Anyone who has experienced the cavernous echoes set up when a large object is moved in a church must find it remarkable that a door could have been broken, and a 450 lb lump of rock dragged over a hundred feet without disturbing either the watchman or the police outside. But even odder things were to transpire.

The first official comments were decidedly tight-lipped. The police confirmed that the Stone had been wrenched out of the woodwork of the Chair, causing some damage in the process. The letters JFS had been freshly scratched into the old gilt on the front of the Chair and it was conjectured that these stood for Justice for Scotland. Rumours circulated that a wrist watch had been found. Attempts had been made to take fingerprints from the Chair, but these proved useless because of the habit of people touching or stroking the Chair 'for superstitious reasons'. The police were looking for a Ford Anglia, with a man and a woman 'speaking with a Scottish accent'. And a warning was given that England's own coronation stone had been threatened by Scottish zealots.

It is to be doubted that one Englishman in a thousand knew that he possessed his own coronation stone. But he did, in the shape of a massive lump of dark granite, supported on a mock Gothic plinth, in a sad little public garden in Kingston, Surrey. Although it cannot compare in historical continuity with the Stone of Scone, it is of very respectable antiquity, at least three Saxon kings having been crowned upon it at King's Stone upon Thames. A police guard was placed upon it but for only a short period, the total English indifference to their own heritage killing at birth any Scottish plans there might have existed to wreak vengeance upon the Saxon stone.

Meanwhile, across the border, opinion was polarizing. Official Scotland condemned the act, or tried to play it down. James Fergusson, Scotland's Keeper of Records, went on record with: 'In Scotland, its presence in Westminster Abbey has not in modern times been regarded with the irritation alleged in some quarters today, and expressed last Christmas Eve by what English law regards as burglary and sacrilege.' The General Assembly of the Church of Scotland decided to delete all reference to the Stone in the record of its debates. And the Lord Provost of Perth, in whose jurisdiction lay the ancient sacring site of the Stone, condemned the outrage 'in the name of Scotland'.

But political Scotland was having a field day. Hector Hughes, MP for Aberdeen North, raised doubts about the authenticity of the relic in Westminster Abbey. 'Many antiquarians believe that it is a mere imitation and that the real Stone of Destiny lies buried in Scone Abbey.' It was a subtle attack which was to be used many times over the following years. John McCormick, chairman of the Scottish Covenant Committee and Lord Rector of Glasgow University – a hotbed of Scottish Nationalism – turned to history for justification. 'The Treaty of Northampton expressly stipulated its return – but the treaty was never observed.' Miss Wendy Wood, a leading Scottish Nationalist, ran up the Lion Rampant on the flagpole in her cottage garden and sent off a telegram of protest to the Inspector of Police in Scotland, demanding that he correct the Scotland Yard description of the act of restoration as theft. Sales of Compton Mackenzie's book *The North Wind of Love* soared: published in 1944, it contained a lively fictional account of a hijacking of the Stone of Destiny. At a crowded meeting of the Scottish National Congress Committee in Glasgow a Dr Mary Ramsay assured her audience that the police would never solve the mystery, for they were trained to track down criminals, not patriots. She also referred mockingly to a bizarre element that had entered the story. A Dutch clairvoyant had informed the police that five people had taken part in the raid. 'I would like to say that he is mistaken in that number. There were accessories before the fact, and there were accessories after the fact. The Nationalists have been discussing ways and means of removing the Stone for years.' A Mr Oliver Brown rose to warn Prime Minister Attlee that he was playing with a most dangerous situation: 'Remember the Boston Tea Party which everyone laughed at at the beginning. Never despise things with small beginnings.'

And outside on that cold January night, somewhere between Edinburgh and Perth, two young policemen promised each other that, should they have the good fortune to stop the car carrying the Stone, 'we would show them the safest way to Perth'.

In July 1981 I wrote to the *Glasgow Herald*, canvassing the opinion of its readers regarding this now historical action. Looking back did they, on the whole, regard the affair as the 'undergraduate prank' with which most of its opponents dismissed it, or as a nascent act of Scottish nationalism. A teacher in Ayrshire scoffed at the idea that the act had any significance. 'I was teaching a primary school when the Stone of Scone disappeared. On Fridays we had a regular "News Discussion" and the children displayed cuttings from daily papers chosen for their importance and interest. A vote was taken on which item was the most important to all of us. Not one pupil voted the Stone of Scone as important.' A retired police officer from Lanarkshire indirectly substantiated that – but bitterly: 'It would be true to say that a number of Scots looked upon the affair as a student prank, but they were people who through ignorance knew nothing of the existence of the "Stone". It would be true to say that their ignorance was caused by the lack of teaching in Scottish schools of Scottish history.' That remark was repeated by others in various forms. '*Our* history didn't begin in 1066 – but you wouldn't think so if you read our textbooks. Everything – but everything – is looked at from the viewpoint of London.'

It was the Lanarkshire police officer who provided me with the information of the pact between himself and his colleague. 'On the instruction of Special Branch the main road from the south to Perth was to be manned during night-time at all junctions with a view to stopping and searching cars. On the first night of many, when my mate and I were discussing just what we as Scots were doing, we shook hands and swore that if we did stop the car with the Stone we would wish the driver luck and advise him the safest way to Perth.' The writer emphasized that he was not a Scottish Nationalist but simply 'an indignant Scot' and claimed that all the police officers with whom he subsequently discussed the matter had stated that they, too, would have acted in the same manner by turning the classical blind eye.

By the end of the month, every well-known Scottish Nationalist had been turned over by the police. The Lanarkshire officer describes an operation which involved the redoubtable Wendy Wood – and incidentally clearly demonstrates the 'Spirit of '45' romanticism which imbued the whole affair.

Wendy knew nothing of the plot, and did not know who was involved but realized that she would be strongly suspected and that her home in Edinburgh would be under constant surveillance. By arrangement with a friend, the skipper of a small coastal vessel, she boarded his ship late at night and set sail from Leith. The voyage round the north of Scotland and through the Western Isles lasted for several days during which time they were shadowed by several ships of the Royal Navy under Special Branch instruction.

Wendy finally landed in darkness on a lonely beach in Wester Ross and made her way to an isolated croft which was raided by the police and army late at night. Wendy kept up her act, and by giving evasive answers kept them chasing all over the Scottish Highlands in a state of utter confusion.

Whatever might be the attitude of the English people, those who directed their lives had very evidently been touched upon the raw and the hunt was on. One of those pulled in for questioning was Ian Hamilton, a young Glasgow law student. His interrogators were unaware that the diary in his waistcoat pocket contained some rather interesting information concerning the interior arrangements of Westminster Abbey, the position of the Stone and the time of police patrols. While waiting to be interrogated, under cover of a newspaper he obliterated the evidence with a moistened finger. After questioning he was allowed to go.

On the evening of 30 December the advertisement clerk in the offices of the *Scottish Daily Record* in Glasgow found the usual pile of replies to advertisements waiting his attention. Working his way steadily through the mail, he came eventually to a small envelope whose contents differed from the rest. They consisted of two copies of a lengthy document, rather grandly described as a Petition to the King, which was cast in terms of what can only be described as fulsome loyalty. 'The petition of certain of His Majesty's most loyal and obedient subjects to His Majesty King George the Sixth humbly sheweth: that His Majesty's petitioners are the persons who removed the Stone of Destiny from Westminster Abbey.' Identifying themselves by describing the watch that had been left in the Abbey, the petitioners outlined their conditions for the Stone's return, of which the central condition was: 'if His Majesty would graciously assure them that in all time coming the stone will remain in Scotland in such of His Majesty's property or otherwise as shall be deemed fitting by him.'

His Majesty did not offer this gracious assurance and, after what must have been an embarrassing period of silence, the petitioners made their next move. On 31 January an anonymous caller telephoned newspaper offices in Edinburgh, saying that news of the Stone of Scone had been nailed to the door of St Giles's Cathedral. This dramatic emulation of Martin Luther fell somewhat flat. Reporters found a crumpled typewritten sheet of paper on the top step of the west door, from which it had evidently fallen. With a note of what seems like desperation, the petitioners now addressed themselves to the Scottish nation as a whole, as represented by the Scottish National Assembly, offering to return the Stone to England, or to retain it in Scotland according to the will of the Assembly. And again, as identification, the writers offered another snippet of information regarding the events of the Christmas morning: 'One of our number was ejected from Westminster Abbey by the watchman, half an hour after the Abbey was closed. Our associate's name was John . . .' The implication that the Abbey's watchman had actually had his hand on one of the conspirators seemed something straight out of a novel by John Buchan. But the police, in a laconic statement in which hindsight can read a tinge of embarrassment, confirmed that 'a man had been on the Abbey premises shortly after closing time on December 23 and was escorted from the building by the caretaker or night watchman'. Did this man, readers must have wondered, also speak 'with a Scottish accent'?

Whether or not he did, nothing developed from the dramatic revelations. The story sank into the background, the British public turning its attention to its chronic economic crisis, the savagely escalating war in Korea, the increasing coldness of the Cold War with Soviet Russia. The news that the police were about to make an arrest in connection with the unauthorized removal of the Stone of Scone was buried, in those newspapers which noticed it at all, in a couple of paragraphs. No arrest was, in fact, made and, in the second week of April, the matter ended on a note of anti-climax. Scottish police were informed that the Stone was to be found in Arbroath Abbey.

The return of the Stone of Destiny to Westminster Abbey was conducted in the same low-key, almost shamefaced manner that had throughout distinguished the attitude of officialdom. Flickering national interest had flared up again on news of the discovery of the Stone, and reporters from most of the national papers converged on Glasgow. In a smartly executed operation involving a dummy run, the police put off the track both reporters and members of the Scottish Nationalist organization who had threatened to wreck the car carrying the Stone. Reporters who managed to follow the real convoy of three cars were stopped some twenty miles outside Glasgow and the police convoy arrived unobtrusively at Westminster Abbey shortly after 8 p.m. on the following night. Only members of the official party were allowed access to the building, a police inspector turning would-be spectators aside with a brusque, 'This is private property. No outsiders allowed in.' The information that the great Abbey of Westminster, the very heart of the then-British Empire, was private property must have come as a considerable surprise to a number of people.

In the days following the return of the Stone there was considerable speculation in legal circles regarding the likelihood of a prosecution. As James Fergusson had pointed out, two English laws had been violated – that relating to sacrilege and that relating to burglary. But discussions between the Cabinet Office and the Attorney-General brought a sensible decision: there would be no prosecution, not even for the clearly provable offence of forcing the Abbey door with a jemmy. And with that assurance came the first authentic account of the events of the night and early morning of 24 and 25 December, told by the leader of the party, Ian Hamilton, to a Glasgow representative of the *Daily Telegraph* newspaper. From this interview, and from subsequent articles in the popular press written by Hamilton himself, it is possible to fill in the gaps in the story of what must be, off the playing field, the last Anglo-Scottish confrontation in history.

Hamilton was the 'John' referred to in the pronouncement that had been nailed up on the door of St Giles's Cathedral. He had indeed been discovered in the Abbey – but on the night before the successful attempt. 'If the opportunity had been ripe then we would have taken the Stone.' But the opportunity was not ripe. In a scene that might have come from contemporary British film comedy, the caretaker apparently mistook him for a down-and-out seeking shelter, gave him a handout but firmly escorted him from the building. He and his companions returned the following night to make their second, successful attempt.

Hamilton had conceived the plan when visiting London the previous September. He returned in October to make a careful survey of the pattern of movements in and around the Abbey, in particular checking the time of police patrols. Back in Scotland, he recruited three other young Scottish patriots – Gavin Vernon, a 24-year-old engineering student, Alan Stuart, another student aged just 20, and Katrina Matheson, a 22-year-old science teacher. She was recruited on a simple, but brilliant piece of reasoning: a party which included a personable young woman would less likely be suspected of nefarious intentions than a group consisting of three young men only.

It is a measure of how much customs have blurred under internationalizing pressure in the intervening decades that Hamilton chose Christmas Eve for the attempt; then Scots and English placed quite different values on the festival. 'We had decided that the night before Christmas was likely to be the most suitable, since at that time the English people would be celebrating their Festival.' It was in the early hours of Christmas morning, when all but a few unfortunates were wrapped in the bosom of their families, that the three men broke into the Abbey, leaving Katrina Matheson in the car outside. The Stone, according to Hamilton, was in two pieces when taken out of the Chair, a fact which made manhandling much easier but was to add immensely to their problems. Hamilton carried the smaller piece out to the car, leaving it to his companions to bring the larger piece. But his piece had barely been placed in the car when a policeman approached and admonished them for being in a 'no parking' area. This was the moment when Katrina Matheson's presence proved of incalculable value, the luckless policeman assuming that they were merely a courting couple: it was presumably from this officer that Scotland Yard received its first information that they were looking for 'a man and a woman with a Scottish accent'.

The two pieces of Stone did not cross the Border, and were not brought together, until nearly three weeks later. Katrina Matheson immediately drove north, leaving her part of the Stone in Birmingham, before carrying on home to Scotland. Hamilton and his two companions dumped the larger piece in a wood in Kent, and it was not until mid-January that he returned with Stuart to pick up both pieces and bring them to Scotland. There, they were repaired and confided to the care of John McCormick while attempts were made to stir the blood of Scotsmen by placing the Stone in Arbroath Abbey.

Our aim was to try and have the Stone brought out into the open for at least a month. We were certain that if it remained for even that short period the Scottish people would be able to demonstrate their affection for it and it would never thereafter leave Scotland. We had hoped that the police would not come between the people of Scotland and the Church when we placed it in the sanctuary of Arbroath Abbey.

There was never an opportunity to establish whether or not Scotsmen would have risen in defence of their heritage, for the police, placing less value on the code of sanctuary than did Hamilton, had no compunction about entering the Abbey and removing the Stone, returning it to its 600-year-old temporary home in England's capital.

But was it *the* Stone? Was it the Stone of Destiny that Kenneth MacAlpin had taken from the Picts and that Edward I, Hammer of the Scots, had taken from the Scots? Or was it a clever substitute? The doubts skilfully raised by the MP for Aberdeen North have multiplied in the interim. The Lanarkshire police officer summed up the matter for me:

During the transportation to Scotland the 'Stone' was slightly damaged, a piece being broken off. On arrival in Glasgow it was taken to the premises of the late Charles Gray, a monumental sculptor, for repair. Charles Gray was at this time an ardent nationalist. While at the premises Mr Gray made several copies of the 'Stone' and up until his death three years ago he would never deny or confirm that the 'real' stone was the one sent back to Westminster. I still like to think that the real Stone is in Scotland.

I received indirect, but anonymous, confirmation of this in the form of a telephone call. The caller refused to identify himself. He had gone to some trouble to track down my telephone number and, speaking with only a trace of accent, which may or may not have been Scottish, referred to my letter in the *Herald* and asked rhetorically, 'What makes you think the original is back in England?'

The last, and certainly the wittiest, word is best left to an anonymous Scotsman writing to the *Manchester Guardian* on 27 December 1950:

Dinna tak on sae aboot the Stane o' Scone. Nae doot the chiels wha hae grippit it are richt bad laddies and, nae doot, they'll soon be ta'en and pit in the talbooth. But man, can ye no see a jook? Whit for a' the lang-nebbit words you set doon in your paper the morn? 'Stupid' 'Ill-conditioned' 'humourless' Man – it's you that are humourless. We hae na had sic a laugh since Bannockburn. We Scots hae been vexed ower lang by English misrule and the reiving o the Stane is jist yin mair sign to show it.

Sae you dinna think much o' this 'miserable piece of Scottish stone' anyway. You would rather have your ain wee bit 'magic' – the Saxon King's Stone at Kingston-on-Thames. Man, dinna fash yerself or look sae solemn – you can hae it. I've aye speired why, efter we Scots hae builded the Empire – India, Burma and ither lands in foreign parts – you English had to make sic a mess o' them. Efter reading the silly, thrawn bit about the stane in your paper, I ken noo.

But the joke is, perhaps, upon the witty Scotsman, for he is writing from a town in southern England – 'In Partibus Infidelium' as he signs himself, bringing to mind perhaps yet another quotation: 'Sir, the finest sight a Scotsman can see is the road to England.'

5

The Crown of St Stephen

'The Hungarian crown should under no circumstances
be handed over to Hungary, but should find its way to
Rome to the Holy Father.'

ROHRACH, *Archbishop of Salzburg*

'It is with a genuine sense of pride that I am able to
return to the people of Hungary this priceless treasure
which the United States has been privileged to shelter.'

JIMMY CARTER, *President of the
USA*

In November 1944 the Red Army was less than ten miles from Budapest,
capital of Hungary. Within the great city was being enacted a scenario that
took place, as the war approached its end, in every city that had been under
the dominance of Nazi Germany: those who had been victims were now
preparing to be masters and those who had been masters were looking to
their skins – and seeing what could be salvaged from the débacle.

In Budapest railway station, towards the end of the month, a train
consisting mostly of goods wagons was being made up. The goods were
decidedly unusual: among them were documents, jewels, gold, historical
manuscripts, share certificates – in short, the treasury of the Hungarian
nation. In the heterogeneous collection was a massive black trunk, securely
locked. It was brought under heavy guard, for this trunk contained not only,
literally, a king's ransom in precious metals and jewels, but also an object
which a sixteenth-century Hungarian jurist defined as the sole fount of
Hungarian legal authority, the thousand-year-old crown of St Stephen. The
train pulled out – carrying with it, among a few other favoured personnel,

the Nazi puppet premier of Hungary, Ferenc Szalasi. Thirty-four years were to pass before the crown returned to Budapest, a generation during which it disappeared completely from public view, became the centre of an international controversy, was transformed into a rallying point for Hungarian refugees, and finally turned up, mysteriously, on the other side of the world.

Stephen, the first Christian king of Hungary, was canonized only a few years after his death in 1045. The eleventh-century concept of sanctity would seem to have been strictly technical. This same St Stephen, upon whose feast Good King Wenceslas annually looks out, was known to have disposed of a political opponent by first blinding him, then pouring molten lead into his ear. But there were special reasons why Pope Sylvester II, who sent him a crown to ratify his assumption of the monarchy, should overlook such peccadillos. The conversion of the savage Hungarians to Christianity would place a shield between western Europe and the Asiatic tribes to the east. And the acceptance of the gift of monarchy from the hands of the pope would give that pope immense prestige in the endless jockeying for power between pope and emperor.

And on his side, King Stephen of Hungary also had excellent reasons to be grateful for the gift of a valuable, but not particularly attractive piece of ceremonial headgear. Pope Sylvester II was widely reputed to be a magician. He had ascended the papal throne in the year 999. Most Christians expected the world to end, with the second coming of Christ, in the millennium, the year AD 1000. Lawyers had even evolved an opening formula for wills: 'Seeing that the world is about to come to an end. . . .' The fact that it did not end the following year produced a universal sense of relief, together with a sense of awe towards those who had guided the planet away from a fate which, though in theory spiritually desirable, most people were anxious to postpone. The fact that Sylvester was a scholar was not particularly important in this context: Europe was full of scholars balancing angels on the point of a pin, debating the precise location of heaven and hell. In twentieth-century terms Sylvester would have been described as an engineer with an interest in astronomy, a combination which was so far out of the common experience as inevitably to lead first to the rumour, and finally the belief, that he had gained the Throne of St Peter, and maintained his position there, by the Black Arts. Deplorable though this might seem to a Christian, it gave a very potent significance to his actions and motives. It is hardly surprising that the Hungarians, but one remove from savagery, should believe that the crown worn by their king possessed occult powers.

Legally, the Crown of St Stephen granted the country a curious and dangerous independence. Situated on the border between east and west, it should have come under the suzerainty of either the Eastern Roman Emperor, with his seat in Constantinople, or the Western Roman Emperor, with his seat in Germany or Austria. By receiving the crown from the Pope, Stephen placed himself and his descendants under the suzerainty of the Pope – a skilful move for, at that distance from Italy, the power of the papacy was expressed mostly in exhortations and, at worst, anathemas.

But Sylvester's act also gave an extraordinary significance to the Crown itself – the physical crown, not simply the symbolic act. Over the next nine centuries, Hungary, set so uneasily between two worlds, reeled from one to the other – now under the dominance of Angevins, now Turks, now Austrians, now a monarchy, now a republic. As the nation went through these phantasmagoric political changes so the metal skull-cap with its cross became the sole symbol of political constancy. So much so that, in 1514, the jurist Stephan Werbocozi formulated the doctrine that whether or not there was a monarch in Hungary, whether he had been deposed, assassinated or exiled, whether the country was technically a monarchy or a republic, the Crown of St Stephen was 'the liege lord'. Law joined piety in giving a unique status to a metal ornament, turning it into a surrogate human being. When in 1848 Lajos Kossuth led the rebellion against the Austrians, it was in the name of the Crown of St Stephen. When nearly a century later Admiral Horthy – 'the Admiral without a navy' – established his Regency, it was, again, in the name of the Crown. And when Szalasi, leader of the Fascist Arrow Cross regime, took over briefly in 1944, he insisted on taking his oath of office in the presence of the Crown. Until World War II, indeed, even academic doctorates were conferred in its physical presence as if, in that circle of gold, enamel and jewels, was the very soul of Hungary.

It was inevitable that so potent a symbol should have been 'stolen' or 'liberated' again and again: to follow its vicissitudes is to follow the stormy career of Hungarian politics over the centuries. In 1301 King Wenceslas carried it off with him to Bohemia, then handed it over to Otto, the reigning prince of Bavaria. Otto shut the Crown up in a casket, then lost it on his endless travels. It was found eventually, in a marsh, with its cross badly bent – a characteristic it retains to this day. (Another explanation for the bending of the cross is that the Crown was once hidden in a cushion – and a heavily built lady sat upon it.) In 1439 the widow of King Albert pawned it to the Emperor Frederick IV, who held it in his court at Vienna until it was regained by Matthias Corvinus. After the terrible battle of Mohacs, which heralded more than 150 years of Turkish domination, the Crown was spirited from one hiding place to another. In 1780, when Joseph II of Austria acceded to the Hungarian throne and supported the idea of uncrowned 'enlightened absolutism' (the sardonic Hungarians styled him 'the behatted king'), he had the Crown placed in the imperial treasury in Vienna. Ten years later, as a concession to Hungarian requests, he agreed to place it in Buda. During the 1848 War of Independence it was buried in what is today Romania, was moved from there to Vienna, thence back to Buda.

The Crown played its last directly constitutional role in 1916 when it was used to crown Charles I, the successor to Francis Joseph. But though its role as a human headgear was never to be repeated, its influence, if anything, grew. A special room was set aside for it in the palace at Buda and a Crown Guard formed, consisting of twenty-four men dressed in green, white and orange and supported by a strong military guard. Here it remained until November 1944 when, together with the regalia – consisting of orb, robe, and sceptre – it began its journey across half the western world.

Tracing the movements of the Crown in the months following its removal from Budapest is particularly difficult for several reasons: Europe was in a state of total chaos, and the Crown became the object of virulent political propaganda. Depending on political viewpoint, its removal from Budapest in 1944 can be seen either as an action designed to protect a Christian symbol of sovereignty from the advancing horde of atheist communists, or as a theft designed to place a valuable national heritage in the hands of the nation's enemies. A deliberate pall of secrecy was drawn over the Crown's whereabouts by those who actually held it: as late as 1973, when without a doubt it was securely locked up in Fort Knox, its whereabouts was still unknown to most Europeans. What follows here is the picture that was built up by the Hungarians themselves as they tried to track it down and bring pressure upon the holder to return. There are a number of internal contradictions which at this distance in time and through the fog of polemics are unlikely to be resolved but, in the main, it is still possible to establish the vicissitudes of the 'soul of Hungary' between November 1944 and late 1947 when it left Europe for America.

In 1956 the villagers of Mattsee in Austria unveiled a simple marble tablet bearing the legend: 'In 1945 the Crown and the Holy Hand [a relic of Stephen] were guarded here. Hungarian Actio Catholica.' In the speech of dedication, the parish priest, Canon Strasser, described how he played host (a singularly reluctant host, one feels) to Ferenc Szalasi and his band of

Arrow Cross men. They had with them the entire regalia and, according to Strasser, handed it over to him. 'Szalasi wanted to hand over the crown as well but I did not receive it.' It is unclear whether Strasser did not wish to receive it, or whether Szalasi changed his mind. In the event, Szalasi and his men continued their odyssey, taking the treasure with them. According to Strasser (in his 1956 speech), 'The crown, together with the other treasures, fell into the hands of the Americans, who took it to Wiesbaden.'

Much of what happened after the halt at Mattsee can be corroborated from American sources. The Arrow Cross contingent was travelling in two trucks. The front truck held Szalasi and his political friends, the second truck contained the treasure, guarded by eight of the Crown Guards. One report describes them as still being tricked out in their guards finery, an inherent improbability. They were under the command of an Arrow Cross Colonel named Pajtas.

At Swarzach, the convoy was stopped by American soldiers and taken to Wiesbaden, interrogation centre for the American 7th Army. The politicos were separated from the Crown Guard and Pajtas, on making his formal respects to the American commander, stated: 'The armoured box containing the crown has been brought from Budapest under my guard. Nobody touched the national treasure before the government convoy reached the Austrian village of Mattsee and the guards of the American camp took us into custody.' On being asked for the key of the box, Pajtas stated that it was being held by the son of the Minister of Defence, a certain Erno Gömbös, who had been Szalasi's adjutant but had sensibly taken the opportunity of decamping before the convoy was stopped. However, he had failed to escape the very efficient drag-net that the Americans had put out for all pro-Nazis and was traced to Landesgericht prison in Salzburg. 'After a long and painful interrogation', according to a Hungarian source, he admitted possession of the key and handed it over. The box was opened, in Augsburg, before Pajtas. It was empty.

Pajtas is dead and it is impossible to reconstruct his motives – why he should have unequivocally claimed responsibility for the contents of the box, knowing it to have been empty. He, too, was 'interrogated' – and one receives the very strong impression that 'interrogation' involved physical duress – and admitted that, under Szalasi's orders, the crown had been buried in a marsh near Mattsee in an oil barrel. This information proved correct. The crown was found, wrapped up in linen, in an oil barrel. It was taken to Frankfurt and placed in the strongroom of the Deutsche Reichsbank.

The presence of the crown and regalia in Wiesbaden was confirmed a few months later by a Belgian journalist, Emil Lagui, writing in a Belgian magazine. He describes how he met a member of the American organization known as MFA & A (organization for the restitution of Monuments, Fine Arts and Archives – see p. 174), a museum expert by the name of Walter J. Farmer. Captain Farmer displayed to Lagui and other journalists 'an old style iron box. In the open box, lined with brown leather, on a velvet cushion there sparkled before us the crown of King Stephen I, the sceptre and great orb.' Some eighteen months later, in February 1947, the Hungarian Finance Minister visited Western Europe, and subsequently submitted a memorandum to his Prime Minister.

The American authorities informed me that they wanted to restore the crown and the regalia to Hungary, to which I replied that there was no obstacle in this – indeed, our mission in Frankfurt had already handed over a request for their return in the previous year. The Americans, however – I don't know for what reason – would like to receive a written request on this matter from the government or from some member of the government. I had spoken with Gyongyosi [the then Foreign Minister] on this question in Paris four days before, and we had agreed that since the question had political bearings, we should ask for your decision in the matter. The opinion of both of us was that since the last part of the Fine Arts Museum Collection was to start for home from Munich within a few weeks, the regalia could be transported home on this occasion.

So far, so good. It is possible to trace the movements of the Crown of St Stephen over some two and a half years, from November 1944 to February 1947, with a fair degree of certainty – Budapest, Mattsee, Wiesbaden, Frankfurt. The Crown then disappears from public view and, in its place, is substituted a large red herring in the form of another crown. Nearly twenty years later the world was astonished to learn that an enterprising Italian burglar had apparently carried off the Crown of St Stephen from the Vatican Museum.

In order to understand why this remarkable story was taken at its face value, it is necessary to backtrack to Eastern Europe in the period immediately following the end of the war. This is the tragic period in modern European history when, having defeated the common enemy of Nazi Germany, allies became enemies under the spur of clashing ideologies. All along the eastern frontier of Europe, from Greece to Poland, the ancient struggle between East and West, taking new form under the names of 'Communism/People's Republics' and 'Free World/Capitalism', broke out anew. Political journalists dubbed it the Cold War, the continuation of direct conflict by indirect means. Hungary was caught within the gravitational pull of the Eastern bloc and, as the Cold War became ever more vicious, Hungary's name became anathema to the 'Western World' – the Western World which, incidentally, held, somewhere, the symbol of Hungarian sovereignty.

It is at this stage that the Roman Catholic hierarchy enters the story. In 1947 Henry Spellman, the American Cardinal, wrote to the American Secretary of State for Defence asking him to handle the delicate business of St Stephen's Crown with particular care. Cardinal Mindszenty, the aged Hungarian prelate who had become the hero of the West with his long-drawn-out defiance of the Communist apparatus in Hungary, had specifically asked that the Crown should be guarded by the American Army – 'or placed in the safe custody of His Apostolic Highness, Pope Pius XII'. The inescapable implication here is that the Crown was still under American control, an implication substantiated by the letter which Archbishop Rohrach of Salzburg had written to Spellman himself, saying that the crown 'should under no circumstances be handed over to Hungary but should find its way to Rome to the Holy Father'.

The hierarchy's interest in the matter was legitimate. From the point of view of Archbishop Rohrach and his fellow Eastern European prelates, the Crown of Hungary was not simply a political symbol but, essentially, a religious one. All coronations are deemed to be at the direct will of God, acting through a recognized intermediary. But of all the crowns of Europe, only this battered, ancient headpiece had come direct from the Vicar of Christ. The totally uncompromising attitude of Pius XII towards Communism, an attitude which even persuaded him to look with some tolerance upon Nazism, further strengthened the hierarchy's belief that this symbol of Christian sovereignty should be placed in the hands of the successor of him who had bestowed it upon Stephen nearly a thousand years before.

The probability is that the Crown did indeed make its way to Rome: in 1951 the American Academy in Rome published a monograph on *The Holy Crown of Hungary*, which was based on an analysis of the crown taken out of Hungary towards the end of the war. Nevertheless, the crown later stolen from the Vatican Library was, in fact, a copy that had been in Rome for many years. Even the most casual acquaintance with the security measures that obtain in the Vatican underlines the burglar's truly remarkable feat. The Library proper is accessible only to bona fide students, each of whom must pass through a highly efficient cordon composed of Swiss Guards and civil police. Any person found wandering round any of the Vatican offices without a pass is summarily ejected. If the burglar made his attempt during the day, then he must have done so under the eyes of a number of people; if by night, then he must have gained access by one of the two gates into the Vatican grounds that are guarded day and night by some of the most formidable soldiers in Europe. The burglar's expertise, in fact, ended with the actual theft. He apparently did not realize that this unique object could not be disposed of as though it were a silver cup won at golf. Two days after the theft the replica was found in a tin box in the garden of a villa in one of the northern suburbs of Rome.

The true crown was meanwhile, almost certainly, in America. In 1951, in response to a number of increasingly pointed demands from the Hungarian Government, the American State Department issued a communiqué: 'The St Stephen Crown, as distinct from the rest of the Crown Jewels and other treasures looted by the Hungarian fascists and taken to Austria does not come under article 30 of the Treaty of Restitution.' Article 30 provided for the restitution of all art objects that had been taken away forcibly. This was not the case with the Crown, the State Department argued, because it had been given up voluntarily for safe-keeping.

The abortive Hungarian Revolution of 1956 gave a wholly unexpected additional weight to the Crown of St Stephen, abruptly transforming a museum relic into a king-over-the-water for the thousands of Hungarian refugees. Those who made their way to America formed a small but highly active and vociferous pressure group that bedevilled the already complex issue. It was the problem of the Ashanti regalia restated in another continent and for another people: if returned, to whom should it be returned? To the Communist government of Hungary, or to its Christian victims across the Atlantic? The State Department said nothing. In 1965 the *New York Times* raised the issue regarding its whereabouts, followed by an article on its financial value. A few months after these articles appeared a journalist, Donald H. May, writing in a local paper, probably hit a bull's-eye with his guess that the Crown was in Fort Knox. In August of the same year the State Department formally admitted that the Crown was on American soil, in the custody of the American government.

By now, the American government must have been heartily regretting the events of that May morning when, through the American 7th Army, Europe's oldest crown passed into the custody of one of Europe's youngest daughters. With the death of Stalin, there was a detectable thawing of the Cold War. East and West had been forced to recognize that, if they were to continue to share the same planet, certain controversies would simply have to be shelved, unresolved, *sine die*. Even the Vatican, last bulwark against change, had discreetly begun to adjust its sights. Cardinal Mindszenty was, if not disowned, told pretty clearly that the Church could not afford the luxury of continued, unqualified support. Janos Kador, Secretary of the Hungarian Communist Party, was actually received by Pope Paul VI. In the relaxing of lethal tension the argument over the possession of a museum piece seemed almost ludicrously irrelevant. In 1974 the *Washington Post*, under the headline 'Cold War Relic', expressed its amazement that the Crown was still in American possession, and when, in that same year, the deputy Prime Minister of Hungary met President Ford on his visit to the USA his insistence that the retention of the relic was hampering the 'normalization' of US-Hungarian affairs was heard sympathetically. All seemed set for a straightforward resolution of the problem when the Americans found themselves hampered by their own legal system.

To non-Americans, the ease whereby litigants can prolong their case for months or even years by appeal after appeal is one of the odder aspects of the American legal system. The Hungarian refugees in the US, and their sympathizers, now made full use of that ability, claiming, *inter alia*, that the US had acquired full property rights in the Crown after being in possession of it for thirty years. This ingenious attempt at justification-in-arrears was blocked by the Supreme Court. So, too, was a move by a Republican senator, Robert Dole of Kansas, who contended that 'The crown's transfer was a matter of such international significance that it may only be accomplished pursuant to a treaty'. On 4 November 1977, thirty-three years almost to the week since the Crown left Budapest, the State Department agreed to return it to Hungary. The actual return was almost an anti-climax. On 6 January 1978, Cyrus Vance, the US Secretary of State, delivered the Crown and the regalia to Antal Apro, Speaker of the National Assembly, in a simple but dignified ceremony in Budapest. Among those who witnessed it was Cardinal Laszlo Lekai, Archbishop of Esztergom, successor many times removed of the same Archbishop of Esztergom who had crowned Stephen King of Hungary in AD 1001.

In its communiqué announcing the decision to return the relic the State Department had emphasized that they were returning the Crown not to the Hungarian Government, but to the Hungarian people, thus neatly avoiding the charge that they were bolstering a Communist revolutionary regime. On their side, the Hungarian Government was decidedly anxious to emphasize the fact that they regarded this symbol of sovereignty simply as a museum treasure: 'The symbolical constitutional significance of the Crown has been completely lost. The country, and all power in the country, came to belong to the people. Nonetheless, People's Democratic Hungary continued to press for the return of the Crown . . . and art treasures of museal value which had been taken out of the country but still belonged to Hungary, now to the Hungarian People's State.' But the people themselves seemed to view their 'museal treasure' in a different light: when it was placed on display, nearly a third of the country's ten million population filed past the relic.

There was to be an ironic codicil to the long saga. The Crown had never been subjected to an authoritative examination. In 1883 and again in 1938 the Crown was examined briefly by experts – so briefly that during the 1938 examination they were actually forbidden to touch it. Neither examination was detailed, or authoritative, enough to substantiate, or dispel, a rumour that was being voiced increasingly in academic circles: this was not *the* Crown of Stephen; it had not, indeed, ever rested upon the brow of St Stephen. In September 1981 a panel of distinguished historians and art experts from five countries, including Britain, met under the direction of Dr Judit Kolba of the Hungarian National Museum, a scholar who had made a special study of the Crown Jewels. The primary purpose of the panel was to decide upon the pressing problem of the restoration and preservation of the regalia. In the past, for example, certain parts of the Crown had been repaired with zinc, which was now eating away the precious metal around it through a process of electrolysis. And during the course of examination of the Crown it was established, beyond a peradventure, that though the relic was of great antiquity and had been in the possession of Hungary throughout its existence, it was not the Crown that Sylvester II sent to Stephen I.

The existing Crown consists, in fact, of two separate headpieces. The lower, or 'Greek crown', was sent to the reigning king, Geza I, by the Byzantine Emperor Michael Ducas in 1074. Geza had refused to accept papal suzerainty and the emperor's gift was an attempt to usurp to himself the papal role, a vivid reminder of the potency inherent in the symbol. The upper crown, or so-called *corona latina*, is a mystery. One theory is that it was a shrine made for the skull of St Stephen, and was later cut down to make the upper part of a closed crown.

And the original crown, the one that Sylvester II *did* send to Stephen? This was returned to Rome, in 1045, after Stephen's death. And disappeared. Unless we suppose that enterprising Italian burglar really did have in his hands the 900-year-old crown of the first Christian king of Hungary.

III
THE WARLORDS

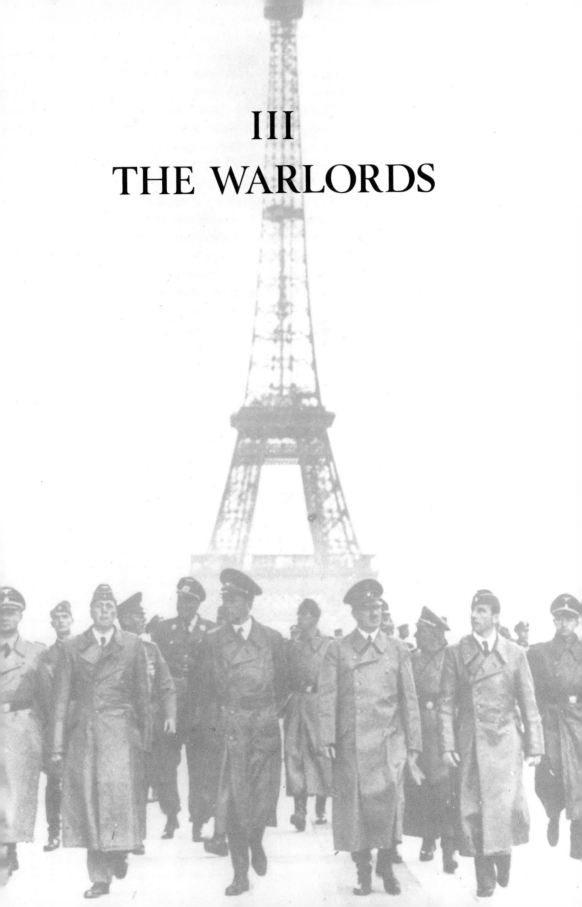

6

Napoleon Bonaparte

'I Francesi son tutti ladri
Non tutti, ma buono parte'

'PASQUINO', citizen of Rome*

The Piazza Navona is the village square of Rome. Its homely name (Turnip Place) shows that it once discharged the function of a vegetable market and, long after it ceased that function, it continued – and continues – to act as the unofficial forum of Rome. The Capitol is for grand ceremonial occasions, the Forum Romanum is a scholar's boneyard, St Peter's Square an extension of the Vatican. Piazza Navona is the place to which tourists and residents both drift, where falling politicians and rising actors practise their waxing or waning crafts, where thieves and singers abound, where cosy family groups taking the air rub shoulders with drug pedlars. It is the place where everybody talks.

On the corner of one of the narrow lanes that lead into the piazza is a marble statue. It is so badly disfigured that, at first glance, one might take it for a religious statue of the kind with which the Christian religion, so obsessed with bodily torment, ornaments its sacred buildings. The disfigurement is, however, accidental, being wrought by time, and not by man. Probably Greek in origin, it represented Hercules strangling Geryon and was dug up and placed on or near this spot in the year 1501. It became the target of graffiti writers – but writers of such high calibre that they bestowed a personality upon the fragment of mutilated marble. The Romans came to know it as 'Pasquino' – the name probably of a witty tailor who had his shop nearby – and what Pasquino 'said' became a major source of Roman gossip, or, indeed, information during the frequent periods of

* In 1509 at least 3,000 epigrams were attributed to Pasquino. In 1957 a scholarly work, *Pasquino e le pasquinate* by Mario dell'Arco, traced the remarkable history of this 'talking statue'.

123

political suppression. During the Napoleonic occupation of Rome, Pasquino became ever more loquacious. And, watching while the soldiers of revolutionary France addressed themselves to what is probably the biggest looting operation in history, he came up with the perfect pun:

> The French are all thieves
> Not all, but most (buono parte).

The hands might have been the hands of soldiers but the directing mind was that of the 26-year-old Corsican general who, somewhat to his surprise, found the weakest but most prestigious country in Europe at his mercy.

On 27 July 1798, there was staged in Paris – appropriately in the Champs de Mars – an elaborate spectacle which deliberately echoed the classical Roman triumph. A contemporary engraving complements the many written descriptions, providing a lively witness for posterity. In the formal setting of the square, backed by a vast grandstand and in front of the grandiose Altar of Victory, can be seen the head of a parade or procession. Leading it are four life-sized statues of horses on a float or car. Immediately behind them are two living dromedaries, and following these is a long file of massive carts and wagons, each laden with prosaic wooden packing cases.

The cases may be prosaic in appearance, but their contents included some of the world's supreme works of art, the heritage of Europe: the Discobolus, the Dying Gladiator, the Laocoön, the Medici Venus – names which are now part of the vocabulary of art. The four bronze horses themselves had stood for five centuries on the portico of the basilica of San Marco in Venice, until their recent removal.

Not shown in the engraving, but commented upon by numerous spectators, were the vainglorious banners proclaiming the fate of these works of art. 'La Grèce la céda: Rome les a perdus: leur sort changea deux fois – il ne changera pas.' They were the fruits of Napoleon's conquest of Italy. 'Plunder', the rest of the world indignantly described them, 'protected heritage' was the complacent retort of the French. 'The French republic, by its strength and superiority and strength of its enlightenment, is the only country in the world which can give a safe home to these masterpieces.' Their twenty-year enforced sojourn in France was to pose the whole basic question of possession based on right of conquest – a question to which the legalistic French had given a neat twist: all the treasures had been handed over, legally, by treaty and thus, legally, now belonged to the French nation.

Napoleon's title as the World's Greatest Looter is one that is subject to considerable competition. In imperial Rome the status of a victorious

The world's greatest looter? Napoleon Bonaparte in characteristic pose. Ingres painted this portrait of the 'Emperor' in coronation robes in 1806.

NAPOLEON AND THE PLUNDER OF ITALY

Napoleon's conquests in Italy were followed by treaties enjoining the handing over of works of art: Italians became honorary Frenchmen ('All men of genius are French no matter in what country they may have been born') as his commissioners sacked Italy to gather 'France's heritage'.

The horses of San Marco (*left*), a major item in these looting expeditions, were removed from Venice under protection by French bayonets in the face of an Italian mob. They are shown *below* in the triumphal procession in the Champs de Mars in Paris in 1798.

A hostile caricature of Napoleon (*right*) – the so-called 'corpse head' in which the face is composed of 'Carcases of the Victims of his Folly and Ambition' while the hat is 'a discomfited French Eagle maimed and crouching' – contrasts with the French view *bottom left*: here the eagle flies strongly ahead, bearing the laurels of victory.

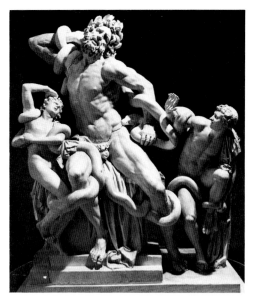

THE FRUITS OF CONQUEST

(*below*) The imperial cortège passes in front of the new 'French' masterpieces in 1810 – among them Raphael's *Transfiguration* (also seen *above left*). The Laocoön group (*above right*), one of the masterpieces of the Hellenistic period, had been rediscovered in Rome in 1506. It was successfully transported to the Louvre after violent riots in

Rome. Napoleon himself made a night visit to the renamed Musée Napoleon (*opposite* – in the centre is the Laocoön, to the left the *Medici Venus*, which had been taken from Florence). Both *Transfiguration* and Laocoön were returned to the Vatican after the defeat of Napoleon, but by then many other treasures had been widely dispersed.

THE FRENCH IN EGYPT

The Battle of the Pyramids (*left*, Napoleon addresses his troops) was not the sole consequence of the French arrival in Egypt. (*below*) Napoleon face-to-face with a mummy. He had appointed Baron Dominique Vivant Denon (*far right*) to lead the scholars and scientists he brought with him in what turned out to be a vital contribution to the birth of Egyptology. The frontispiece to Denon's *Description de L'Egypte* (*below far right*) takes in telescopically the antiquities adjoining the Nile, looking south from Alexandria. The Grand Gallery of the Great Pyramid of Cheops – one of the Seven Wonders of the ancient world – was also depicted in the book (*right*), which was first produced in 1809. Denon was by then Director-General of Museums in France.

Denon gave shape to what otherwise might have been a formless plundering campaign; he was the guiding spirit behind the Napoleonic policy of acquisition based on conquest. In this allegorical painting in the Louvre the results of this single-minded policy surround him.

general – and his possible fitness for the imperial purple – was measured by the number of slaves dragged in his triumph, the quantity and quality of looted hardware made from precious metals heaped up in the wagons following, the looted bullion which, turned into coin, would be tossed into the mob and so buy prestige. When the emperors themselves removed to Constantinople they regarded Rome simply as a bran tub: each visit of the emperor to his titular capital was marked by a diminution of that capital's treasures, whether it was the golden tiles of the Pantheon or the remains of holy corpses in the catacombs. Plundering in the Dark Ages and early Middle Ages tended to be strictly practical, the victorious general being more interested in that which could be eaten, worn, or turned into coin than in that which merely ornamented or informed. With the Renaissance the plunder of art was revived with much else: the status of a prince was now measured by the bibelots and gewgaws with which he stuffed his court, as much as by his overt power. Isabella d'Este prettily requested from Cesare Borgia, despoiler of her sister-in-law's court at Urbino, antique statuary which he had obtained from that same court: Cesare was graciously pleased to grant her request. Learning received its accolade: in 1624 Pope Urban VIII graciously received, as a gift, the superb Palatine Library that had been the pride of Heidelberg and had now fallen as prize to the Catholic generals of the Counter Reformation. Gustavus Adolphus turned his barbaric court at Stockholm into the simulacrum of a cultural centre by stuffing it with the proceeds of a continent-wide robbery. The generals of his daughter Christina timed their attack upon Prague in 1648 in order that their cultural-hungry mistress could devour the accumulated treasures of the Emperor Rudolf.

Napoleon has formidable competitors for his title. But where he stood – and stands – alone is that he was the first successfully to identify his tastes with those of his nation. His illustrious forebears plundered upon their own behalf, to enhance their own personal prestige or for their own, personal, pleasure. Napoleon plundered for France. In 1796 a petition signed by most of the leading French artists took upon themselves, and their Gallic fellows, full responsibility for the act: 'The more our climate seems unfavourable to the arts, the more do we require models here in order to overcome the obstacles to the progress thereof. The Romans, once an uncultivated people, became civilized by transplanting to Rome the works of conquered Greece. Thus the French people will, by seeing models from antiquity, train its feeling and its critical sense.' The argument that education justifies robbery is an odd one and has now, on the whole, been rejected. But the assumption that a strong nation has a natural right to the cultural goods of a weaker was one that was to flourish well into our own time.

It had always been Italy's misfortune to have her fate settled by foreigners. In the closing years of the eighteenth century the dominant power on the peninsula, so far as there was one, was Austria, with its firm foothold in the plain of Lombardy. Uneasily sharing that plain was the 1,200-year-old Republic of Venice, the *Serenissima*, precariously holding on to its independence while being careful not to offend the imperial forces of Austria. To the south the King of Naples, the Duke of Tuscany and, the oldest monarchy of them all, the Papacy, shared or bickered over what remained.

Napoleon's impact upon this creaking, tottering structure was as decisive as that of a demolition contractor upon a derelict house. He was just 26 years of age. Two years earlier, he had so distinguished himself at the siege of Toulon that his commanding officer had given a piece of advice to the Minister of War that proved remarkably prophetic. 'Reward, promote this young man – otherwise he will do it for himself.' In 1795, he saved the Convention from a dangerous royalist rising, was promoted second in command of the Army of the Interior. A Corsican by birth, he spoke fluent Italian and was the natural choice as commander for the army that the Directory had resolved to send into Italy to make a flanking attack upon Austria. In a series of brilliant campaigns that were distinguished as much by an almost suicidal courage as by military genius – at the bloody passage of the bridge of Lodi he charged in person up to the mouths of the enemy's guns – he fought the Austrians to a standstill in a little over a year. He began his campaign in April 1796 and signed the treaty of Campo Formio with Austria in October 1797. And it was during these action-filled eighteen months that he initiated his vast campaign of plunder.

Napoleon Bonaparte's decision to add cultural plunder to military triumph arose partly from his desire to impress his adopted fellow countrymen. But mostly, one suspects, it arose from that awareness of history which was later to lead him to assume an imperial crown – a legal absurdity which he was to make into reality (and incidentally provide a model for endless petty 'emperors'). Italy, weak though she was and at the mercy of whatever strong outsider cared to enter her frontiers, still carried the magic of the great name of Rome. Napoleon, conquering this symbol of power, took symbolic possession of its treasures rather like a savage eating the heart of a noble enemy in order to ingest his powers. Uneasily aware that what might seem symbolic possession to Frenchmen would look uncommonly like theft to non-Frenchmen, he deftly evaded the charge by making ancient Italians honorary Frenchmen. 'All men of genius are French no matter in what country they may have been born.' With the comforting assurance that they were simply gathering in France's heritage, his commissioners set about sacking Italy. They were led by Dominique Vivant Denon.

A man who began his career as keeper of antique gems for Louis XV, who became successively a favourite of Madame de Pompadour and Josephine Bonaparte, who practised as a diplomat and finally acted as art director, adviser and general cultural arbiter for Napoleon might fairly be described as a professional survivor. But there was more to Denon than a capacity for boudoir and cabinet intrigue, far more.

Baron Dominique Vivant Denon was born into an aristocratic French family. His portrait shows a man with a cheerful, battered face that gives no clue to the remarkable power that he must have had over women. During his career as diplomat, he added Catherine the Great of Russia to his conquests – or, to be exact, he survived Catherine the Great's conquest of him, no mean feat for any male who came within the orbit of that predatory monarch. Fortunately for him, he was away from France, comfortably established in Florence during the early, lethal days of the Revolution. His absence probably saved his life, but not his fortune. With considerable courage he returned to France to find that his inheritance had been confiscated, he himself was on the proscribed list and was reduced to destitution. But in addition to an ebullient nature and boundless self-confidence he had one outstanding talent: he was a brilliant draughtsman and sensitive painter. He survived by selling drawings and small paintings for tiny sums.

But it was this humble and humiliating experience of peddling his work that was to provide him with the first rung of the ladder leading out of the gutter. His work attracted the attention of the immensely popular revolutionary painter, Jacques Louis David, and through the painter's patronage he began his slow climb back into the ranks of power. It was now revolutionary, not aristocratic power, but a man like Denon knew how to operate the levers, whatever their colour, once he was within reaching distance. It was said that he owed his introduction to Napoleon to Josephine and that it would be indiscreet to enquire too closely into the basis of their relationship. It may be so, but Napoleon had his own skills for choosing those who would execute his demands. He was impressed by the burly aristocrat who had the manner of a courtier, the face of a pugilist, considerable talent for pornographic drawings – but had also been a member of the French Academy.

When choosing his savants to accompany him into Egypt, Napoleon included Denon, a fact which was to have immense effect not only upon Denon's own career, but upon the as yet unborn science of Egyptology. Egypt struck him with the force of a revelation. Where his predecessors, and many of his contemporaries, saw either a world of black magicians or a rundown African country peopled with a supine peasantry, he homed in unerringly on that aspect which would provide a key to the past – Egypt's architecture. Like all cultured Europeans, his touchstone for architectural beauty had been the monuments of Greece and Rome. He was overwhelmed by the austere beauty of the Egyptian style 'with no extraneous ornaments or superfluity of lines'. His passion to record overcame the natural fear of a civilian travelling with an army on campaign. The French were marching up to thirty miles a day, continually under attack. Frequently Denon would have only a matter of minutes in which to record the scene before him, often under fire. He describes how on one occasion he remained in the saddle for sixteen hours, sketching, sketching, sketching, his face excoriated by wind-blown sand, blood seeping from his eyelids and obscuring vision. Back in France he scooped the vast official publication by issuing, in 1801, his own two-volume book, *Voyages dans la basse et la haute Egypte*, which was promptly translated into all major European languages and became an immediate bestseller.

This was the man destined to give shape to what would otherwise have been a formless plundering campaign, a man quite unscrupulous when need be, adept at palace intrigue but also deeply knowledgeable and utterly dedicated to the agreeable task of making France the cultural capital of the globe. Formally, he became the first Director of the Musée Napoleon – later known as the Louvre from the building it occupied. Informally, he was the guiding spirit behind the policy of acquisition based on conquest. He was in a situation that would have been the envy of any museum curator who was able to stifle the pangs of conscience – to have at one's total disposal all that was best in portable European art.

The process started in Italy in May 1796, when treaties were signed with the dukes of Modena and Parma. In the treaties were clauses enjoining the handing over of stipulated works of art. Next it was the turn of Milan, then of that incomparable treasure house, Rome itself. The treaty signed by the wretched Pope Pius VI in June allowed for the handing over of five hundred manuscripts from the Vatican Library and one hundred 'pictures and busts'. These were to be chosen by the commissioners and they obviously knew what they were about in the matter of statuary. Among their choices were the busts of Marcus and Junius Brutus and the Laocoön.

The Laocoön forms one of those links between past and present that have a potency out of all proportion to their intrinsic beauty or value. It was discovered in Rome in 1506 by a man who was digging a well on the Esquiline. It says much for his classical education that he immediately recognized it from Pliny's description, even though it had been hidden from human sight for over 1,400 years. Michelangelo was one of those who examined it, agreed that it was indeed the statue described by Pliny and refused requests to 'restore' it, the first known example of the feeling that the past existed in its own right and that it was impertinent for the present to alter it to fit its own predilections. The Pope had claimed the statue and it had been in the Vatican ever since. Its removal, together with other famous pieces of statuary, excited the rage of the Romans. Their opinion of their bishop might be equivocal, but seeing the traditional enemy, France, carrying off the very symbols of Rome heated the ever-volatile mob to explosion. There were violent riots in the city – but the prizes were nevertheless removed.

The commissioners were less successful with their choices of manuscripts from the library. The awe-inspiring size of the 300-year-old Vatican Library might have daunted even professional librarians forced to make a choice. The commissioners evidently had little or no expertise in the matter. A French scholar suggested that they take, in its entirety, the collection bequeathed to the Vatican by that formidable blue-stocking, Queen Christina of Denmark. She had, herself, purchased it in Paris – a variation from her usual tactics for the acquisition of cultural material – and there would be a certain logic in re-acquiring the collection. The commissioners ignored the suggestion and adopted the easy way of taking every manuscript written before the year 900 on the assumption that the older the manuscript, the more valuable it was. This was not necessarily true in terms of intrinsic value, but the cavalier act eroded the very base of Roman historiography, hampering future generations of scholars, for by no means everything was returned after the Napoleonic adventure.

In April 1797 the Commissioners turned their attention to Venice.

Napoleon's relationship with the state that still bore the proud title of Serenissima Republica was equivocal. In a burst of rage he had said, in his native Italian, 'Io saro un Attila per lo Stato Veneto' – I shall be an Attila for the Venetian State – a phrase which proved to be a very useful piece of propaganda for the Venetians. But it would be a gross distortion of history to cast him in the role of ravening Hun destroying what he could not understand. Hindsight has given to Venice, the last independent republic of Italy, a nobility which its contemporaries would have had very considerable difficulty in recognizing. Napoleon was able to make good use of the resentment felt towards Venice by the cities on the mainland which she held in subjection: at least two major cities, Crema and Bergamo, were induced to rebel against their Venetian masters, confident in the support of the French 'sons of liberty'. Napoleon also had legitimate political and military reasons to launch a direct attack on Venice, had he so wished, for Venice had both given asylum to Louis XVIII – though shabbily withdrawing it under French pressure – and allowed the Austrians free passage across her territory.

But initially, the young commander seems to have been reasonably well disposed to the island republic. It is from one of Venice's ambassadors, Gian Contarini, that posterity has received a priceless portrait of Napoleon as he steps on to the stage of international history. It was shortly after the first successful, whirlwind campaign in Lombardy that Contarini visited him at Crema and found, in place of a ravening, raging tyrant, a young man living on his nerves. He was stretched out, limp with fatigue. 'He seemed serious and thoughtful and to the direct question "Are you tired?" the General answered, "Yes, I am very tired." ' But not too tired to put the fear of death into the Venetians: not too tired to force this ancient republic to commit suicide in the most ignoble manner. Over the following year the Venetian Senate, like an unskilful fox, doubled and redoubled upon its tracks until it fell into the jaws of the hounds. The Venetians, the most accomplished politicians in a nation of politicians, fell victim to the greater skill of the 26-year-old Corsican. But the republic deserved a better epitaph than that uttered by its last Doge, Lodovico Manin, who, as the hounds moved in, immortalized himself with the almost tearful remark, 'We shall not be safe in our beds tonight.' On Friday, 12 May 1797 the Great Council of Venice voted itself into extinction and for the first time in a thousand years Venice was occupied by foreign soldiers.

The French made their headquarters in the beautiful monastery of San Giorgio Maggiore, on the island of the same name, and inaugurated 150 years of squalor and degradation for a complex that included some of the most superb architecture of Renaissance Italy.* The terms of the treaty of

* Even after all foreigners had been driven from Italy, the national Italian government continued the degradation by keeping the monastery as a barracks. It was only in 1951 that a wealthy industrialist,

Campo Formio, which Napoleon signed with Austria five months later in October 1797, provided for the handing over of Venice to Austria. The Austrians did not arrive to take possession of the city until January 1798, and during the months of their stay the French turned to the systematic looting of the city.

It is arguable that the cowardly abdication of responsibility of the last doge and his senate saved Venice. It was ringed round by the heavy artillery of the French on the mainland, and of their warships outside the mole. If the Venetians themselves had had no compunction about lobbing a shell into the Parthenon in 1687, there is no reason to suppose that Napoleon would have jibbed at lobbing shells into Piazza San Marco in 1797. But the absence of any governing body put the city wholly at the mercy of the victorious French. Until the twentieth century, all victorious armies looted as a matter of course – loot was the major reason why the underpaid private soldier put his body voluntarily at risk. But the looting of Venice, like that of Rome, was carried out in the name of the revolutionary French people, formally, in an organized manner. And completely illegally. The Treaty of Milan, which allowed for the removal of art treasures, was signed on 16 May – four days after the Venetian state had ceased to exist, a curious oversight on the part of the legalistic French. Even today, the full extent of loot taken from the city is not known, so heterogeneous was the collection, from private as well as public sources. But two major works can stand as representatives for the rest, one because it was never returned, the other because it reflected the very soul of the city. The one was the *Marriage at Cana* by Veronese and the other was the group of four bronze horses from the front of the basilica.

Veronese painted his enormous picture with one place only in mind, the immense refectory that Palladio had built for the monks of San Giorgio. It filled one entire wall, and with its gorgeous colouring and swirling movement must have given just the right balance to the architect's cool and lofty structure. The commissioners had to cut the immense painting in two in order to get it out of the hall for which it had been designed. On the credit side of the act is the fact that it probably saved the picture because the refectory was degraded, along with the rest of the building, into a barracks. But it was destined to stay in Paris.

The Horses of San Marco sum up, in their eerily beautiful forms, two millennia of cultural plunder. Venice herself had plundered them – from Constantinople after the infamous sack of 1204. But Constantinople, too,

Count Vittorio Cini, restored the complex in memory of his son. It is now known as the Fondazione Cini and functions as a cultural centre.

had obtained them by violence or, at least, force majeure, either from Rome or Greece. And if they came from Rome then Rome, too, had obtained them by strongarm methods, for they are undoubtedly Greek in origin, though of what date and by what hand is likely to be a matter of continuing debate. In 1204 Venice joined the 'Crusaders' to attack and sack Constantinople, Christian bastion in the east. The Venetian commander, with a Venetian's eye to a valuable work of art, claimed the Horses and in due course they were placed above the portico of San Marco. There they looked so right, so integrally a part of the basilica which was itself the heart of Venice that they became an alternative symbol of the republic, rivalling even the Winged Lion. As a doge of Genoa remarked when, uncharacteristically, Venice sued for peace after one of her many wars with her Ligurian rival: 'Truly you will never have peace if we do not first of all rein those unbridled horses which are on top of the palace of your evangelist.'

The horses remained, unharmed, high above the square, for nearly 600 years until a day in December 1797. Six weeks after the signing of the Treaty of Campo Formio, they were lowered from the front of the basilica. Again, as in Rome, French commissioners had to go to work protected by French bayonets from the anger of an Italian mob. The contemporary illustrations of the event point up, accidentally or inescapably, the contrast between the serenity of the beautiful creatures, and the restlessness of the crowd, as they made their way in stately procession across the piazza. They were joined by other treasures – including the Veronese – and went down the coast to Ancona, then onward to Leghorn, where a great convoy was being built up of loot from all over Italy. Thence they travelled up the Rhone, then inland to Paris by canal. Curiously, it seemed that no official preparations had been made for their reception. A group of savants declared themselves horrified at the idea of 'precious relics arriving like coal barges and unloaded at the Quai du Louvre like boxes of soap'. The reception on the Champs de Mars – with most of the exhibits still resting in their packing cases – was therefore arranged.

There was no lack of protests at this grotesque result of peace treaties. The sculptor Canova addressed himself directly, sardonically, to Napoleon: 'May your majesty at least leave some things in Italy. These ancient monuments form a chain which cannot ever be transported.' A noble protest came from a Frenchman, Quatremere de Quincy. Why did not France cherish her own incomparable treasures, he demanded. If the symbolism of Imperial Rome was needed, then why did France not instead exploit the ruins of Provence. Passionately he goes on to protest again the ruination of 'that great laboratory, Rome'. Instead of plundering like barbarians, 'We should reassemble there once more all those monuments which misguided enthusiasm has removed from the city.' But he was ignored as revolutionary France went on its triumphant way.

Italy was the first and richest of the cultural treasure chests, but as the conquering army swept through Europe, so the wagon trains rumbled back to France bearing the heritage of half a dozen nations. Denon masterminded the operation from Paris, ably supported by scholars of the status of Daru, the historian of Venice, and Henri Beyle, better known to posterity as Stendhal. As befitted a writer, Stendhal was particularly interested in the contents of libraries, greedily helping himself – but careful to ensure that the abductions were covered by treaty and so were 'legal'.

Germany suffered particularly badly. The commissioners descended upon Aachen, that prestigious prize that had been the seat of the first great emperor of the West, Charlemagne: not content with the marble pillars from the Hochminster, in their lust for possession the commissioners dragged back to Paris the very tomb of Charlemagne (though this too was not without its irony: the tomb had once belonged to a Roman of the second century). Cologne was plundered of stained glass, Berlin of paintings, Potsdam of gems and a world-famous collection of medallions. Individuals lost as heavily as states: the Duke of Brunswick lost seventy-eight paintings – Raphaels, Titians and Rembrandts among them – as well as his entire library, an operation happily supervised by Stendhal. Religious foundations, with their treasures accumulated over centuries, were particularly vulnerable. A lapsed Benedictine monk proved a useful ferret for nosing out manuscripts and early printed books from monasteries in the Rhineland.

Notoriously, collectors have thick skins. Not all the plundered material finished up in the state's collections or, indeed, even got back to France. An English art dealer, William Buchanan, compiled an interesting little essay on the morality of art collecting. Innocently entitled *Memoirs of painting*, it described the attractive collections that had been built up from the sales of these expropriations. In France, many of the choicer items – of jewelry in particular – never got beyond Josephine's fingers: if she did not want them, her friends and courtiers did. Here, in the court of the Empress (for such she now was), the ugly, unequivocal face of the continent-wide campaign was demonstrated. Some sort of case can be put up for adorning the capital of a victorious nation with the treasures of the conquered, but there is no other word but 'theft' to describe the steady stream of pictures and jewels that made their way into the homes of Josephine Bonaparte.

The official destination of most of these treasures was the Louvre. Built originally as a fortress, then transformed into a royal residence, over the past century it had evolved into a species of warren, housing government favourites. There was little or no control over them. The vast, beautifully proportioned rooms were casually divided and subdivided: holes were knocked into walls, doors or windows filled in as and when the tenant decided. Denon's major task as first director of the Musée Napoleon was the cleansing of this Augean stable, evicting the squatters to make room for the incoming treasures. It was a slow job and would have been even slower if Napoleon had not taken a hand. On one of his visits he noticed, apparently for the first time, the vast number of insecure-looking chimneys protruding from the windows of one of the great rooms. Fearful for the safety of his conquests he peremptorily ordered the eviction of the squatters.

Napoleon's own view of the aesthetic, as opposed to the propaganda, value of the treasures he had swept into the French net was displayed unequivocally by his instructions regarding Veronese's masterpiece, *Marriage at Cana*. It had at last been hung in the refurbished great picture gallery, one of the few rooms capable of absorbing so vast an impact. Napoleon decreed that his wedding to Marie-Louise of Austria should take place in this megalomaniac chamber and there was a tremendous scurry to rearrange pictures and furniture in order to accommodate the 6,000 people expected. The size of the *Marriage at Cana* was an embarrassment. 'Since it cannot be moved – burn it', was Napoleon's soldierly decision – one which, fortunately, Denon ignored. There seems to have been no overall attempt to sift the valuable and rare from the beautiful but common. The famous golden Palo d'Oro from San Marco in Venice was saved from the melting pot only because it was believed to be of base metal. But other objects, including two papal tiaras, were destroyed to finance the endless wars.

On 6 April 1814, Louis XVIII, the 59-year-old brother of the guillotined king, ascended the rickety throne of France. He was the classic example of the Bourbon who had learned nothing, and forgotten nothing. On 8 May he announced, unequivocally, his intention to return the looted treasures: on 4 June he announced, unequivocally, his belief that these treasures inalienably belonged, now, to the French people. His words are a masterpiece of deviousness: 'The glory of the French armies has not been tarnished, the monuments to their bravery remain, and the masterpieces of arts belong to us from now on by stronger rights than those of victory.' What, if anything, did it mean? What stronger rights were there than those of conquest – apart from the minor detail of the original owner's rights of possession?

Across the Channel, the English – who had fought the hydra of Europe to a standstill – were justifiably suspicious that here was the birth of a myth, the myth that the troops of Napoleon had never, really, been defeated. The London *Courier* spoke for the nation. The writer – evidently somebody based in Paris – drew attention to the fact that as the army of occupation was withdrawing, so the disbanded officers of Napoleon's army were returning to Paris, swaggering round. What 'right' was the king referring to, the writer demanded. 'The right of conquest? Then have they not twice lost them? Do they persist in enforcing that right? Then why do not now the Allies plunder France of every article worth removing which she possessed before Bonaparte's time? They are entitled to do this by the example of Bonaparte's practice, now so eagerly sanctioned by the Parisians.'

England, as leader of the coalition against Napoleon, had the duty of ensuring the restitution of the stolen objects. The Prime Minister, Lord Liverpool, substantiated that: 'It is most desirable in point of policy to remove them if possible from France as whilst in that country, they must necessarily have the effect of keeping up the remembrance of their former conquests and cherishing the military spirit and vanity of the nation.' And if that were not enough, then the Hero of Waterloo himself threw his weight in on the side of justice. As the Paris correspondent of the *Courier* wrote on 4 October:

Things have taken suddenly a very different appearance here. To the great astonishment of everybody, and when there was least reason to expect it, the Duke of Wellington came to the diplomatic conferences with a note in his hand, by which he expressly required all works of Art should be restored to their respective owners. This excited great attention, and the Belgians, who having immense claims to make, had been hitherto most obstinately refused, did not wait to be told to take back their own. The brave people are already on their way to return with their Potters and their Rubens.

They had lost, among much else, the great altarpiece *Adoration of the Lamb*, by Van Eyck. It was eventually returned to them – though they were to lose it again in the era of Hitler.

Napoleon returned, the Hundred Days intervened: Napoleon was packed off, finally, to St Helena and the Allies took up the bickering over who owned what and what should be returned to whom. It is at this stage that the French introduced a dizzy moral twist to the story, a twist best summed up by Stendhal's indignant remark, made at the end of the affair, when – by application of rule of thumb – most of the looted property had been returned. 'The Allies have taken 1,150 pictures. I hope I may be permitted to observe that we acquired them by treaty. On the other hand, the Allies have taken *our* [author's italics] pictures without treaty.' No matter that these treaties had been signed with a gun in the hand, no matter that, even taken on the French evaluation, the Treaty of Milan, for one, was invalid; the luminous French intellect, with its passion for logic chopping, managed to draw a cloud of uncertainty over the whole issue: because these treasures had been obtained by treaty, they belonged to France. Only by bearing this twist in mind does the long-drawn-out and bitter controversy in Paris make sense.

The Prussians were the first to act, with Teutonic military directness. Ribbentrop, the representative of King Frederick William (and ancestor of Hitler's hapless Foreign Minister), marched into the Louvre, tackled Denon personally and demanded the return of all Prussian material. Denon fobbed him off, in his turn, demanding authorization from the French Government. Exasperated, Ribbentrop called up a troop of Prussian hussars and threatened to carry Denon off along with the disputed objects. He gave way and Ribbentrop collected not only the property of his own state, but that of a number of other German princes – all of which was scrupulously sent on to its owners.

The action set off an avalanche: the Dutch, Belgians, Spanish, Italians all hastened forward to present their demands and to identify their property. Denon fought back skilfully, using every weapon in his legal arsenal to delay or to obscure the issue. He was convinced that, behind these demands, lay the jealousy of England: 'England has in truth nothing to claim, but since she has bought the bas-reliefs of which Lord Elgin plundered the Temple at Athens, now thinks she can become a rival of the [Louvre] and wants to deplete this Museum in order to collect its remains.' And his suspicions seemed to be substantiated beyond a doubt when he heard that William Richard Hamilton, one-time secretary of Lord Elgin, was leading the English delegation in Paris.

It is worthwhile looking in some detail at the career of W. R. Hamilton, who appears, disappears and re-appears throughout this period like the demon or good fairy (according to taste) in a pantomime. He is frequently confused with his namesake, Sir William Hamilton, the diplomat and archaeologist who was some forty years older than himself. Like Sir William, he spent considerable time in Naples; like Sir William, he became deeply interested in Greek art and architecture; like Sir William, he wrote learned treatises on his subject – Sir William was a fellow of the Society of Antiquaries, while W. R. was one of the founding members of the Royal

Geographical Society. Their principal distinction is that Sir William was married to Emma, Lady Hamilton and W.R. was not.

Hamilton was born in London, the son of a clergyman, in 1777. An accident at his public school, Harrow, lamed him for life, limiting – but certainly not ending – his activities in the field. He was 22 years old when he became secretary to Lord Elgin, and so became involved in the affair of the Marbles. In 1801 he was sent on a mission to Egypt, just after the French withdrawal following the battle of Alexandria, and it was then that he gained the undying enmity of Denon and other French savants. Contrary to the treaty imposed upon them, the French had tried to smuggle the Rosetta Stone out of Egypt (from the French viewpoint, any given treaty was deemed to operate in only one direction). Hearing of the attempt young Hamilton, with considerable courage and dash, got together an escort of soldiers and rowed out to the transport to which the Stone had been taken and, after a tense scene, succeeded in removing it. Like Denon, he too introduced his fellow-countrymen to the mysterious world of Egypt, though his *Aegyptiaca, or Some Account of the Antient and Modern State of Egypt* was never as popular as Denon's book. He did, however, make a solid contribution to Egyptology by translating the Greek portion of the Rosetta Stone, observing prophetically that the Stone would provide a key.

In his suspicion of Hamilton, Denon did him an injustice. He had, in fact, been commissioned by no less a person than the Prince Regent to obtain some of the choicer items in the Louvre for the rival organization, the British Museum. But in a memorandum to the Earl of Bathurst, Hamilton vigorously rejected the idea:

We must necessarily give up the idea of procuring for ourselves any of the chef d'oeuvres from the Louvre. It would throw odium upon our exertion to restore stolen goods, and those French who are the most exasperated against the general measures of restitution already make use of this argument against our pretended disinterested exertion in the cause of justice . . . If accompanied with any proposal to our own benefit the whole will fall to the ground, and the French will remain undisturbed proprietors of what they are now afraid to lose. And they will have the additional gratification of owing it to our mismanagement.

The French remained unconvinced that the English were not making hay while the sun shone. As the Paris correspondent of the *Courier* pointed out, it was singularly unfortunate that English troops had been used to guard the Louvre when the Apollo Belvedere was removed from the Museum. 'The Duke of Wellington has explained that his sending a guard of the 53rd Regiment to the Louvre was an accident which he neither could nor sought to avoid. It happened to be the turn of the English to provide the guard for that day, and the Duke had no discretion.' The fact that Hamilton was a personal friend of the sculptor Canova added further grounds for suspicion. Canova was in Paris as the representative of the Pope, to obtain restitution of material taken from the Vatican. Pius VI had given the sculptor considerable leeway. According to Castlereagh, the British Foreign Secretary and Hamilton's immediate superior:

The French when they plundered the Vatican, ignorantly brought away some works of little or no value. These Canova has authority to cede to the King [Louis XVIII] or to sell, to facilitate the return of the more valuable objects. But it is quite clear that no sum of money could secure to the Prince Regent any distinguished work from His Holiness's collection.

Denon thought otherwise. The cultural rivalry between the two nations that had taken form in Greece, developed in the sands of Egypt, now flowered in Paris, epitomized in the conflict between Hamilton and Denon. Injudiciously, Denon leaves the record of a singularly unedifying squabble he had with Hamilton in the Louvre. Hamilton had begun by criticizing the assembling of so much mixed material under one roof. Denon contemptuously dismissed his criticism as showing the perception of a schoolboy. Hamilton retorted that central Paris was, for all practical purposes, a brothel where no serious student could possibly work. Denon said so was London . . .

It is only fair to add that not all non-Frenchmen were convinced that the cause of art, and of art history, was best served by returning the looted works to their places of origin. Andrew Robertson, a young Scottish miniature painter who was living in Paris at the time, reported a conversation he had with Sir Thomas Lawrence, the painter. 'He said that every artist must lament the breaking up of a collection in a place so central for Europe, for everything was laid open to the public with a degree of liberality unknown elsewhere.'

Robertson was in Paris throughout the period from the Hundred Days onward. In his letters to his family he gives a vivid picture of life in the capital, and the very real sense of indignation, of outrage, that the Parisians felt at the stripping away of 'their' artistic prizes. He noticed that the Louvre was now crowded with common people. 'There used to be nobody. I saw fury and despair in their looks like the brewing of an insurrection.' The upper classes were even more indignant. He met Baron Grosz on the same day.

He would scarcely speak to me and when I introduced Mr Salt he turned away –
said a time of vengeance would come. France was the garden and the cradle of the
arts . . .

The stripping of the Louvre is the chief source of public irritation at present. The
long gallery of the museum presents the strongest possible image of desolation, here
and there a few pictures giving greater effect to the disfigured nakedness of the
walls. I have seen several French ladies in passing along the galleries suddenly break
into extravagant fits of rage and lamentation. They gather round the Apollo to take
their last farewell, with a most romantic enthusiasm. There is so much passion in
their looks, their language and their sighs, in the presence of this monument of
human genius, that a person unacquainted with their character or accustomed to
study the character of the fair sex in England, where feeling is controlled by
perpetual discipline, would be disposed to pronounce them literally mad.

One is bound to wonder whether the pleasure displayed on the return of the
treasures equalled the despair apparently evinced by their departure.

The London *Courier* reprinted Canova's exultant letter: 'We are
beginning to drag forth from this great cavern of stolen goods the precious
objects of art taken from Rome.' The Horses of San Marco were already on
their way back to Venice. They had had a varied stay in Paris, housed first in
the Invalides, then placed on gate piers at the entrance to the Tuileries and
then finally hoisted up as part of a triumphal group on the Arc du Carrousel.
They were removed from the arch by Austrian and English engineers, to the
accompaniment of hostile demonstrations from a large crowd. Just as,
seventeen years earlier, French bayonets had kept back a protesting crowd
of Venetians as the beautiful creatures were moved out of Venice, so now
Austrian bayonets kept back the protesting crowd of Parisians as they began
their return journey south on 17 October 1815. Their journey back took
nearly two months: it was not until mid-December that they arrived at
Mestre and, placed on rafts, were triumphantly ferried across the lagoon
and, after a brief inspection for damage, were hoisted back to their old
position on San Marco.

It was in his *History of Painting in Italy* that Stendhal bitterly criticized
the Allies for taking away the looted material without benefit of treaty, and
calculated that they had taken 1,150 paintings. This was only a small
fraction of the whole. There was, in fact, a grand total of: 2,065 paintings,
130 statues, 150 bas reliefs, 289 bronzes, 16 Etruscan vases, 1,199 enamels,
271 drawings, 471 cameos, 37 wood carvings, 105 ivory vases, 76 'precious
objects' and 294 'divers objects'. Although the most valuable works had
been concentrated in Paris, many had been distributed throughout France.
They were, in effect, lost to sight and remained in their provincial museums.

Others had been sold: the Tsar, for example, had bought the Hessian collection of paintings that Josephine Bonaparte had 'acquired' and, having paid good money, declined to give them up. Short of launching a war upon Russia to obtain the treasures, there was nothing much that Hesse could do. Some had been so treated that it was impossible to remove them from their new settings. The marble pillars which had been taken from the cathedral of Aachen had been structurally built into the Louvre. There were bitter complaints that some of the items that were returned had been so badly restored as to be almost worthless. One advantage (if advantage it can be counted) that came out of the upheaval was the allocation of monetary values to works of art: intended as a rule of thumb guidance for purposes of compensation, this was the foundation of the present system of pricing.

'La Grèce la céda: Rome les a perdus: leur sort changea deux fois – il ne changera pas' – the boastful banners on the Champs de Mars had brought their own hubris. Within five years of Napoleon's exile to St Helena, the treasures had been restored. A century and a half later the commissioners of another entrepreneur of violence, Adolf Hitler, were busily gathering them in again.

7

Adolf Hitler

i The artist's dream

'Between October 1940 and July 1944 my organization accomplished the greatest art operation in history.'

ALFRED ROSENBERG at the Nuremberg Trials, 1946

'Whenever you come across anything that may be needed by the German people, you must be after it like bloodhounds. It must be taken out of store and brought to Germany.'

HERMANN GOERING, speech to the Reich Commissioners for Occupied Territories, 1942

On 4 July 1945 James P. O'Donnell, correspondent for the American *Newsweek* magazine, was rather reluctantly exploring the underground headquarters in Berlin where Hitler had met his death nine weeks earlier. In his brilliant reconstruction of Hitler's last days, *The Berlin Bunker*, O'Donnell describes the vile squalor of the bunker on that July day. Even under the best circumstances this concrete tomb, sunk deep in the garden of the Reich Chancellery, was a cramped and cheerless place: now, two months after it had been abandoned, it beggared description. The Russians had moved all the corpses – both those of the murdered Goebbels children and the self-murdered adults – but the place still stank. It was littered with rubbish, and the floor was inches deep in stagnant water. Uneasily aware of the possibility of booby-traps O'Donnell suppressed the temptation to go souvenir-hunting. Walking through the water, however, he kicked up what appeared to be a large parchment map. On examining it more closely he

149

found that it was not a map but 'an architect's sketch for the post-war remodelling of the Austrian city of Great Linz'. He dropped the map back on the floor but, some twenty-four years later, while interviewing Hitler's architect Albert Speer, he mentioned the incident. Speer remembered the sketch perfectly.

Ah yes [he replied]: On my last day in the Bunker, seven days before Hitler's suicide, the nostalgic Fuehrer hauled out that blueprint and began to reminisce. His lifelong dream of rebuilding the Linz of his childhood had been assigned not to me, but to my colleague, Professor Hermann Giellser. [But] at our melancholy farewell meeting Hitler talked for almost an hour about Linz. Perhaps this was because it was a mutual link with our own past.

In 1981 I met, by appointment, another Austrian: in a London hotel. Professor Herbert Steiner was visiting England to lecture on the subject of right-wing terrorist organizations. The subject was appropriate because Professor Steiner, as an adolescent, was the victim of the most finished of all right-wing terrorist organizations, and has spent most of his life combatting its offspring. An Austrian Jew, he was eleven years old when, in 1933, Austria was harnessed to the German war machine in the *Anschluss* masterminded by Hitler. And he was sixteen when his parents were taken away and subsequently murdered. He himself just succeeded in escaping to England.

He returned to Vienna in 1945. 'I went upstairs to the flat of our neighbours. Hanging on their wall was a painting that used to hang over my bed. In the flat of another neighbour, I saw our carpets. Another neighbour kindly gave me some tea – I noticed that the silver teaspoons were ours. As soon as the Gestapo arrested my parents our neighbours had descended upon the flat and stripped it!' He shrugged with enormous tolerance. 'It could have happened anywhere, I suppose.'

The purpose of our meeting was to discuss one of the most dramatic, cliff-hanging rescue operations in history, the salvation of the art treasures, looted by Alfred Rosenberg's organization, that were buried in a saltmine in Austria. In 1963 Steiner founded the *Dokumentations-archiv des oster-reichischen Widerstandes* (Archive of the Austrian Resistance Movement), of which he is currently the Director. Like most Britons, I had assumed that the Austrians and the Germans had been the only peoples in Europe that had never produced a Resistance movement. 'That's true of Germany – the so-called Werewolf movement never got off the ground. But Austria . . .! There were at least 2,700 Austrians condemned to death between 1938 and 1945 for political reasons.' It had been members of the Resistance movement who had risked their lives to save the treasures of the Alt Aussee saltmine.

During our conversation, we turned naturally to the creator of the holocaust. 'Hitler was making plans for the gallery at Linz right up to the end. You know he fancied himself as an architect, don't you? And a painter!'

As it happened, I had recently seen some of Hitler's paintings. They were by no means as bad as I had expected. The wartime British propaganda that turned Adolf Hitler, the failed artist, into Adolf Schickelgruber, the house-painter, has percolated deep into the British subconscious. The idea that house-painting is, of itself, worthy of contempt is a depressing comment on British valuation of the crafts, but it was effective propaganda, turning the Tyrant of Europe into a figure both comic and contemptible. Though Hitler's work lacks the dash and flair for colour possessed by his arch-enemy Winston Churchill, some of his architectural sketches convey a cool dignity that is by no means unimpressive. It is a sobering thought that, had Vienna's Academy of Fine Arts maintained a less demanding standard for its entrance examination, Europe might have possessed one extra reasonably competent architect, and one less political dictator. And Hitler the Artist did, after all, leave one highly effective legacy – the theatrical trappings of Nazi uniform and insignia which have been adopted by some right-wing groups, mainly in the USA, to give a touch of dignity to threadbare political concepts. The Nuremberg Rallies were turned into stupendous Wagnerian spectacles that inspired the committed and affected even the neutral and hostile. 'I had spent six years in St Petersburg before the war in the best days of the old Russian ballet – but for grandiose beauty I have never seen a ballet to compare with it', wrote Sir Neville Henderson, the British ambassador, after seeing one of these explosions of light and colour and marching men. According to Hitler's biographer, Joachim Fest: 'Each detail was tremendously important to Hitler. Even in the Festivals with their vast blocks of humanity he personally checked seemingly trivial points. He approved every scene, every movement, as he did the selection of flags or flowers, and even the seating order for guests of honour.' Hitler the Artist designed for Hitler the Politician the presentation box in which Nazism was offered to the world. It was only when the box was opened that the corruption inside was evident.

Adolf Hitler was born, in 1889, in Braunau am Inn, but the little town played no part in his life, for the following year the family moved to Upper Austria and in 1894 settled in Linz, the provincial capital. At the turn of the century, Linz had a population of around 50,000. It seems to have been a comfortable little town, strongly class-stratified and with a genteel interest in culture, music predominating: the adjectives used to describe it by those who knew it before World War II include 'dowdy', 'dull', 'stuffy', and 'provincial'. It is notable that the inner ring of the Hitler court in the days of his ascendancy, with its cream teas and banal conversation, accurately reflects this provincialism. Hitler left the town, for ever, when he was eighteen, but it retained a very powerful hold upon his imagination. In the last traumatic years of the war it became his Shangri-la and he would return again and again to the theme of how he would retire there, accompanied by no one but Eva Braun and his dog Blondi. He even expressed his intention of being buried there, and not in state in Berlin.

In October 1907 the eighteen-year-old Hitler sat for the drawing examination of the Academy of Fine Arts in Vienna: its laconic assessment of his work – 'Few heads. Sample drawings unsatisfactory' – changed the course of his life and, arguably, the history of Europe. In indignation, the young man insisted on seeing the Director of the Academy, who suggested that he should study architecture instead. It was a perspicacious remark. Years later, the professional architect Albert Speer recorded his favourable impressions:

When buildings were in question, Hitler repeatedly displayed his ability to grasp a sketch quickly and to combine the floor plan and renderings into a three dimensional conception. Despite all his government business and although he was dealing with anywhere from ten to fifteen large buildings in different cities, whenever the drawings were presented to him again – often after an interval of months – he immediately found his bearings and could remember what changes he had asked for.

During the course of conferences with these top-level professionals, he could also illustrate his point with almost professional skill, dashing off drawing after drawing to do so. And Speer further makes the point: 'in these conferences he usually behaved with civility and restraint. He asked for changes amiably and without any note of insult – entirely in contrast to the domineering tone he took towards his political associates.' In recommending that the gawky, gangling eighteen-year-old from Linz should study architecture, the Director had therefore shown considerable insight. But the young man did not possess the minimum academic qualifications necessary to enter the course and he drifted out of sight towards a quite different goal.

Thirty years after that inconclusive interview in Vienna, on 12 March 1938, Adolf Hitler stood on the balcony of Linz Town Hall, addressing a vast and tumultuously rapturous crowd. He had crossed the Austrian border, at his birthplace at Braunau, earlier that afternoon in the wake of German tanks. This was the beginning of the so-called Anschluss, but all indications are that it was not until his almost hysterically welcoming reception at Linz that he decided, finally, upon incorporating Austria into the Greater Reich. The reception at Linz would have delighted the Walter Mitty that lurks in every man – to have come back, as supreme arbiter, to the home-town he had left as a failure long before must have been deeply satisfying. But Linz had a greater significance: it was the first non-German town he had visited as Chancellor of the German Reich and the unequivocal triumph of his visit boded well for the future. In a sense, therefore, Linz was the foundation stone of the new European empire and as such deserved very special treatment.

The rebuilding of Linz was planned on a gigantic scale: it would outshine both Budapest and Vienna and, with the Fuehrer's own mausoleum at its centre – a mausoleum designed by himself – it would become the very heart of the Third Reich. And, held in that splendid setting like a rare and fabulous jewel, would be the world's greatest art gallery.

Hitler's plans for the rebuilding of Linz were of many years standing: Speer found one of these sketch maps dated 1925, a period when the Nazi party was little more than a gang of organized brawlers – testimony alike to Hitler's confidence in the future and the part that Linz played in his imagination. But the plans for the art gallery seem to have been conceived only in 1938, triggered off by the visit that he made to Italy in the summer of that year. Ever since coming to power he had been collecting paintings on a somewhat desultory basis, 'advised' by his court photographer Heinrich Hoffman. Master and man shared the same unsophisticated, provincial taste with a similar liking for sentimental genre pictures and 'heroic' sculpture. That provincial taste was to lead to the weeding out of all 'degenerate' art from German galleries and the absurd 'Exhibition of Degenerate Art' which, intended as an indication of what was wholly unacceptable to a vibrant new Germany, was in fact an excellent collection of all that was best in modern art. But Adolf Hitler's visit to the Uffizi in Florence in the summer of 1938 appears to have opened his eyes to the provincial nature of the collection being built up in Linz. During the last months of peace, about the time he was preparing to unleash global war, the Chancellor of the Third Reich found time to organize the foundations of the world's richest gallery.

The title given to the operation was 'Sonderauftrag Linz' (Special Operation Linz). Hindsight gives it the appearance of a ruthlessly efficient machine directed towards one end: in reality, it grew on an ad hoc basis.

When making high-level appointments, even those which dealt literally with matters of life and death, Hitler preferred to divide power between two, three or even more rivals, their internecine fighting establishing automatic checks and balances. So, with Sonderauftrag Linz, there were two main appointments: Hans Posse, an art expert, and a collecting agency under the supposed control of the Nazi 'philosopher' Alfred Rosenberg. In fact, Rosenberg himself was controlled by the bizarre figure of Hermann Goering, Posse operated his own system of collection, and in between every light-fingered official who could get away with his own share of loot, or every sycophant who hoped to curry favour with the Fuehrer by conducting his own freelance operation, confused the issue further.

Hans Posse was Hitler's Denon, the dedicated expert to whom the ethics of acquisition were totally irrelevant. He had been the Director of Dresden Art Gallery, had been dismissed by the local Gauleiter for his lack of interest in Nazism and was reinstated by Hitler on the recommendation of a Berlin art dealer, Karl Haberstock, who had himself grown rich on interpreting his all-powerful patron's preferences. Professionally, Posse was quite incorruptible. Albert Speer describes, with admiration, Posse's reaction on being shown Hitler's favourite paintings by nineteenth-century German artists: 'Objective and incorruptible, he turned down many of these expensive acquisitions – "scarcely useful" or "not in keeping with the status of the gallery, as I conceive it".' And Hitler, whom opposition would usually rouse to screaming fury, docilely accepted this expert's opinion. On 26 June 1939, a little over two months before the outbreak of World War II, Dr Hans Posse was formally commissioned to build up the new museum at Linz. All party and state officials, whatever their rank, were ordered to assist Dr Posse in whatever was required to fulfil his mission.

Napoleon's commissioners had sought to legalize their plundering by operating under treaty: Hitler's agents sought to achieve the same result by dividing desirable material into two: that which was 'confiscated' from the State's internal enemies and that which was 'safeguarded' from the State's external enemies. Property which could not be conveniently slotted into either category was bought but, in most cases, the purchasers were using reichsmarks that were worth less than a quarter of their face value. The extraordinary lengths to which high-ranking Nazis were prepared to go to 'legalize' the acquisitions are demonstrated by the anxious correspondence which Hermann Goering had with Germany's Industrial Representative in Holland. Goering had acquired a number of paintings from a Dutch dealer – half shares of which belonged to the dealer's English partner, an enemy alien: 'I would be glad if you would tell me how the share of the enemy alien's property is to be paid, so that the pictures may become my legal property.'

Dr Posse's first mission was a delicate one – to Austria. Unlike subsequent additions to the Reich, Austria was a free partner and wholesale plundering was out of the question. There was, however, an 'enemy of the State' within the Austrian borders – the Jew: in 1938 there were some 300,000 Jews living in Vienna alone. Their property automatically fell forfeit to the State, in Austria as elsewhere, and outstanding among such property was the art collection of the banker and landowner, Louis de Rothschild. It took Dr Posse over four weeks simply to inventory the total Jewish haul, and make his recommendation. Not all the booty was destined for Linz: Posse proposed that 57 out of 269 important paintings should be distributed among Austrian galleries. Hitler subsequently reduced the total, but a considerable number of the paintings found their way into the national collections, evidence of Austrian ambivalence regarding the morality of 'confiscation'. Non-Jewish property, particularly that held by the State, was in the main protected.

But there were exceptions. The regalia of the Holy Roman Empire, including the so-called Crown of Charlemagne, was removed from the Imperial Treasury, Posse using the argument that a fifteenth-century decree of the Emperor Sigismund had enacted that the regalia should be housed in Nuremberg. And to obtain a particularly coveted painting from a private family he conjured up the distant threat of violence that lay behind all the legalism. The painting was the great Vermeer oil, *Portrait of an artist in his studio*: it belonged to Count Czernin, who was neither a Jew nor, by any stretch of the imagination, an 'enemy of the State'. The Count had many times refused handsome offers for this masterpiece: nevertheless, after first resolutely refusing to sell, he abruptly capitulated and accepted a sum far less than he had refused in the past.

The kind of pressure that was probably brought to bear upon Czernin is well illustrated in Madeleine Duke's novel *The Bormann Receipts*. Although fiction, the novel is based upon fact: the looting by state officials of the art collection belonging to Mrs Duke's father. The title of her book is significant: it was Bormann who received the collection. For behind Dr Posse, behind the dozens of art experts and soldiers and architects who made up Sonderauftrag Linz, was the brutal devious figure of Martin Bormann. To the general public he was quite unknown: only those in the inner ring of power realized, by 1940, that this mole-like creature had worked his way in to stand at the Fuehrer's shoulder. Whoever wished to approach Hitler must needs first approach Bormann: whatever Hitler decreed, passed through Bormann. Very early on, this master of survival saw just what the Linz project meant to Hitler, and from then until the very end it was he who controlled the details – and the purse-strings. Dr Hans Posse committed the ultimate *trahison des clercs*. But there is a certain poignancy in the fact that this genuine scholar was obliged to dance to the tune of a man described contemptuously by Speer as 'a peasant', a crude bully who knew nothing and cared less about art; who treated his subordinates like cattle; whose favourite pastime was the seduction of the office girls in his power. But who enjoyed unrestricted access to the ear of Adolf Hitler.

Meanwhile, in Paris, Alfred Rosenberg was setting up the organization proudly called after himself, in the acronymic jargon of the day, ERR – Einsatzstab-Reichsleiter Rosenberg. And Reichsleiter Rosenberg's Administration had one simple objective: the looting of Europe's art.

In 1946 Airey Neave, then twenty-nine years of age, was one of the court officials at the Nuremberg Trials. One of his duties was to serve the indictments, personally, upon each of the accused in his cell and he later published a book on the experience. His portrait of none of the accused is particularly friendly, but when he comes to describe Rosenberg his pen is dipped in a virulent contempt:

He was by far the most boring and pedantic of the accused at Nuremberg. His cell stank, and he was covered in breadcrumbs. I imagine that the boots of our party must have sounded like a firing squad for, as the cell door opened, he was trembling from head to foot. He had the expression of a sick spaniel. He looked then, as he had been over the years, a dreary flop. I was startled to hear that he had once been an art master. His appearance was that of an off-duty undertaker in a Boris Karloff film.

Rosenberg owed his fame to a single book, *The Myth of the Twentieth Century*. The clearheaded Josef Goebbels called it, inelegantly but expressively, an 'ideological belch'. Even Hitler described it as being a mish-mash, a jumble of ill-assorted, undigested facts: he told Speer that Rosenberg's idea of 'an Aryan church' was pure nonsense. Nevertheless, the book sold at least a million copies – and this is an estimate not of Rosenberg's publishers but of the Nuremberg prosecutors. The very fact that it was 'an undigested mish-mash of ill-assorted facts' made it an ideal expression of Nazi philosophy, such as it was. On its shoulders, Rosenberg emerged as the philosopher of Nazism and, in due course, as the editor of the official voice of Nazism, the periodical *Volkischer Beobachter*.

In the privacy of his tea-table conversations Hitler mocked Rosenberg and his work: 'The *Volkischer Beobachter* is as boring as its editor.' In a spirit of what appears almost to be mockery he adorned Rosenberg with sonorous titles – 'Commissioner of the Fuehrer for the Safeguarding of the National Socialist Philosophy'; 'Commissioner for the Central Control of Questions Connected with the Eastern European Region', and the like; but by 1940 Rosenberg had been sacked from, or edged out of, every worthwhile party post. Why therefore did Hitler choose such a man for his art-looting operation?

Albert Speer provides a partial answer. In Spandau prison, brooding over the wasted years, he remarked upon one outstanding characteristic of the man who led Germany to destruction. 'Somebody ought to write on Hitler's dilettantism some day. He had the ignorance, the curiosity and the temerity of the born dilettante . . . a genius of dilettantism. He also had a profound sympathy for all dilettantes – non-academics such as Houston Chamberlain and Walter Darre, not to speak of Rosenberg. They were all dilettantes.' But at best the explanation can be only partial for Hitler's capricious mind is beyond rational analysis: it is no more possible to explain fully why he put Rosenberg in such a position than to explain why he tolerated Hermann Goering as chief of the Luftwaffe long after it had become evident that he was incapable of fulfilling the role.

The collecting headquarters of Sonderauftrag Linz was in Munich, within comfortable distance of Hitler's mountain retreat at Berchtesgaden. The gradually accumulating material was stored in the Fuehrerbau, safely below ground. In the early part of the war Hitler made regular visits to inspect new material, choosing what was to go to Linz and the less coveted material that was to go to favoured German galleries. As pressure increased upon him, so his visits became fewer and fewer until, in the latter part of the war, the treasures piled up in the Aladdin's cave were seen by nobody except their custodians. Hitler was kept closely informed, however: Bormann arranged for all major works of art to be photographed as they were acquired: poring through the handsomely bound volumes became one of Hitler's few recreations. Ironically, the volumes survived to become evidence for the prosecution at Nuremberg.

The ERR's approach to collecting reflected Nazi philosophy – in that, at least, Rosenberg discharged a function. The further East, the less valuable, was a working rule of thumb. Hitler had virtually no interest in the products of the Russian subhumans. Poland and Czechoslovakia were another matter. Even though the Poles and Czechs themselves might be deemed *untermensch*, their art was worthy of collection because, so the theory ran, they had been executed either under German influence or actually by German craftsmen.

An excellent example of the operation of this theory was the fate of the superb Hohenfurth altarpiece. Painted in the mid-fourteenth century for the Hohenfurth monastery in Bohemia, it was removed by the Czech government during the Sudeten crisis of 1938. It was seized by the Gauleiter of Bohemia in 1941 as a 'birthday present' for the Fuehrer. Dr Posse later justified the confiscation partly by arguing that Germany was merely re-acquiring a great German work of art and partly by adopting the same 'curators' argument' that Wallace Budge had used to justify the seizure of Egyptian antiquities: the coveted work of art would be better preserved, and would be seen by more people, than in the obscure place for which it was designed. 'Ethnic justification' was also advanced in support of the seizure of the great Veit Stoss altarpiece in Poland: Veit Stoss was a citizen of Nuremberg and the altarpiece, though commissioned by the King of Poland, therefore belonged to Nuremberg – whither it was duly transported.

There was one further difference between ERR's operations in Eastern and Western Europe. In the East confiscation – with or without justification – was automatic; in the West, 'purchase' was the more common means. Hitler expressly forbade confiscation from French state galleries, though making it clear that in the final peace treaties France would be expected to cede certain of her treasures as 'reparation'. The private collections, both in France and the Low Countries, were fair game. Here, however, the Nazi obsession with legalism created a complex system of wheeling and dealing. German art dealers, such as the smooth, bland Karl Haberstock, made immense fortunes at the same period in which the German armed forces were embarked on a life and death struggle, in which the German civilian population was beginning to experience the full horror of mass bombing. But not only German agents were to benefit financially from the German Fuehrer's passion for acquisition: in all the occupied countries – notably France and Holland – native art dealers rose to the bait of unlimited funds. What Hitler did not require was immediately snapped up by his paladins.

The ERR established its headquarters in Paris, taking over the small museum known as the Jeu de Paume in the Tuileries. Into this centre poured cultural material confiscated, 'bought' or simply looted: and to this centre as to an emporium came favoured members of the Nazi hierarchy, jackals come to pick up what the lion did not want. The fighting Wehrmacht protested vigorously. The Hague Convention specifically forbade all confiscations of the property of defeated enemies, except that deemed essential for the prosecuting of the war. The ERR had, in effect, turned the Wehrmacht into a robber's accomplice. The protests were rejected, for did not Reichsleiter Rosenberg possess, on the highest possible authority, the right to 'transport to Germany cultural goods which he deems valuable'? And if any army commander was disposed to dispute the matter with the Philosopher of Nazism, behind him stood the vast and formidable figure of Hermann Goering, Marshal of the Third Reich, Successor-designate to the Fuehrer. For Goering regarded the ERR as his private collecting agency. Unlike Hitler, with his petit-bourgeois tastes, his limited education, the fat chief of the Luftwaffe was a man of wide culture and experience, a connoisseur of knowledge and discernment. And he was engaged in building up, in his palace of Karinhall, an art collection that would by far have outshone that of Linz had the Thousand Year Reich continued into its third decade.

ii Maecenas

Of all those who directed the affairs of Germany between the years 1933 and 1945 only two might, reasonably, have been expected to make their marks in an ordinary society. They were the architect Albert Speer and the First World War flying hero Hermann Goering. Speer sold out for professional advancement and Goering demonstrated, to the last degree, the truth of Acton's dictum, 'Power tends to corrupt and absolute power corrupts absolutely'.

Goering's childhood was odd enough: born, in 1893, of a decent middle-class family, his mother became the mistress of an aristocratic bachelor in whose splendid castles the young Goering grew up. But he had a normal adolescence and a brilliant young manhood. During the war he became a member of the famous Richthofen Squadron, gaining the highest possible award for bravery, the *Pour le Merite* medal, and when he joined the Nazi party in 1922 he introduced a much-needed note of gallantry and good breeding to a party of scruffy mediocrities. Able, immensely energetic and with social contacts denied his lower-class colleagues, Goering was second only to Hitler in the task of turning a mob of brawlers into a government. He was as totally amoral as any of his colleagues. But he also had a very human streak that allowed him to make contact both with representatives of foreign governments and with the ordinary German people. 'Of all the big Nazi leaders, Hermann Goering was for me by far the most sympathetic. He was himself a typical and brutal buccaneer, but he had certain attractive qualities and I must frankly say that I had a real personal liking for him', remarked Sir Neville Henderson, Britain's ambassador to Germany. And in Germany, the ordinary man in the street responded in a similar way to the bluff bonhomie and the very real courage. 'If a single bomb falls upon Germany, you may call me Meyer', he boasted unwisely. The bombs fell in their thousands of tons, and he was indeed called Meyer behind his back. But he was still cheered and congratulated when he made his appearance in the bombed cities whose condition was so much his responsibility.

It was, nevertheless, a façade. His constitution undermined by drugs, his political standing and influence totally destroyed by the collapse of the Luftwaffe, from 1943 onward he withdrew more and more from reality. This is the period when he adopted the manners and appearance of one of the more dissolute Roman emperors, creating for himself ever more bizarre uniforms, appearing in sweeping robes of crimson velvet, smothered with jewels. He seemed to find, indeed, not simply a solace but an anaesthetic in the handling of gems. Count Galeazzo Ciano, the Italian Foreign Minister, describes how, when Goering was nervous and on edge during some particularly important negotiations, his aides brought him a small vase filled with diamonds. 'He placed them on the table and counted them, lining them up, mixing them together and calmed down completely.' He frequently carried gems in the capacious pockets of his clothing, taking them out, abstractedly pouring them from one hand to another when talking.

Initially, Goering's plans to establish an art gallery received Hitler's approval. As early as 1933, the two had agreed that Goering should lay the foundations for a comprehensive collection which would, in due course, go to the State. Goering had formal plans drawn up, and announced that the transference would take place on his sixtieth birthday – in 1957. But as Hitler's plans for his own gallery gradually crystallized, so the two became rivals. In theory Hitler, as supreme dictator, had everything on his side: in fact, Goering, though outwardly agreeing, was in an ideal position to circumvent his leader's plans. As the pressure of war mounted, and Hitler took ever more direct control, so his opportunities for physical movement dwindled: rarely was he away from one or other of the centres of control. Goering, on the other hand, was able to travel widely, should he so wish: certainly he made not less than twenty visits to France, most of them to Paris, in a little over three years, theoretically on 'visits of inspection', in fact to pursue that collecting of art which had become an obsession with him.

Goering's invariable goal in France was the Jeu de Paume museum, the collecting centre for the ERR. The spineless Alfred Rosenberg succumbed without a fight but he had, in fact, little choice between following the wishes of an omnipotent – but distant – Fuehrer, and a scarcely less powerful and very present Reichsmarschall. And Goering made it easy for him. On 5 November 1940, in his capacity of Reichsmarschall, he divided the loot that was pouring in to ERR into four main categories. The first was for the Fuehrer; the second was for himself; and the third and fourth were to be divided between Germany's universities and public galleries. It was scarcely Rosenberg's fault if the distinction between Categories I and II was only too frequently blurred, or that the chalked letters AH on those items intended for the Fuehrer should have been changed at some stage to HG.

It is possible to gain from two, mutually hostile, sources an inside picture of the operations of ERR. Unknown to Rosenberg, to Goering or to any of the German staff, a dedicated French patriot was at work within the very heart of the organization. Rose Valland was an art historian who, from her specialized position, realized very clearly early on just what was the significance of the activities at the Jeu de Paume. On the face of it, it seems curious that the German administration should have placed someone of Madame Valland's background in so delicate a position. Subsequent research has unveiled the somewhat melancholy reality of French collaboration with the occupying forces, and it is to be assumed that the officials at ERR simply accepted Madame Valland's application for employment at its face value – just another French citizen accepting the reality of political change. They could not have made a more embarrassing mistake. Madame Valland had two objectives: to delay or otherwise sabotage the workings of the organization and to keep records of the various movements of the looted works.

On the other side of Europe, in Goering's rural palace of Karinhall, was another dedicated woman, Fraulein Gisela Limberger, Goering's Second Secretary, painstakingly keeping account of those treasures that eventually arrived in Karinhall. Between the establishment of ERR in the autumn of 1940 and its dissolution in July 1944, some 21,000 works of art were taken in. Of these, Goering had 237 paintings, 15 stained glass windows, 28 statues and 51 pieces of furniture – from France alone. Like Hitler, he disliked modern painting, but was canny enough to realize that there was an international market for it. In the summer of 1941 – at about the time that Operation Barbarossa launched the biggest military adventure in history – he was negotiating with a Swiss art dealer in Lausanne to exchange a number of French impressionist works for the medieval German paintings that he loved.

He also seems to have made a spirited attempt to get hold of the Van Eyck altarpiece, *Adoration of the Lamb*, just 150 years after it had been wrested from Napoleon. The Belgian authorities had sent the great painting to Pau in the Pyrenees for safekeeping. Goering sniffed it out and put pressure on the Vichy Minister of Culture, Abel Bonnard, to acquire it. There are conflicting accounts of the subsequent movements of the altarpiece. The journalist, Willi Frischauer, who interviewed many of the surviving residents of Karinhall immediately after the war, believed that the altarpiece had been housed in a special room in Karinhall. On the other hand, it undoubtedly turned up, with other Linz treasures, in Austria after the war. The probability is that Goering did indeed 'own' this incomparable work for two or three years and it was then evacuated, with other Karinhall treasures, to Berchtesgaden in the last months of the war.

As early as 1943 Goering boasted to Rosenberg, 'I have now obtained, by means of purchase, presents, bequests and barter, perhaps the greatest private collection in all Europe.' Backed as he was by the unlimited funds of the State, he was prepared to buy where necessary. But one of his most effective means of acquisition was through 'presents'. Like some Oriental potentate who had to be propitiated with rich gifts, he expected those who required his favours to make presents in cash or kind that would enable him to expand his collection. Goebbels recorded, with indignation, how in 1944 the Mayor of Berlin contacted him, asking what would be a suitable present for the Reichsmarschall's birthday. But even Goering could be embarrassed. Over-zealous paratroopers cleaned out the treasures that had been stored in the monastery of Monte Cassino for safekeeping. Italy was still technically an ally, and the Marshal expressed his anger in blistering terms – but somehow the chests containing some of Italy's most precious works of art remained in Germany.

Towards the end of the war, Speer and a companion were invited to dinner with Goering at Karinhall. 'The meal was not too lavish, but I was rather taken aback when at its end an ordinary brandy was poured for us, while Goering's servant poured his, with a certain solemnity, from a dusty old bottle. "This is reserved for me alone", he commented without embarrassment to his guests, and went on about the particular French palace in which this rare find had been confiscated.' After the meal, he took them on a tour of the building, proudly displaying the treasures ranging from rare wines to Gobelin tapestries. The anecdote revealed two things about

Goering: his total indifference to the opinions of his peers – and the fact that he was collecting to satisfy his own pleasure. Hitler, like Napoleon, looted for his country: Goering looted for Hermann Goering. Had he, and the Nazi state, survived until his sixtieth birthday it is highly unlikely that he would have denuded Karinhall of its treasures for the State – or turned it into a State Museum. For Karinhall was more than a place: it was an idea in a shrine.

Karinhall has gone now, destroyed with the distorted system that had given it birth. Willi Frischauer saw its ruins in 1945, just before the Iron Curtain clanged down across Europe, separating wartime allies:

Today, like ghosts in an eerie prehistoric landscape, two dirty lion figures, their marble ears and mane chipped and broken, rise from the dim light of an evening in the Schorfheide – behind them a waste of masonry and rubble. Now and then a shot rings out as soldiers of the Soviet Occupation Army hunt the stray deer which have survived the destruction of Karinhall. The lions and a slab of stone with the Goering family crest are all that remains of the elaborate portal through which Goering took his bride in 1935.

Goering acquired the estate, forty-five miles north-east of Berlin, in 1933 – the year that the Nazis finally emerged as the legitimate government of Germany. The Reichsmarschall promptly set aside 100,000 acres of forest, heath and lakeland as a reserve – where, amongst other activities, he successfully experimented with re-introducing bison and elk. The original house was simply a hunting lodge, but from 1933 onwards no year passed without some major alteration, some extension being made to it. All the Nazi paladins seem to have fancied themselves as architects and Goering was no exception, according to his German biographer Ernst Gritzbach, in designing everything himself. The estate was named after his first wife, the Swedish Karin von Kantzow, who had saved his life at risk of her own and whom he had abandoned on her death bed in Sweden to attend a political meeting in Germany. She became a cult figure with him. As soon as he acquired the estate, he built an immense mausoleum in the grounds and transported her body thither. On the day of his second marriage, to the actress Emmy Sonnermann, he visited the coffin as soon as he had returned to the house with his new bride. She accepted the situation with tranquillity – for not the least remarkable thing about the hedonist Hermann Goering was that he was deeply loved by two beautiful and virtuous women.

The catalogue of the works of art at Karinhall is a roll-call of European culture: Tintoretto and Rembrandt, Velasquez, Van Dyke, Leonardo da Vinci, Chardin, Goya, Cranach, Hals, Boucher, Rubens – all were represented. To the dazed eye of Sumner Welles, who was taken on a conducted tour of the place, there were 'hundreds of paintings'. Speer describes rooms filled with jewelry cabinets. There were rare tapestries and carpets, porcelain, silver, gold. And everywhere there was rare and exquisite furniture, representing four centuries of European culture from the Renaissance to the nineteenth century, scattered about as everyday objects. Even the private rooms must have resembled public galleries: over Goering's vast four poster was an equally immense statue of Europa. 'It would be difficult to find an uglier building or one more intrinsically vulgar in its ostentatious display', was Welles's opinion.

The end came in April 1945. For weeks beforehand the treasures had been packed and had begun to be transported south, away from and ahead of the terrifying advance of the Soviet armies. The only safe place was the so-called Mountain Redoubt of Berchtesgaden. It was in a chalet there, on 9 May, that Goering was captured and taken to the headquarters of the American 7th Army. Apart from one trainload of treasures that was intercepted between Karinhall and Berchtesgaden, all the rest was buried in cellars in and around the Alpine Redoubt.

The war ended: a shattered continent started to piece itself together, and there began what must be the largest treasure hunt in history. A generation later, it is still in process, involving the children and, in some cases, the grandchildren of the original participants.

iii Treasure hunt

On 18 December 1945 the drab courtroom at Nuremberg was briefly enlivened by a film show. The audience, with varying emotions, watched as reproductions of paintings and sculpture were projected on the screen. Joshua Reynolds's painting of Lady Spencer, Michelangelo's *Madonna and Child*, part of the Van Eyck altarpiece, were among those which brought a touch of life and colour into the room. Also circulating were thirty-nine handsomely bound volumes, each containing photographs of looted objects. 'Neither the British Museum, the Louvre, the Metropolitan in New York, nor the Tretiakov Gallery in Moscow could present a comparable catalogue. Even if they pooled their treasures they would fall far short of the art collection that Germany had amassed from the other nations of Europe', said the prosecuting counsel. Then, turning to the bound volumes, the counsel quoted from a letter that accompanied one of them. It was from Rosenberg, at that moment sitting on the front bench of the dock and

Adolf Hitler spent his formative childhood years in Linz, the provincial capital of Upper Austria. Through the period of his rise to power he carried with him a fervent wish for the grandiose reconstruction of the town – a plan which eventually found focus in 'Sonderauftrag Linz' – Special Operation Linz – and the looting of Europe's art treasures. (*above*) Hitler looks wistfully at the ambitious model for the Greater Linz that he planned: the photograph was taken a few days before his suicide. (*left*) A detail of the model showing the museum at Linz which, stuffed with looted treasures, was going to be the greatest art gallery the world had ever seen.

'THE GREATEST ART OPERATION IN HISTORY'

The moment of looting. A painting by Tintoretto is inspected by a Nazi officer before being transported to Germany (*opposite below*). The appalling dangers to which these superb but fragile works were exposed is revealed as Signorelli's *Crucifixion* is dumped casually on its side after being taken from the Uffizi Gallery in Florence (*opposite above*) and paintings taken from Monte Cassino are carried into the Vatican for 'safekeeping' (*below*).

TREASURE HUNT

The Allies move in. Goering's 'treasure' included fine wines (*below left*). MFA & A (Monuments, Fine Arts and Archives) officers inspect loot from Polish churches deposited in a salt mine (*below*), while General Eisenhower examines silver in another mine (*left*). The Crown of Charlemagne (*right*), removed from Austria to Nuremberg, was found in 1945.

THE BEST-LAID PLANS . . .

The Nazi looting organization was by no means a homogeneous operation: on the contrary, it fragmented as powerful and unscrupulous men grabbed what they could. Pre-eminent among them was Goering, using greed and sophisticated taste, backed by his powerful position in the Reich. Most of his plunder was housed in his mansion at Karinhall, but as the Russians advanced westwards in the last weeks of the War, they were given new and temporary homes. (*right*) Eyeball to eyeball, the loot and its liberator, at Berchtesgaden. (*below*) A washroom at the former Luftwaffe headquarters at Konigsee. (*left*) Twenty years after the War, paintings were still being stored in the cellar of Hitler's former headquarters in Munich.

listening in profound embarrassment to his own, fulsome words, addressed to Hitler, hoping 'that this short occupation with the beautiful things of art which are nearest to your heart will send a ray of beauty and joy into your revered life'.

The Nuremberg trials brought home formally the extent of the looting operation. But long before that, details of the bizarre story were surfacing as the Allied armies liberated more and more areas of occupied Europe. In October 1944 the *Times* correspondent in Rome provided the first clear picture of the extent of German looting in Italy. At least 500 items were missing from Florence alone. A fortnight before the city fell to the Allies two SS officers turned up, presented themselves to the Italian superintendent of art works in Tuscany and demanded the collection of a carefully compiled list of paintings and statuary from the Uffizi, Pitti and Bargello. 'These were all taken by the Germans under the pretext of moving them to greater safety. But they did this more in the manner of crackers of cribs than of persons solicitous in the cause of art.'

The survival of some of these supreme works of art can only be called miraculous. The writer Eric Linklater, then serving in the army, describes how he awoke one morning in a barn to see a number of rolled canvases stacked around. One, on being unrolled, proved to be the *Primavera* of Botticelli. They found shelter in the Italian home of Sir Osbert Sitwell, the castle of Montegufoni. In his biography of the Sitwells John Pearson describes how, in distant England, Sir Osbert had been painfully awaiting news of the fate of his home, caught up in the battlefield. 'I suppose Montegufoni is in the battle line this week. We shall probably see the usual photographs of "Montegufoni liberated" and the usual heap of stones and Guido offering a lemon to the forces.' But the mansion survived, with its priceless contents:

I heard yesterday from an old comrade in arms, General Alexander, that Montegufoni my Italian castello is untouched. And it has been used to put all the great Italian pictures in by the Italian government. So I have had, as distinguished guests, Venus rising from the sea and Primavera and the Duke and Duchess of Urbino by Piero della Francesca and many saints and popes. I am so happy about it. It's just the use I would like to have the house put to.

Other works of art were less fortunate. In Berlin, paintings by Rubens and Van Dyck and at least one Michelangelo sculpture were destroyed when the flak tower in which they were temporarily housed was bombed.

But there was an even greater threat, as was made clear in a report, in May 1945, published by the London *Daily Telegraph*. The writer was Cornelius

Part of Goering's collection at Berchtesgaden, to which it had been moved and where he was captured on 9 May 1945.

Ryan, later to gain international acclaim as the author of war histories which, though covering vast panoramas, were minutely documented. In 1945, however, he was still an unknown writer and the probability is that most of the *Telegraph*'s readers dismissed the report as one of the highly coloured stories which were continually surfacing in the immediate postwar period. According to Ryan, an immense cache of art treasures had been discovered in a saltmine in Upper Austria and, as though that were not drama enough, the report ended with the information that the Germans had intended to destroy the mine and its contents and had placed eight enormous bombs, all ready to be exploded at the touch of a switch. This incalculable blow to civilization had been prevented, at the last moment, by a band of 'Free Austrian' fighters.

Ryan's report was correct both in details and general circumstances, an impressive example of newspaper reporting under very adverse conditions. Over the next few months stories of first-hand experiences began appearing in newspapers and magazines – perhaps the first examples of the deluge of 'wartime stories' which was about to swamp the Western world. A Major Edward Adams contributed to an American Army publication, *The Quartermaster*, a remarkable account of how he, with a French colleague, had spent months tracking down hidden treasures. Other similar stories appeared in British and American periodicals, the whole forming a kind of mosaic picture which the reader had to assemble for himself.

As early as September 1945, however, there had existed an authoritative and comprehensive account of the looting of the treasures, their concealment, and subsequent restitution. Hard on the heels of the fighting soldiers of the Allied invasion there came an organization entitled the Art Looting Investigation Unit of the US Office of Strategic Studies. Eisenhower, the Commander-in-Chief of the Allied armies, had been persuaded that the restoration of the looted material was a matter of great political importance.

It is not wholly clear why the Americans should have taken the lead in this matter. Elsewhere, in Italy in particular, British experts seconded to the Monuments, Fine Arts and Archives section of the Restitution Control Branch of the occupying forces did much good work. It is probable that, because Bavaria and Austria became part of the American zone, and because much of the loot was hidden in these areas, the task of investigation naturally fell to the Americans. Whatever the reason, by 15 September the ALIU had produced a number of 'Consolidated Interrogation Reports' which, based on the interrogation of the German officials involved, gave a detailed and comprehensive picture of the looting operation.

The reports were secret in 1945. A copy of report No 2, dealing with Goering's activities, came into the hands of Willi Frischauer in 1950. It was still secret. Nearly twenty years later a copy of Report No 4, dealing with Hitler's plans for Linz, came into the hands of two journalists, David Roxan and Ken Wanstall. It was still secret. In an interview in *The Times* in September 1964, David Roxan disclosed that, though they had received somewhat reluctant permission to publish from the American National Archives and Records, they were bluntly refused permission to see, much less publish, material in the other reports: 'They were maintaining as much secrecy as they possibly could. I cannot think why. These reports – they were of interrogations of various people by art experts – were made twenty years ago.'

Willi Frischauer assumed that the reports were kept secret because 'of an avalanche of requests for restitution, many of which were simply speculative and spurious'. This is a possible explanation, but a more likely one was the profound embarrassment caused by the discovery of just how much collaboration must have been taking place between the German invaders and the citizens of the occupied countries for Sonderauftrag Linz to be quite so effective as it had been. In autumn 1945 'collaboration' was an obscene word. It was assumed, in general, that all citizens of German-occupied countries had been, de facto, heroes: that all citizens – apart from a handful of corrupt individuals – had nobly resisted the Nazi terror. The discovery that this was not the case, that in France and the Low Countries in particular a lot of art dealers had made a lot of money from the invaders, was something deemed best kept quiet.

The Consolidated Interrogation Reports show how, under the mounting pressure of the Allied bombing campaign and faced with the threat of invasion, those responsible for the safekeeping of the looted material retreated with it deeper and deeper into the Reich. The ERR had already taken over the extraordinary mountain castle of Neuschwanstein – created by the mad King Ludwig of Bavaria – as a main storehouse, and it assumed ever more importance in the latter months of the war. The American Major Adams inspected it, with a French colleague, immediately after the capitulation of Germany. 'Our preliminary survey of the castle took nearly an entire day. The cache turned out to be about 6,000 items of fine paintings, sculpture, silver, archaeological relics, antique tapestries, furniture, oriental carpets and a large collection of rare books. Half of it was in its original crates. The rest of it was stored in orderly racks or bins in locked rooms.' The MFA & A team found an excellent administrative suite in the castle, complete with reference library, photo laboratory, conservation laboratory and workshop. Ironically, the team was able to give much-needed employment to the locals, twenty labourers, an electrician and a carpenter being taken on to sort and pack the wealth of objects.

The bizarre King Ludwig II would have enjoyed the surrealist collection housed in his mountain-top castle, but the material in the saltmine at Alt Aussee surpassed even this. The saltmines of Upper Austria are amongst the oldest in Europe: the Romans knew and exploited them. That at Alt Aussee was immense, with chambers leading out of chambers. It had been chosen as a potential storage place for works of art because its depth would have protected it even from the 'block-buster' bombs then in use: its remoteness enabled it to be sealed off under a strong SS guard and the cleanliness and dryness of its atmosphere ensured that even delicate objects could be stored indefinitely without detriment. Initially, it had been used as a safe deposit for artifacts taken from Austrian museums and galleries but, as the bombing raids on Munich increased in frequency and intensity, Hitler ordered material to be moved out of the Fuehrerbau into the mine. It says much for the dedication of the German workers that thousands of fragile objects were moved, under conditions of a wartime winter along appalling mountain roads, with little damage. By April 1945 some 10,000 paintings (including the Van Eyck altarpiece), 68 pieces of sculpture (including Michelangelo's *Madonna and Child*), as well as thousands of prints, drawings, coins, books and various objects, had been moved to Alt Aussee.

Safe, that is, from allied bombs. In early April however, there arrived at the mine a number of heavy wooden crates stencilled with the legend 'Marble – do not drop'. Inside each box, however, was one of the great bombs to which Cornelius Ryan had referred. They were taken underground, and placed at certain strategic points.

There can be no doubt about the purpose of these bombs. But did Hitler himself order preparations for what would have been the greatest act of vandalism in history?

'He may well have done so', Herbert Steiner told me. 'After all, he was prepared to take the State down with him. The direct order would have been given by Bormann, however, and it was carried out by Gauleiter Eigruber.' As far as can be established, Eigruber received a typically ambivalent instruction from Bormann, simultaneously ordering him to ensure that the treasures in the mine came to no harm – but also did not fall into Allied hands. The creation of a vast booby trap was Eigruber's response to an impossible directive. What happened next is confused, with some of the details contradictory. 'You must remember', Steiner said, 'that there were two or three resistance groups working in the area – and they were not all necessarily in sympathy with each other. One was led by a Communist, Sepp Plieseirs. He was a local man who had been in a concentration camp and established a partisan group of about a dozen men. Another one was led by an ex-PoW called Geiswinkler who volunteered to be parachuted into the locality. It is said that Eigruber's mistress, a local girl, learned about the preparation to blow up the mine and passed it on to one of the groups.'

However the operation was organized, there is no doubt that western civilization owes a profound debt of gratitude to a certain Karl Sieber, a German art expert who, wearing an incongruous uniform, worked on the treasures as they poured into the mine. It was largely through Sieber's good offices – undertaken at a time when such action would be construed as treason and punished accordingly – that the Austrian resistance workers were able to block off the mine with a series of controlled explosions. Almost immediately afterwards an American infantry division arrived, were appraised of the situation, and put a guard upon the mine until a detachment of the MFA & A relieved them of responsibility.

The problems of restoring looted treasures after the Napoleonic wars had been relatively straightforward. Most of the objects had been housed in one or other of France's museums and were of known provenance. Nevertheless, scores – and probably hundreds – of items were never returned. The problem of tracking down Nazi loot was immense: there were at least 200 official caches in and around southern Germany and an untold number of decidedly unofficial caches – separately looted items, many of which would be used for bargaining on the black market in the desperate period immediately after the war ended. The looters, both official and private enterprise, of the Napoleonic wars had all emanated from France. The homelands of those who acquired, in whatever manner, looted Nazi treasures were scattered around the globe: as they returned home, they took their acquisitions with them, confusing the picture still more. Most were never seen again, or simply turned up as private possessions in art sales. But occasionally some stolen object was so well known that, though it might disappear for decades, eventually it would surface, creating an international furor. A remarkable example of this was the discovery of two miniatures by Antonio Pollaiuolo, missing from the Uffizi since 1944.

In December 1962 an art restorer, Dr A. A. La Vinger, appeared on Los Angeles television in a routine programme. Towards the end, he made the point that many people possessed valuable works of art and were quite unaware of the fact. Listening to the programme was a waiter of German origin, Johan Meindl, who recalled that he had two ancient-seeming oil paintings hanging on the wall in his modest flat. He took the paintings to La Vinger who, in due course, established that they were indeed the missing Pollaiuolos. He estimated their value at some $250,000 and, delighted at the publicity this would bring him, broke the news to the press. Whether or no he would, ultimately, have benefited it is not possible to say, for he died the following week. But around the unfortunate Meindl's head there burst an international storm. Louisa Becherucci, an art expert attached to the Uffizi, promptly made the journey to Los Angeles and, satisfying herself that these had been the property of the Uffizi, alerted her government. The Italian Premier, Fanfani, cabled the American President Kennedy: an embarrassed Department of Justice persuaded Meindl to store the paintings in Los Angeles Museum until their future had been decided – and the world's press descended upon him. In one week, the unfortunate waiter had first had his hopes raised with the prospects of a sale of a quarter of a million dollars, was subsequently informed that the Italian government had no intention of establishing a precedent by paying for stolen property, and ended by being regarded as a species of international crook. How had he come by these rare works of art that belonged to one of the world's most famous museums?

The answer was not long in coming. Meindl was a Bavarian who had emigrated to America after the war. During the war he and his wife came to know an elderly lady, Josephine Berkman, who once worked for the German Ministry of Art. It seemed that she fell ill, Meindl and his wife took care of her and, in 1946, in gratitude she gave them the paintings. But where had Josephine Berkman acquired them? Here the trail is lost, for she died before the Meindls moved to America. The probability is that they were acquired by Goering – as a present for his baby daughter, it is believed – and must have come into Fraulein Berkman's hands during the chaotic transfer of material from Karinhall to Berchtesgaden or Alt Aussee. The two tiny paintings could easily have been slipped into a pocket – or a handbag.

Italy suffered more than any other country from the attention of looters both official and unofficial. There is scarcely a village church that does not possess at least one art object worth stealing. The centre of every historic city is adorned with every variety of sculptured material, from titanic marble statues to cast or carved embellishments of buildings, little of it protected, as the current Italian government has found to its cost. And some of the fiercest, most destructive fighting of the war took place in and around Tuscany, containing probably the highest concentration of cultural objects in the world. Much was destroyed, but much, too, was simply left unprotected. In 1950 I was travelling in the mountainous country behind Lucca and, losing my way, sought shelter for the night in a ruined Franciscan monastery. It had once been an enormous building, sheltering more than a hundred people. Now it held only two men, friars both, acting as caretakers and living in the vast kitchen. Initially they were not particularly welcoming, for my accent betrayed my origins and the monastery had been destroyed by the RAF and not the Luftwaffe. But they thawed out, shared their poor meal – a thin vegetable soup – and gave me a bed for the night. The bed was an old, battered iron frame, set up in a sea of books for, apart from the kitchen, the library was the only remotely habitable room in all that huge building. I spent two hours, torn between ecstasy and horror, prospecting through the piles of books and manuscripts, and found among them a manuscript of the *Divine Comedy*. Codices of Dante are by no means rare but each is, by definition, unique. I took it down in the morning and showed the two friars, but they only shrugged and went on with their housework. There was nothing they could do, and as late as 1950 what was probably a fortune in bibliographical material lay at the mercy of anybody with a ladder and a lack of scruples.

There was little that Italians could do about spontaneous looting. But in response to the massive operation set up at an official level by the Germans, the Italians developed what must surely be the world's first Ministry for Treasure-Hunting – and one which proved so effective that it has been adapted to combat modern art thefts. The Minister was a Florentine, Rodolfo Siviero, who was first alerted to the scale of the problem by the then Vice-President, the philosopher Benedetto Croce. After the collapse of Italian resistance in September 1943, at least half the country was under the direct control of the Germans. Croce, a Neapolitan, was concerned by the rumour that art treasures from Naples that had been lodged for protection in the monastery of Monte Cassino had been moved 'for safeguarding' by the Germans. Where had they been taken? How many more of Italy's treasures were being similarly 'safeguarded'? Croce contacted Siviero, who was at that time head of an espionage unit working with partisans behind the German lines, and arranged with him to keep track, as far as possible, of the movements of art objects in the north of Italy.

After Italy became a 'Co-belligerent', in the military jargon of the day, the Allied Military Government co-operated in the tracking down and recovery of stolen art objects, setting up a Fine Arts Sub-Commission. It was headed by an American colonel, Professor Ernest de Wald, and a British officer of the same rank, Ward-Perkins, later director of the British School of Archaeology in Rome. Professor Ward-Perkins had a similar experience to that of Eric Linklater, as he described to a journalist, Conrad Allen. It was in the Sitwells' castello of Montegufoni. 'I walked through the french windows and stopped dead with a gasp. Right in front of me, propped up against the wall, was Velazquez's magnificent portrait of Philip IV on horseback. Next to it was a Madonna by Giotto and, peering over it, another by Cimabue. Next to the two Madonnas was the famous *Battle of San Romano* by Paolo Uccelli.'

Paradoxically, the ending of the war increased Siviero's problems. Now formally attached to the Italian Foreign Ministry, he was one of the experts who examined the treasure troves at Alt Aussee and Berchtesgaden and had little difficulty in identifying items taken from the Uffizi and the Pitti. But he immediately encountered a legal problem regarding their restitution. As an ex-member of the Axis Powers, Italy could not claim reparation as of right and it was not until 1948 that the peace treaty was modified to allow Italy to claim back her own. But even now Siviero encountered a bizarre legal twist, very similar to that which French savants had employed in an attempt to retain material obtained by 'treaty'. A considerable number of the objects had not, indeed, been looted in the traditional sense, but purchased. No matter that the transaction itself was made under pressure, or that the sums paid were far less than would have been obtained in the open market: receipts existed, contracts had been signed. A number of German scholars even protested to President Truman that what had been paid for by German taxes belonged to Germany.

Under the Adenauer administration, the Germans tended to adopt a more conciliatory attitude, but tempers still flare. In 1975, a major row developed over a ceiling by the eighteenth-century Italian painter, Sebastiano Ricci which, Professor Siviero claims, the Germans obtained under duress – although money changed hands. The ceiling originally adorned the Mocenigo Palace in Venice and, in the early part of the war, was taken to Rome for safekeeping. Hitler put pressure on Mussolini who, in turn, ordered his Foreign Secretary (who also happened to be his son-in-law) Count Ciano to authorize its sale. Long after the war, the ceiling went on display in the West Berlin State Museum whose director, Professor Henning Bock, argued that it had been bought legally. 'Lies, all lies', Professor Siviero is reported as saying.

VI The Horses of San Marco, though almost as symbolic of Venice as the Winged Lion, nevertheless sum up two millennia of cultural plunder. Venice herself first plundered them from Constantinople, where they had long before arrived from ancient Rome or Greece.

The Germans have consistently refused to collaborate in returning missing works of art. But for the pressure and diligence of the Allies, we would have recovered almost nothing. Four years ago, the ceiling turned up in Berlin, insolently displayed in a state museum – an ugly testimony that Nazi-Fascist practices are still paying off. This masterpiece should be back in Venice on the ceiling of the Palace for which it was painted.

One can only regret that there was no Rodolfo Siviero to protest at the French retention of Veronese's *Marriage at Cana*, the other Venetian treasure which never found its way home.

Siviero's detective work played a leading part in the affair of the Pollaiuolo miniatures. As it happened, he was already on their trail in Europe, together with a number of other missing Uffizi pieces, when he was informed of La Vinger's approach to the Italian consul in Los Angeles. According to Californian law, Johan Meindl was the legal owner of the miniatures, having been in possession of them for more than fifteen years, and was therefore entitled to sell them for what he could get. But the evidence of theft produced by Siviero convinced Meindl's lawyer that a lawsuit was unlikely to end in his client's favour and he, in his turn, persuaded the waiter to surrender the paintings without compensation. The contact proved a fruitful one for Siviero and Italian art generally: Meindl provided him with the name of a butcher still living in Munich through whom a remarkable selection of Italian Renaissance paintings – including works by Bronzino, Lorenzo di Credi and Correggio – were recovered.

Under Rodolfo Siviero's direction, the Italian government had recovered some 3,000 major works by 1966 and, in that year, reduced Siviero's Recovery Office budget from £17,000 annually to £6,000. The Ministry of Fine Arts proclaimed itself satisfied that only eighteen works were still unaccounted for – including the famous head of a faun which Michelangelo sculpted as a youth. Italian art experts disagreed emphatically, insisting that the real number was at least 700, and publishing a list to prove their case. So basic a contradiction argues that the total number is not, and probably never will be, known.

The majority of missing art objects are relatively small – paintings designed to hang in a room or ornaments to stand in it. The fact that the Russians could lose the room as well – and that its whereabouts are even now unknown – is indication of the problem facing any would-be treasure hunter.

The room is the famous Amber Room of Tsarskoe Selo, consisting of some fifty-five square yards of exquisitely carved amber panels, backed with silver

X   Whose heritage now? Days of carnival in St John's, Antigua, where the inhabitants once worked as slaves on the sugar estates described in the Codrington Papers.

foil and conservatively valued, in the 1960s, at some £20 million. It was originally made, in or about 1709, for Frederick I of Prussia, who gave it to Peter the Great. Peter set it up in his Winter Palace in what was then St Petersburg, but his daughter Elizabeth moved it to the Summer Palace of Tsarskoe Selo, a few miles outside St Petersburg. It survived the Revolution, was opened to the public and achieved worldwide fame. The Germans captured the Palace in 1942 and completely gutted it, removing the entire Amber Room. In 1949 the Soviet Government followed Italy's lead and set up a special Commission to track down plundered Russian treasures, and the Amber Room was high on the list. It was traced, with little difficulty, to Koenigsburg (now called Kaliningrad) but there the trail became confused.

There is little doubt that the Amber Room was officially 'confiscated', for even the most enterprising freelance looter could not have organized the labour and transport to dismantle, pack and move the heavy, fragile panels. The Room's fame, and the fact that it was of German origin, ensured that it engaged the attention of German officials at the highest levels, almost certainly at the direct orders of Hitler. The so-called Brown Tsar of the East, Erich Koch, Gauleiter of East Prussia, was probably the person who co-ordinated the operation.

The Amber Room was destined for the Prussian Fine Arts Museum in Koenigsburg – which incidentally had one of the world's most famous amber collections – and was certainly on display there in September 1944. Packed in twenty-four massive boxes it was probably taken by train further west in October. And then disappears from history. According to some accounts, it was buried in one of the ubiquitous saltmines and is still there. Other reports place it in a private castle in Saxony, and even in an abandoned brewery in Koenigsburg. At one stage, the Soviet Commission entertained the idea that it had been sunk while being shipped west via the Baltic, and later the Soviet Government believed – or affected to believe – that it was secretly being held by the West German Government. But as the Soviet Government also affected to believe that the Allies connived at the escape of Adolf Hitler, it is difficult to know what credence to give this assertion. At the time of writing, the whereabouts of this massive, now incredibly valuable, treasure is as great a mystery as it was in the autumn of 1944. Unless, of course, it is back in Russia – which is by no means unlikely. The Soviet Embassy in London declined to provide the author with any information, but referred enquiries to the Ministry of Culture in Moscow. No reply has been received to a letter addressed to the Ministry.

The total number of missing objects from all over Europe almost certainly runs into thousands. In addition to those taken from official collections, whose existence would be recorded, is the unknown number taken from homes whose owners were 'liquidated' in the concentration camps and which change hands clandestinely. The uncertainty provides a rich harvest for con-men and criminals. 'They turn up with a picture said to belong to Goering – and that immediately puts an additional value on it,' an English art expert told me. 'Chances are that it is a fake anyway – but the buyer can't do a thing about it.'

And most tragic of all are those thousands of items whose whereabouts are indeed known – but whose owners are not. These, too, were the personal treasures of the victims of Nazism which came into the hands of the State after the deaths of their owners. And the meticulous, efficient bureaucracy processed them and protected them: none who saw the collection of rings and gold dental fillings in the strong room of the Reichsbank will ever forget the macabre evidence of national schizophrenia. In 1960 I travelled between Cologne and Heidelberg with an English banker whose task was to unravel the affairs of such victims. 'I've been at it since the war: it'll keep me going until I retire.'

Austria, where the process started, has one of the largest art collections of this nature. Some 8,000 art treasures, taken from private Austrian collections during the war, were returned by US forces after the war. In 1952, they became the responsibility of the Ministry of National Works and Monuments and in 1969 a law was passed stating that all items remaining unclaimed by the end of 1970 would become State property. At 31 December in that year, the collection had been whittled down to 657 oil paintings, including canvases by Frans Hals, and several hundred assorted pieces of silver, bronze, ceramics, coins and books.

IV
THE THIRD WORLD

8

City of Blood

'The King of Benin is fetiche, and the principle object
of adoration in his dominions.'

CAPTAIN JOHN ADAMS, *Remarks on
the country from Cape Palmas to the
Congo*

'Our educational system has failed to take cognisance of
the cultural matrix of our people.'

Federal Ministry of Information, Lagos

In August 1980 a film entitled *The Mask* was given a private showing in
London. Made by the Nigerian actor and producer Eddie Ugbomah, it was
intended for general release only in Nigeria. Guests at the preview were
given a handout whose text, purporting to be factual, explained how in 1815
one of the 'colonial masters' who were ruling Nigeria with a rod of iron 'was
about to return to England after his duty of slavery and stole the mask of
Queen Adesua of Benin to take with him'. The mask was given to Queen
Elizabeth I [sic], who in her turn gave it to the British Museum. 'In 1979
Eddie Ugbomah wrote the story of how the mask could best be recovered.'
The film which accompanied the handout was a more or less preposterous
farrago, deplorably influenced by the James Bond films, in which a Major
Obi, a black James Bond, is personally commissioned by the President of
Nigeria to get the mask back at all costs – though if detected, he will of
course be disowned. Slugging and slaying his way from Lagos to
Bloomsbury, leaping in and out of female-occupied beds, outwitting venial

Nigerian officials and brutal British police, Major Obi succeeds in his mission and is last seen driving off, girl in one hand and mask in the other, for a triumphant return to Nigeria.

Despite its nature, however, *The Mask* succeeds in touching reality at two points. There is, in the British Museum, a beautiful ivory mask of a woman and the Nigerians do indeed want it back very much indeed, together with a number of other pieces of sculpture taken from the city of Benin in 1894. And they want them back so badly as to have threatened, at one stage, to 're-examine' Nigeria's political relationship with Great Britain – the colonial power that ruled Nigeria until 1960.

In January 1897 J. R. Phillips, Her Majesty's Acting Consul-General for the Oil Rivers Protectorate, was in a tempting position for an energetic and ambitious young man. His immediate chief, Consul-General Moor, was in England, discussing what should be done about the King of Benin. In Phillips's files was the copy of a despatch which Moor had sent to the Foreign Office eight months earlier: 'An expeditionary force should be sent about January or February to remove the king and his ju-ju men for the sufferings of the people are terrible.'

Young Mr Phillips was in entire agreement with his chief's energetic policy. It was a shame and a humiliation to every Briton that the vile custom of human sacrifice as practised by the King of Benin should not have ceased as a result of the treaty signed in 1892 but should have increased – indeed, was now practised on such a vast scale as to lead to speculation about whether there would be any citizens left to sacrifice. There was, also, the violation of another clause of the treaty enjoining free trade with neighbouring states – including those 'protected' by Great Britain. Again and again Consul Moor, his predecessors, and now his loyal assistant had emphasized to the Foreign Office that Britain's honour required immediate and effective action. But the voice of the Foreign Office, as supplied by Lord Salisbury, was timid and uncertain: 'The King of Benin may have to be dealt with, but it should be set about with care and with a sufficient force, and in our own time.'

In the absence of Consul Moor, Phillips came to a certain decision. His reasons were never known. It was commonly assumed that his decision to lead an expedition into Benin was the product of ambition: evidently he thought it would be a great boost to his career if, in the absence of his superior, he could singlehandedly solve the nagging problem of the King of Benin. Fatally, he tried to disarm possible Foreign Office censure by leading a pacific, *unarmed*, visit instead of a proper military expedition. On 3 January 1897 Acting Consul Phillips, with seven British officials, two British traders and an impressive carrier force of 200 left the consular base of Sapele. Twenty-four hours later almost every man was dead, two survivors – Locke and Boisragon – escaping to bring the news to an appalled District Commissioner at Sapele on 7 January. The British Empire struck back immediately and, with overwhelming force, a punitive expedition under Admiral Sir Harry Rawson seared its way through the Benin Empire and captured Benin City.

They found a city which, to European eyes and European sense of smell, seemed to be one great charnel house. 'The one lasting impression of Benin in my mind is its smell', Commander R. H. Bacon recorded. He was the Intelligence Officer with the expedition and later published his memoirs under a title, some version of which was used by virtually every European writing about nineteenth-century Benin City: *Benin: the City of Blood*. 'Crucifixions, human sacrifice and every horror the eye could get accustomed to, to a large extent, but the smells no white man's internal economy could stand. Four times in one day I was actually sick for them, and many more times on the point of being so. Every person who was able, I should say, indulged in human sacrifice, and those who could not, sacrificed some animal and left the remains.'

But Benin City was not all rotting corpses. As the British went about their almost housewifely task of cleaning up and restoring order – on one occasion pulling out a living adolescent boy from a pit of decomposing human bodies – they began to make perhaps the most remarkable art discovery of the nineteenth century. 'Buried in the dirt of ages', Bacon recalls, 'were several hundred brass plaques, suggestive of almost Egyptian design, but of really superb castings.' The embossed figures upon the plaques seemed to leap out at the observer, vibrant with energy. The figures, usually, were of Africans – evidently important men flanked with attendants – heavily armoured and carrying enigmatic symbols. But amongst these figures were some of indubitably European origins, as seen through African eyes: men in doublet and hose or sixteenth-century plate armour, bearded and long-haired, usually shown smaller than the dominant Africans, carrying clumsy weapons that were obviously stylized muskets.

But the plaques were not the only extraordinary objects. In the king's compound were 160 huge metal heads, stylized rather than portraits, hollow and with a hole at the top into which fitted immense, intricately carved tusks, some of them evidently of extreme age. There were portrait heads and statues, carved ivory figures of animals, and a recurring motif of a fish identified as a mud-fish. Many of the objects were so thickly covered in human blood that the details were quite obscured, but by the time they had been cleaned it became evident to the leaders of the expedition that they had stumbled upon one of the great mysteries of Africa. And it speaks much both for the skill of the unknown artists, and for the sophistication of the finders, that – though relatively few of the objects were made of intrinsically valuable material – they were recognized as being of potentially immense commercial value. They were collected, photographed, transported to the coast and from there to Europe, where they were to make an immense impact, overturning many a comfortable theory of the African's inherent inferiority, but also posing even greater problems. How old were they? Who had made them? Above all, what was their significance? These were not works of art in the European understanding of the concept.

Britain's relationship with the Kingdom of Benin was wholly different both in its origins and course from its relationship with the other great West African peoples, the Ashanti, with whom it had come in contact. Within a generation of becoming aware of each other's existence Britain and Ashanti met on a collision course. Britain and Benin, by contrast, maintained a parallel course for centuries, and it was only in the dying days of the Benin empire that the British empire in effect moved in to fill a vacuum.

It was the Portuguese who, in 1472, first entered the Bight of Benin and then began cautiously exploring along the maze of great rivers that formed a delta emptying into it. The generic name they gave these rivers – 'slave rivers' – is indication of one of their two main goals, the acquisition of slaves for sale first in Europe, and then for the plantations of the New World. But they had an ideological objective, too – the search for Prester John.

Like the quest for the legendary Philosopher's Stone, the search for the legendary Prester John produced very real by-products. The legend haunted the medieval Christian imagination, becoming stronger as the Muslim tide grew more threatening. Prester John was an African Christian king so great as to disdain the ordinary title of 'king', styling himself simply 'priest' – Presbyter John. He counted seventy-two monarchs among his subjects. In war, he could place a million men in the field, and in peace there was no dissension among his subjects. Before his great palace there hung a marvellous mirror in which he could see all that was happening throughout his vast realm. And some day this great Christian prince would arise in the rear of the hordes of Mohammed and sweep them into the sea.

Prester John's country was variously located. Traditionally, it was associated with Ethiopia, that strange land of black Christians that was older even than Rome. But gradually news came, via the caravels exploring the Bight of Benin, of a black empire, ruled over by a semi-divine person styled the Oba, somewhere up one of these great rivers.

Whereupon, the king [John II of Portugal] and his cosmographers of the kingdom, consulting Ptolemy's general map of Africa and the charts of the coast drawn up by his explorers, and considering the distance of 250 leagues towards the east where the people of Benin affirmed the state of this Prince Ogane [the Oba] to be, they found that he must be Prester John, for both were concealed behind curtains of silk, and both held the Sign of the Cross in great veneration.

Such is the account given by a Portuguese cosmographer. Both these infallible indications were founded on misconceptions: the 'curtains of silk' was a messenger's attempt to convey the remoteness of the Oba even from his people, and the cruciform shape of certain objects venerated by the Benin was purely fortuitous – though this was later to produce the basis of a horrific misinterpretation: impressed by the Christian obsession with crucifixion, the people of Benin adopted the custom.

What the first Portuguese did, undoubtedly, find was a highly sophisticated civilization ruled from a city whose size impressed them all. Even Commander Bacon, in the nineteenth century, suppressed his revulsion sufficiently to recognize that 'the town was not without beauty of a sort. Plenty of trees and green all round, the houses built in no set fashion, but each compound surrounded by bushes and shady avenues.' The first Portuguese and Dutch descriptions of the city are almost lyrical. For a Portuguese captain, Lourenço Pinto, the city was bigger even than Lisbon:

All the streets run straight and as far as the eye can see. The houses are large, especially that of the king which is richly decorated and has fine columns. The city is wealthy and industrious. It is so well governed that theft is unknown and the people live in such security that they have no doors in their houses. The artisans have their places carefully allocated in the squares which are divided up in such a manner that in one square there are altogether 120 goldsmith's shops all working continuously.

These were, in fact, brassworkers and not goldsmiths and the fact that Pinto made such a mistake is evidence of the status enjoyed by these craftsmen, the most important body in the kingdom after the nobility.

And at the centre of this empire was the Oba.

In the absence of written records, Benin chronology before the coming of the Europeans is extraordinarily difficult to establish. The nearest equivalent to a genealogical tree is the 160 brass heads, each with a great tusk placed in it, discovered and taken away by the expedition. These heads represent the Oba, and take back the dynasty to some time in the twelfth century. But a community had been established on the site of Benin City for years – perhaps centuries – before. All that is known for certain is that, some time during the twelfth century, the people of this town sent to the town of Ife asking them to provide a sovereign ruler – a procedure by no means unknown to more sophisticated peoples. The ruler thus provided was to found a dynasty, and under these Oba the Benin empire came into being, absorbing other city-states.

It was in attempting to account for the power of the Oba, and to describe the relationship – incomprehensible to a European – between human and animal sacrifices, art, government, and religion, that the Portuguese coined the word 'feiticarias'. Translated as 'fetish', it was to enter most European languages as a very useful portmanteau word to be applied to any operations of the native African religions that could not be explained in terms of the world's recognized major religions. Thus, in the nineteenth century, Captain John Adams tried to describe the relationship between the Oba of Benin and his people.

The King of Benin is fetiche, and the principal object of adoration in his dominions. He occupies a higher post here than the Pope does in Catholic Europe for he is not only God's vice-regent on earth, but a god himself, whose subjects both obey and adore him – although I believe their adoration to arise from fear, rather than love as cases of heresy, if proved, are followed by prompt decapitation.

Adams's qualifying clause was the typical – and reasonable – reaction of a European to the practice of human sacrifice: it did not – because it could not – occur to him that the victim was entirely willing, regarding the swift stroke of the executioner's axe as an honourable means of passage from one world to the next by a messenger from the Oba himself. From the earliest days of their association with Benin City, the Oba were regarded as possessing supernatural powers. In a sense, they become prisoners of those powers, emerging from their great palaces only once or twice a year to make direct contact with their people, delegating their direct powers to high officials who, inevitably, usurped yet more.

In 1769 a French sea-captain, J. F. Landolfe, left a lively account of an audience he had had with the reigning Oba. Landolfe wanted to establish a 'factory' for slaves and other natural products in the lesser city of Ughoton and, after working his way up through subordinates, was eventually summoned to a meeting. It took place at 11 p.m. – probably because the Oba

Carved ivory tusks from Great Benin:
its customs, art and horrors, *published in 1903.*

wanted to make it personal and private. Landolfe was conducted to the
palace by an impressive guard of twenty-five armed men and two couriers.
All were dismissed and he was left alone, in a room lit by two oil lamps, with
the Oba and an interpreter, the latter remaining prostrate throughout the
interview. Landolfe was much impressed by the Oba, who had then been
reigning for over fifty years, describing him as an immensely dignified, grey-
headed man, upright and vigorous despite his sixty-five years. At the end of
the interview, servants plied Landolfe with port and rum, served out of
crystal, and afterwards the Oba showed him the ivory warehouse which
held, Landolfe calculated, more than 3,000 great tusks. In a subsequent
meeting of the great Council, his request was ratified – and then sanctified
by the sacrifice of a man. Brought on by two tall men clad from head to foot
in grey, the victim seemed quite calm, Landolfe thought. The two
executioners clubbed the man simultaneously in front and behind and his
head was then cut off, the blood being caught in a pan.

The bronze, ivory, brass and wooden objects produced by the craftsmen
of Benin were all 'fetish'-linked in some manner with the religion whose

197

centre, or expression, was the Oba. It was at first generally assumed that the Benin metalworkers had learned their craft from the Portuguese, an assumption based on little more than the fact that Portuguese soldiers figured widely in the representations. But though the supply of metal was substantially increased by the advent of the Portuguese, and though that advent of energetic foreigners would naturally stimulate the craftsmen, metalworkers of a very high standard were following their craft long before. According to Benin tradition, bronze casting was learned during the reign of the sixth Oba of the present dynasty, that is, some time during the first quarter of the fourteenth century. When an Oba died, a formal head was cast in bronze. Originally, this was a means of maintaining a link between Benin and the sacred city of Ife, where the Oba originated: at death, the Oba's head would be removed from his body and sent to Ife and a bronze head returned to Benin in its stead. In due course, the bronze heads formed the furnishings of an altar erected to the memory of the deceased Oba. In his survey of Benin art history, Phillip Dark calculates that the last Oba to have cast heads of his predecessor would have been the Oba deposed by the punitive expedition in 1897: Ovonramwen, who came to the throne about 1888. 'Thus, before 1897, heads would have been made for thirty previous Oba.'

The city of Benin was divided into two by a broad street, which a seventeenth-century Dutchman described as being 'seven or eight times broader than Warme Street in Amsterdam'. In the smaller half of the city lived the Oba and his court, and in the other the town chiefs. The craft workers were organized into their own wards. The largest group was the blacksmiths, occupying four wards, their shops taking up entire streets. Wood and ivory carvers shared the same wards, while the aristocrats of the crafts were undoubtedly the bronze workers. So well organized was the craft, and so vital to the cultural life of the people, that it continues almost unchanged into the twentieth century, making it possible to trace, through its modern counterpart, the system which prevailed, with some modifications, over centuries. Each of the ten sections into which the bronze-workers were divided was headed by an hereditary chief, and specialized in one particular aspect of the work: 'When casting objects for the Oba's ancestor altars, the first and senior chief is responsible for full figures in the round. The bronze staves used to decorate the altars of past Oba are made by the sixth chief. The fourth chief casts bronze bells.'

It is perhaps unfortunate that the first official visitor to Benin City should have been the traveller and writer Sir Richard Burton. Burton reached Benin City in August 1862 and it was from his official despatches and, even more, from the colourful accounts he wrote for *Fraser's Magazine* that the British public got their first clear picture of the black empire of the Oba.

It was not a very attractive picture and, from the first, Burton touched on that theme of human sacrifice which was to be the leitmotif of British-Benin relationships over the next half century. 'One of the first objects that met our sight was a negro freshly crucified after the African fashion sitting on a stool with extended arms lashed to a framework of poles', he wrote to the Foreign Office a few days after arriving in the city. 'I fear it was in honour of our arrival. We then marched over the space before the King's palace. It was strewn with human skulls and bones like pebbles. Our first visit to the palace showed us the body of a fine young woman fastened to the top of a tree – a Fetish for rain.' Of the people themselves, he was wholly contemptuous. 'I determine the Beninese to be with the sole exception of the Mpongwe or Gabons the most pilfering race I had visited on the West coast of Africa.'

Over the next thirty years this casual assessment developed into a chorus of condemnation. The invention of photography brought to British breakfast tables pagan Africa in dramatic and horrid form. One photograph in particular took the public imagination and was reproduced again and again in books on 'darkest Africa'. Starkly outlined against a dreary, cloudy sky is a ladder or lattice of crossbars lashed between two sturdy trees: suspended on that lattice with arms and legs brutally extended and lashed is a human figure, probably female. Traveller after traveller reported that the appalling custom of female crucifixion, almost unknown before the nineteenth century, was now almost epidemic. The trader, Cyril Punch, whose eyewitness accounts of Benin provided the staple for a number of writers in England, claimed that the Oba once said to him 'that he was sick of it all but that he could not discontinue the customs of his ancestors'.

In his history of the slave trade, *Black Mother*, Basil Davidson returns again and again to the theme that, in the first years of contact between blacks and whites on the West African coast, there was no indication whatever of the condescension and contempt on one side, and sense of inferiority on the other, which bedevilled that contact throughout the nineteenth and much of the twentieth centuries, down to our own day. The distortion, Davidson believes, was produced by the slave trade itself. Alan Ryder, Professor of History at Ibadan University, provides a similar picture of changing and deteriorating relationships between the peoples of Benin and Britain, though ascribing that change to a different cause.

They [the first consular reports] draw a picture curiously at variance with that presented by earlier European visitors and chroniclers, most of whom had described a state in which civilization and the art of government had progressed further than in any other known kingdom of Guinea. Fundamentally, the change in attitude between these writers, and their Victorian successors, must be ascribed to a general shift in the standpoint from which nineteenth-century Europeans viewed and judged other races, to the development, that is, of 'scientific racialism'.

Some British officials were inclined to agree with Cyril Punch, regarding the Oba as a prisoner of custom. In 1892 the Vice-Consul, Henry Gallwey, reporting to the Foreign Office, stated: 'The King struck me as being very ready to listen to reason, but he is tied down by fetish customs and, until the power of the fetish priests is done away with, the trade of the Benin country will continue to be a very doubtful source of profit.' Whatever the causes of the changing viewpoint, whether the slave trade had indeed a mutually corrupting effect, or whether British writers viewed the same situation from another perspective, the result was the same. And when Vice-Consul Gallwey added the ingredient of 'trade' a most potent brew had been made: it was Britain's moral duty, as well as conducive to financial gain, to 'do something' about the Kingdom of Benin. Vice-Consul Phillips prepared to make his bid for fame.

A few years after the punitive expedition, there was published in Halifax, England a handsomely produced volume under the title of *Great Benin: its customs, art and horrors*. Its author, H. Ling Roth, combined an interest and considerable expertise in art history and ethnography. His book, though limited to an edition of some 320 copies, is something of a landmark. For Roth, the people of Benin were neither benighted savages sunk in bloodlust, nor noble primitives corrupted by the white man, but a highly civilized people following a parallel course of development to that of the European. He made no attempt to process his material in order to tell a coherent story but, in effect, produced a species of commonplace book, drawing upon a wide variety of sources for the purpose. Many of them were published. But many, too, were first-hand contacts who provided him with lively eyewitness accounts – outstanding among whom was the indefatigable Cyril Punch, trader and traveller extraordinary.

Through Roth's compilation it is possible to gain an impression – unaffected by hindsight – of the impact the punitive expedition and its horrific discoveries made upon Victorian Britain. The surgeon with the expedition was Felix Roth, the writer's brother, who kept a diary from 4 p.m., 6 February, when he landed from HMS *Theseus*, to 22 February, when Admiral Rawson and his staff retired from the destroyed city. The early part of the diary reads like a contribution to the *Boy's Own Paper*, with its account of bridge-building, road-making and, in general, making-do in a tough country. The tone changes with their arrival in Benin City.

It is a misnomer to call it a city: it is a charnel house. All about the houses and streets are dead natives, some crucified, some sacrificed on trees, others on stage erections. . . . In front of the king's compound stakes have been driven into the ground, and cross-pieces of wood lashed to them. On this framework live human beings are tied, to die of thirst and heat, to be dried up by the sun and eaten by the carrion birds, till the bones get disarticulated and fall to the ground. At the base of them the whole ground was strewn with human bones and decomposing bodies, with their heads off. Three looked like white men, but it was impossible for me to decide, as they had been there for some time. . . . The bush, too, was filled with dead bodies, the hands being tied to the ankles so as to keep them in a sitting posture. It was a gruesome sight to see these headless bodies about, the smell being awful. . . .

The last days of Benin seem to have been spent in an orgasm of slaughter. Among the art objects, Roth found a considerable number of crosses, some merely cruciform in shape and others based on the familiar Christian cross. It was the prevalence of these crosses which led another doctor with the expedition, identified simply as 'Dr Allman', to speculate that 'the custom of human crucifixions, as practised by the natives, was derived from the representations of the Crucifixion of our Saviour, introduced probably by the Portuguese'. In an article in the *Lancet*, Allman stated that he had found 17 pits, each some 12 feet wide and 40 feet deep, seven of which were filled with rotting bodies.

Dr Roth provided his brother with a lively description of that aspect of Benin in which the writer was particularly interested – the discovery of the Benin carvings. 'Every house had its alcove of various dimensions [containing 'fetish' carvings and sculptures]. A large part of the loot was found embedded in the walls, and occasionally in so testing the walls the soldiers put their hands into human corpses built up in them.'

Surgeon Roth described the more important objects in detail, and a brother officer took a remarkable photograph showing members of the expedition posed in the midst of an immense collection, heaped up in one of the compounds. But within a few weeks of the taking of this photograph, the priceless collection was already being scattered, first shipped to England and then sold as a contribution towards the cost of the expedition. Ling Roth describes how the Keeper of Antiquities at the British Museum hastened to secure what he could and was able to obtain most of the plaques, but little else. 'Not only was the national institution deprived of its lawful acquisition, but at the same time another government department sold for a few hundred pounds a large number of castings which had cost thousands to obtain, as well as much blood of our fellow countrymen.' A number of British buyers, among them the formidable General Pitt-Rivers, picked up some of the items for private collections, but most appear to have gone abroad, German academic institutions being particularly active. At a British Association meeting in Ipswich, a disgruntled speaker remarked that: 'If an Englishman wishes to learn anything about the coloured peoples under British sway without actually visiting them, he had to go to Berlin to do so.'

Ling Roth was considerably in advance of his day in believing not only that British officials should 'have a thorough knowledge of the native races subject to them', but also that the art forms of those subject races shed brilliant light upon their customs and characters. He was acutely aware, too, of the problem that is in the forefront of modern anthropology but rarely if ever occurred to those entrusted with the running of the Raj: 'Unlike the Tasmanians or the ancient Peruvians the West African will never be wiped off the face of the earth, but intercourse with the white man alters his beliefs, customs and ideas and proper records of these should be made before we destroy them.'

As it happened, by a quirk of fashion Benin art became of immense commercial value and was therefore protected from casual vandalism. But this merely substituted one problem for another. William Fagg, doyen of African art historians, describes the change thus:

When I was travelling in Yorubaland [northern Nigeria] with Kenneth Murray 28 years ago we rarely sought to collect an object which was still in ritual use unless it was certain that it would be at once replaced, preferring to do our little bit to keep tradition alive. More recently, since about 1960, the delicacy of our approach to collecting has been quite superseded by the advent of the *African* [author's italics] dealers who collect indiscriminately, mostly for export. What was needed to meet this threat was for a task force to be sent to any area on which the dealers were about to descend and to pre-empt those works which were needed for museums.

In addition to those native dealers intent upon turning a common heritage into personal profit were the employees of the new international corporations, and the thousands of soldiers of 'peace-keeping' forces who found themselves in Africa following the break-up of the old empires. Many – perhaps most – of these individuals were simply picking up souvenirs in the immemorial manner of expatriates. But a substantial number of them had a lively awareness of the current value of once-despised 'native art'. The much-castigated colonial government of Nigeria did attempt to stem the tide. In 1953 an ordinance was enacted, placing all antiquities under government protection and defining 'antiquity' as 'any object or relic of early times before the advent of the white man'. But it had little practical effect and Nigerian antiquities, together with similar material from all other African countries, continued to pour into Europe and America.

The sovereign Republic of Nigeria came into being in 1963 and from the beginning has been in the vanguard of the African campaign to obtain the return of their treasures. The Nigerian philosophy was clear and succinct: 'Our educational system has failed to take cognisance of the cultural matrix of our people' – an official African statement which curiously echoes the Scottish policeman's complaint about the educational system of his own country (see p. 104). And, like that policeman's complaint, the statement goes on to link the awareness of national history and national identity with the physical presence of certain objects: 'These antiquities are the only authentic objects which illustrate and illuminate the course of our development. This is vital to us as a people as it enables us to establish our identity, and hence restores our dignity in the community of nations.'

The ordinary operation of commerce has widely scattered the Benin antiquities, placing them in private as well as public ownership. As recently as June 1980 the collection of a Dutch millionaire was auctioned in London, making nearly £750,000 for twenty-three items. There is little that the Nigerian or any other African government can do about material in private collections, for no European or American government, no matter how sympathetic, is going to confiscate or compulsorily purchase antiquities that have been acquired on the open market and in good faith. Since the punitive expedition placed them on the market, some of these objects have changed hands at least half a dozen times, their value increasing inexorably on each occasion. But the Nigerian government can, and does, place a very easy target in their sights – the museums of Europe and America, in particular the British Museum, the national collection in the largest of the old colonial empires.

Until the mid 1970s, the Nigerian campaign was conducted decorously between museum officials. Then Lagos was designated as the venue for the great pan-African cultural exhibition, Festac 1977. And very rapidly Festac 1977 achieved a political dimension as white nations perceived its value as a contact point with oil-rich Nigeria. The American contingent numbered 2,000, and though most of these were travelling either at their own expense or financed by black American organizations, they were led by Andrew Young, at that time the US Ambassador to the United Nations.

Nigeria adopted as symbol that same ivory mask which the cinematic Major Obi was later commissioned to obtain by hook or by crook. It is difficult to avoid the suspicion that the choice of this unique object was a more or less deliberate attempt to put a cat among the pigeons, for of all the Benin treasures in public ownership in Great Britain this is at once the most valuable and the most vulnerable. The Nigerians requested, not its return, but its loan. The British Museum temporized, first requesting an insurance bond of £2 million and then arguing that it was, in fact, too delicate to be moved out of its carefully controlled environment. Nigerians were profoundly irritated on both counts: the vast size of the requested bond seemed part of the artificial rigging of the international art market, and the argument that an artifact was best preserved outside the environment that had created it seemed, to say the least, disingenuous. 'It could be fair to infer that the Museum suspects Nigeria is now not competent to safely handle the property it carved and preserved from the sixteenth century until some 79 years ago when it was plundered. Until around 1897 the carving was not being stored under conditions of "controlled temperature and humidity", yet it did not deteriorate', is the opinion of an irate Nigerian writer, Asong Ndifor.

'Ironically, the place where the ivory was carved is in fact the worst place to house it – the temperature and humidity is all wrong', is the firm contra-opinion of John Picton. He was deputy-director of the Museum of Mankind when I interviewed him, and took me on a tour of the Aladdin's cave of treasures that lies behind the public rooms. Not so long ago, the Ethnographic Department of the British Museum somewhat resembled an up-market junk shop, crammed away as it was on an upper floor behind that classical frontage in Great Russell Street. But the Department, like most of our museums, has been a major beneficiary of our current obsession with antiquities. Trendily but accurately renamed the Museum of Mankind and housed in its own imposing Edwardian building, it is no longer just an academic repository to which the public is allowed grudging access. The incredible wealth of material is still within reach, but tucked away behind the scenes: what the public sees are selections displayed like those of an expensive jewellers. But it is an indication of the Museum's more liberal attitude that a request to view, though emanating from a non-specialist, resulted in a highly informative tour conducted by an academic who was fascinated by his subject.

The Museum's collection of bronze plaques is housed in a series of battered, singularly unglamorous Civil Service-type wooden cabinets. They dominate their drab surroundings. My guide pulled open one draw at random. It was obviously very heavy, though it contained only one plaque – the king holding two writhing, spitting leopards by their tails – and the impact upon a European was immediate and immense. Gazing down at that vibrant creation in its cheap wooden drawer one could understand just how it was that the members of the punitive expedition realized that they were engaged in a remarkable discovery.

We moved into an adjoining room lined with industrial metal shelving. On the floor, tucked away in the semi-darkness, were the great brooding heads of the Oba – minus their carved tusks. But these too were in the Museum, though housed in another temperature-controlled room. 'Ivory is best kept at a temperature of 65°F and a stable humidity: the average temperature of West Africa is around 85°F.' The ivory mask which has been at the centre of controversy was housed in its own special glass case in one of the public rooms. The young female attendant took me straight to the exhibit when I asked. Had there been many queries? No, I was the first who had ever specifically asked for it. Why did she immediately know what I was looking for? 'Because she's so beautiful. I go back and look at it again and again.' She spoke with a slight Cockney accent: quite evidently, the ivory mask represented a culture totally alien from her own. But, just as evidently, the genius of the unknown sixteenth-century artist had allowed him to transcend the limitations of space and time, reaching out to touch the mind of a young woman separated from him by four centuries and three thousand miles.

Section 3, Sub-section 4 of the British Museum Act of 1963 specifically prohibits the Trustees of the Museum from disposing of objects 'vested in the trustees as part of the collections of the Museum'. Dr Picton was sympathetic towards those African states, Nigeria in particular, who were demanding the return of their cultural treasures. 'They do have a point – but at this stage I can't help feeling that their energy would be far better devoted to stopping illegal exportation, which still goes on at a scandalous rate.' It is common knowledge among Europeans using Lagos airport that quite a small 'gift' of cash will induce customs officials to look elsewhere if the traveller wants to take an antiquity illegally out of the country. Despite the energetic attempts by the Federal Ministry of Information to educate their own people in the significance of these artifacts, it is probable that relatively few ordinary Nigerians see anything particularly important in objects that still play a role in everyday life. At the Africa Centre I was told the story of two Nigerian graduates in Lagos who watched while bronzes were being packed for illegal export. They were shocked. Because of the illegality of the act? 'No, because they were ashamed of what the West would think of Nigerians still producing such primitive material. There's this deep dichotomy still – some now aware of their heritage but many, only too many, probably only too glad to exchange a Benin bronze for three flying ducks.' It is not a dichotomy peculiar to Africans: in remote country districts in Europe one only too often encounters locals gladly exchanging their 'clumsy' handmade artifacts for the plastic and steel products of the twentieth century. But it underlines the complexity of the problem.

And finally there is the deep suspicion, voiced to me by more than one museum curator, that demands for restitution of cultural treasures are governed as much by political as by cultural considerations. 'It's a useful means for some local lad to make his name – or for his government to put pressure on the UK for something quite unconnected with it.' I found some evidence to justify this cynicism when I wrote to the Nigerian High Commission in London, asking for a statement on Nigeria's current attitude to Britain's retention of the bronzes. Receiving no reply to my letter, I telephoned and eventually spoke to one of the cultural attachés. 'There is no problem', my contact said firmly. 'They have all been returned.' I was astonished. Had I missed the cultural scoop of the century? Had the British Museum broken its own regulations, cleared out its scores of Benin objects – some of enormous financial value – and not a word of this had been made public? Further questioning elicited the fact that my contact had been misled by the sale of the Dutch collection which had recently taken place: the Nigerian government had bought four of the items. My contact refused to discuss the matter. 'There is no problem. They have all been returned.' I wondered if, perhaps, my interview technique was at fault but shortly afterwards a BBC reporter interviewed me on the subject of this book. She, too, had telephoned the Nigerian High Commission to obtain the official Nigerian attitude. 'Do you know what they said? "We are all going to lunch." I said, "Can I come after lunch?" They said "We shall be too busy." And tomorrow? They rang off!'

Although we did not know it at the time, our real-life experience was closely paralleled by that of the fictional Major Obi. Towards the end of the film, *The Mask*, he arrives at the High Commission for help to get the relic out of Britain. 'The High Commissioner says he is too busy to think of that now as he is in the middle of an important private meeting. Private commerce takes precedence over the cultural heritage.'

9

The Corporate Memory

'What I consider personal family documents have got to
be sold.'

SIR SIMON CODRINGTON, quoted in
The Observer, 14 December 1980

'History is not private property.'

LOWENTHAL and HOGGART, *ibid*

During the 1970s a publishing phenomenon of immense proportions hit
America and then moved across the Atlantic, subsequently enjoying the
ultimate twentieth-century accolade of being turned into a television series.
Roots by Alex Haley was a totally new departure in history and biography,
for it was the attempt of a black American to trace, despite the lack of
documentation, his origins on the West Coast of Africa whence his ancestors
had been deported as slaves. Although the book was vigorously attacked for
its cavalier treatment of facts, its enthusiastic reception on both sides of the
Atlantic by both blacks and whites is testimony alike to the sense of
rediscovered pride among the descendants of slaves, and of guilt among the
descendants of those who enslaved them.

Between the mid sixteenth and late nineteenth centuries about twelve
million black Africans were shipped as slaves across the Atlantic. Perhaps
two million of them fell sick and died during the terrible Middle Passage.
The ten million who survived created vast wealth for a relatively small
number of people and, in due course, contributed substantially to the
populations of North and South America and, above all, the West Indies.

This was the biggest forced migration in history. In the normal course of
events, migrations on such a scale can keep track of their own history.

Because the entire community migrates, it takes its memory along with it – its priests, shamans, minstrels, chroniclers. But that vast migration from Africa carried nothing with it. Family was sundered from tribe, individual wrenched from family. The appalling death rate created a further gap. The 12 per cent death rate is the overall average: in some individual cargoes the death rate could be as high as 70 per cent, effectively cutting off the survivors from contact with their origins as they were distributed across a continent.

Roots was an attempt to bridge this racial amnesia and, though the book might be suspect academically, it – and the reaction to it – is the surface foam of deeply moving waters. The same impulse that led the Nigerians to announce that their antiquities were a means of establishing their corporate identity was at work here. The black peoples of the New World were looted of a heritage which, though intangible, was quite as real as the looting of the concrete heritages of the Ashanti or the Benin.

But there is also a concrete dimension to their loss, a fact which was made very apparent in the autumn of 1980 in the controversy over the sale of the 'Codrington Papers'. A discreet announcement in the trade press had originally identified these papers as being simply 'the property of a gentleman', but in the small world of scholarship such anonymity could not long be preserved. It became very soon known that the gentleman was Sir Simon Codrington of Dodington Hall, Shropshire, who had instructed the London firm of Sotheby's to auction a collection of documents relating to the islands of Barbuda and Antigua. The Codrington family had run vast sugar estates upon Antigua for over two hundred years, farming them with slaves who, it was claimed, had been bred by them upon Barbuda for the purpose. The documents, consisting of correspondence between the family and their agents in the Caribbean and various estate records over the period, provided unique genealogical and biographical information on the black population who now form the majority of the population of Antigua and Barbuda.

A substantial proportion of these documents had been sold in 1951 without attracting any particular attention, except by interested experts. But the climate of opinion had changed drastically in the intervening thirty years. It so happened, too, that during the very same period that the papers were placed on the market in 1980, representatives from Antigua were in London conducting negotiations for the island's final political severance from the United Kingdom and its emergence as a sovereign state. Vigorously they protested against the sale of the papers, arguing that they formed an integral part of Antiguan history and should at least be offered to

Among the treasure the British found in the palace of the Oba of Benin in 1897 was this leopard made of ivory studded with copper and dating from the late eighteenth or early nineteenth century.

'GREAT BENIN: ITS CUSTOMS, ART AND HORRORS'

(*below*) When the punitive expedition captured Benin City, its Intelligence Officer recalled, it found 'crucifixions, human sacrifice and . . . smells no white man's internal economy could stand' — but also masterpieces of Benin craftsmanship: bronze heads and statues, carved ivory figures of animals, bronze plaques. The plaques *left* were in fact sold back to Nigeria in 1950.

(*opposite*) The Oba of Benin in the distinctive coral collar and headdress which is seen in Benin bronzes.

PAST – AND PRESENT

Bewildered Westerners, trying to work out the complex relationship in Benin between art, human and animal sacrifices, government and religion, coined the word 'fetish' in an attempt to explain both the relationship and its operation.

(*below*) An ancestral altar of the Oba of Benin shows the king supported by his attendants. On the ground at the right is a formal head of the Oba: one was made on the death of each Oba and a chronology can be constructed from their number.

The head of a Queen Mother (*left*), dating from the sixteenth century, is an excellent example of the precision and sensitivity of the Benin bronze workers, while *opposite* is an only-too-common example of the degradation of 'native' arts for purposes of tourism. This stall 'represents' Nigeria – but every emergent country can show something similar.

The Christian
Remembrancer
VERSUS
THE
Anti-Slavery
Society.

ENGLISHMEN, read and reflect upon the following extract from the Christian Remembrancer for February 1831, a work long distinguished for its able support of the *real unadulterated* principles of the Christian Religion, in contradiction to the "seers of visions, & dreamers of dreams" who pervert the word of God to their own vile and infamous purposes. "Let not your own prophets and your divines"(your Evans's & Bennett's) that be in the midst of you, deceive you." *Jeremiah*, xxix. c. 8.

A short comparison of the respective conditions of the British Peasant and African Negro will perhaps, alter the opinion of some of our readers who may have been misled by unfounded assertions, or blinded by pre-existing prejudices.

Slave!	Free Born Briton!
1. The Slave is provided with a comfortable house, of which he cannot be deprived, and good clothing suited to the climate; he is allowed a portion of land and time to work it which enable him to maintain himself, his children must be provided with good and wholesome food by the master, he never wants a hearty meal for if the produce of his labour fail through bad seasons, his owner feeds him and provides for all his wants.	1 The British peasant from his daily labour, must the rent of a miserable hut and provide food and cloth, for his family. If work fails, or times are hard, he cannot pay rent, he is turned out of his house, his family must starve beg or steal, and perhaps end their days in a workhouse.
2. The Negro goes to his daily labour a little after six and toils about nine hours, he has the evening undisturbed and he sleeps soundly without a thought for the morrow.	2 The poor man generally labours longer and harder, and when he lies his head upon his bed, *if he has the fortune to possess one*, he knows that *if the morrow gives him on employment, he and his family get no food.*
3. If he is sick, he has a doctor to attend him, who is paid by his master; medicines are provided for him which cost him nothing, and soap and wine, and every thing else which his situation requires are supplied him free of expence, and his wife and family are well fed and want for nothing	3. If sickness disable him from pursuing his daily labour, he can have no medical advice, no physician, no food, no soap, no wine, nor any other comforts indispensable for his situation, save from the grudging humanity of a parish doctor, or flinty hearted overseer, and even that not always, besides, his wife and children must pass their cloths to procure bread. Their only source is the hospital. Their only prospect of relief the grave!!
4. When the Negro dies, he leaves his wife and children without anxiety for their future welfare, he departs with the consoling reflection that want cannot assail them, and that the evils of poverty can never reach them.	4. The death of the poor man is the scene of human sufferings. His friendless wife and wretched children add bitterness to his dying moments. His honest heart bursts at their future lot. He sees them stop themselves of the covering that should protect them from the inclemency of the winter blast, to afford him some little relief.

ENGLISHMEN! The above are the statements, not of a West India Planter, but a Christian Writer, not the advocacy of a hired agent but the indignant expression of a defender of the Truth a minister of the Gospel who would not have you deluded by the base fabrications of an interested and dishonest faction. The character of the Christian Remembrancer conducted & supported as it is, by some of the most distinguished members of the Church of England, forbids the supposition that they could be actuated by any improper motives in advocating the cause of an honorable and much calumniated body of men — again therefore I repeat, read, mark, & weigh well the contrast, & say whether *the Chapels of these anti Slavery demagogues are not converted into arenas for factious discussions.*

London, August 8th, 1832.

Turner & Co. Printers, Wood Street, one door from Cheapside.

TO WHOM DOES HISTORY BELONG?

In the winter of 1980 Sotheby's auctioned the so-called 'Codrington Papers' – documents relating to the vast Caribbean sugar estates owned by the Codrington family for over two centuries. Some argued that these records should now go to the descendants of the slaves who worked the estates – the people of Antigua. The heated but fascinating and by no means one-sided debate that followed is described in Chapter IX.

(*left*) Life as a slave favourably compared to that of a British peasant in a document from the Papers. (*opposite above*) Carting sugar for shipment. (*below*) Punishments for slaves on West Indian plantations. By comparison the slaves on the Codrington estates were well treated. (*opposite below*) Dodington Park, home of the Codrington family and – for many years – of the papers: ironically, their sale was partly intended to help with the cost of upkeep to the house built with plantation profits.

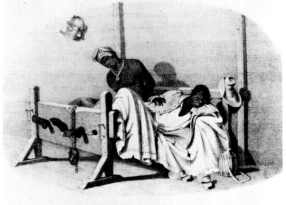

As the once-subject peoples of the European imperial powers have come to independence, the controversies about the ownership of cultural treasures have greatly increased. In 1982 Sri Lanka composed a long list of items whose return was demanded in order to build up a national museum in Colombo. (*left* and *below*) Sri Lankan objects in the British Museum: the bronze statue of the goddess Tara (*left*) was acquired from the collection of Hugh Nevill in the late nineteenth century, the carved ivory plaques (*below*) are eighteenth century.

the new republic on preferential terms, instead of being auctioned off to the highest bidder. They even raised £40,000 among their compatriots for the purpose, an impressive sum for a total population of 77,000. The debate entered the national press, becoming a heated controversy: in what sense did these papers – undoubtedly created by and for the Codrington family and legally owned by them – actually belong to them in a moral sense? 'History is not private property', declared Professors David Lowenthal and Richard Hoggart. 'It belongs to the offspring of those who tilled the soil as well as to those of their landlords.' To this Sir Simon responded that money was vitally needed for repairs to Dodington Hall, the ancestral home. Altogether, it was a classic demonstration of conflicting but equal interests.

The story outlined by the Codrington Papers reflects the rise and fall of the British Empire before it realized it was rising, and before it realized that it was falling. The Codringtons themselves were established members of the English aristocracy (a John de Codrington was standard-bearer to Henry V during the Agincourt campaign) with their seat at Dodington in Shropshire. The family became divided during the Civil War and the younger son, Christopher – a Lieutenant-General in the Royalist army – left for Barbados in 1649. Twenty-five years later his son, also known, confusingly, as Christopher, moved across to the tiny neighbouring island of Antigua. The Spanish half-heartedly claimed it, but it had lain, virtually uninhabited, since it had been granted in 1632 by Charles II to Lord Willoughby. Fresh water was hard to come by, and there was none of the mineral wealth that was luring Europeans elsewhere.

But the island was well adapted to produce another form of wealth – a tall, bamboo-like plant which, when crushed, exudes a delicious and very sweet liquid. Sugar cane. Christopher Codrington had already cultivated the crop with great success on Barbados and it was he who now introduced what was to be Antigua's only industry for the next three centuries. In 1674 he bought 725 acres on Antigua, building his house on the curiously named Betty's Hope and establishing the island's first sugar plantation. He also leased for 'one fat pig per year when asked' the minute neighbouring island of Barbuda, a fact which was to have considerable significance some three centuries later.

Sugar was the great growth industry of its day. Twenty years after Codrington established his plantation exports to England alone had risen from half a million tons a year to $2\frac{1}{2}$ million tons. The soil and climate of Antigua were ideal for the production of this white gold: construction of reservoirs overcame the lack of springs and rivers. There was only one shortage and that was labour. The Spaniards had wiped out the docile aboriginals of the islands and no European was going to travel 4,000 miles to labour under a tropical sun. There was, however, a vast reservoir of labour on the African coast. In his book *Black Mother* Basil Davidson succinctly demonstrates the cause and effect of the establishment of the sugar industry. 'In 1515 came the first shipment of slave-grown West Indian sugar and, in 1518 as though by the sheer logic of the thing, the first cargo of African slaves shipped directly from Africa to the West Indies.' All that Sir Christopher Codrington had to do was to plug Antigua into the pipeline.

By the early nineteenth century the West Indies were commercially of even greater importance to Britain than was famed India. India might mean elephants and jewels and nabobs and splendour: the West Indies meant cash. Hard cash. 'There were comparatively few merchants in Great Britain in 1761 who, in one connection or another, did not trade with the West Indies and a considerable number of gentry families who had interest in the sugar islands.'

The Codringtons were among them. They had never been exactly penurious but now, rapidly, they grew wealthy, wealthy enough to follow the tradition of their class, tear down their old manor house and build a splendid new palace in its stead, commissioning Wyatt to design it. They were not wholly absentee landlords: from time to time Codringtons lived on Antigua at Betty's Hope. But, in the main, they continued to follow the tradition of their class, spending in Europe the money gained in the Caribbean. From first to last they were good businessmen, expecting and receiving minute information regarding the conduct of their affairs on Antigua. And out of this arose the Codrington Papers.

That part of the collection which was sold in 1951 consisted in the main of letters. 'In some ways it is regrettable that such an unusual record should be broken up in the sale room', the distinguished philatelist Robson Lowe noted at the time. 'It is the longest continual run from a British colony and covers a longer period than any other recorded find.' Before the collection was dispersed, Robson Lowe was able to calendar the items and even this skeletal outline tells a remarkable story.

In 1688 the Post Office set up a packet letter service between London and St John's, Antigua, the letters going first to Falmouth and then onward by packet boat. The journey took between five and seven weeks: storm, shipwreck, piracy and war were all occupational hazards. One of the letters in the collection actually had the legend 'Opened by Enemy' written upon it. Presumably the vessel carrying it had been captured by French privateers and the French, with curious chivalry, forwarded the letters. But despite the hazards, for over 200 years the service continued, the boat leaving once a month from Falmouth, carrying around 1,500 letters and one or two official passengers.

And at the other end, in the small, claustrophobic island in the sun expatriates waited hungrily for the mail. A contemporary account, written about 1840, describes the scene in St John's at about the time the boat is due.

The packet from England is signalized and away they scamper to the post office, almost before the mails are landed, to the utter consternation of the poor postmaster and, with anxious eyes and clamorous tongue, crowd the office door. At length, two or three burly sailors, followed by the commander of the packet – a lieutenant in the Navy, are seen approaching the spot bearing upon their broadbuilt shoulders the long-looked-for mail bags, well secured in their leather envelopes. . . The letters are at length sorted. Happy now does that individual feel whose name begins with an 'A' for they always conduct this business alphabetically. A silence ensues, the letters are distributed and, too anxious to know their contents, their several receivers open them on the spot.

The same writer presents, with considerable skill, a pen portrait of a prosperous planter, a man of substance who might, perhaps, have been one of the Codrington agents:

A fine, portly looking man whose complexion rivals in colour the chateau margaux he so liberally indulges in: a pair of gold-rimmed spectacles surmounts his well-formed nose, a substantial-looking umbrella is stuck under his arm, while in one hand is born an open letter and in the other a voluminous silk handkerchief and a gold snuff-box. 'Not bad, though' he mutters to himself as he carefully looks out for the lapses in the stone platform which runs along the front of the post office. 'My last ten hogsheads brought 78s per cwt and my agent tells me the sugar was not so good as the former shipment or he would have got higher prices. I must look to what my manager is doing; he must exert himself more.' So saying, he gains his 'top-gig' and, carefully stepping in, he tells John to gather up the reins and hasten home. This is a resident proprietor of a sugar estate – a man with whom the world has long dealt well.

The correspondence sold in 1951 covered the years 1743 to 1851. Most of the letters are passing between one or other of the heads of the family either in Shropshire or London, and their agent or attorney on Antigua. For the modern reader, the casual way in which human beings dispose of human beings comes as a profound shock initially. Thus in 1812 Langford Hodge, the Codrington attorney, is writing to Sir Christopher: 'A family of negroes I purchased for you the other day came to solicit me to purchase the remainder of their Family which was to be sold. I bid for them and I am glad to say they are now your property.' Prices varied considerably over the years, but always remained relatively very high: on average, a boy was worth three oxen. Samuel Redhead, an estate owner in his own right as well as a Codrington agent, tells Sir William that a blacksmith cost £36, while he paid £189 for 'seven fine young women'.

According to the Reverend William Moister, a missionary writing about the year 1880 after the emancipation of slaves, 'In most instances the slaves were treated with extreme rigour, their food and clothing always coarse and sometimes insufficient: their daily tasks of labour unreasonably arduous and the punishments administered for real or imagined faults cruel in the extreme.' If this is the general case for the West Indies the slaves of Antigua were singularly fortunate in their treatment. The same Samuel Redhead wanted to purchase the freedom of a female in Barbuda who had borne him a son. He either did not succeed on this occasion or transferred his attention to another of Sir William's slaves, for ten years later one Godfrey Davis is writing in person to Sir William, asking for the freedom of his mulatto half-sister, 'one of Sir William's slaves who has borne many children to Mr Redhead and now wishes to retire'.

It is evident that, throughout, the Codringtons were extremely good masters. A certain George Edward Codrington – who, despite his resounding English name, is a black slave – writes spontaneously to Sir William: 'Believe me, my kind master, if God gives me Health and Strength I will do all that is in my power to return that Kindness which I have received from you and all yours Kind Hearted and Noble Family when I were in your care through London, at free expense, with the blessing of God and all therein.' Even before emancipation, slaves enjoyed considerable economic freedom: 'Quashey, a Slave of Sir Henry Martin, lately died possessed of cattle and £500 of money. And your head carpenter here, Wm Gay, I have no doubt is worth considerable property. He keeps his horse and gig, has a free wife living with him.'

Indeed, so close is the identity of interest between black slaves and white freemen that it is proposed to recruit blacks into the army for the defence of the islands against the French. In March 1797 Samuel Athill – who in time became President of the Council of Antigua – reports that the government has sent out Sir Ralph Abercrombie to raise a regiment of 500 blacks and mulattos. Athill is critical of the proposed level of payment: 'Mr Bousettin has a contract to supply half, at £70 sterling each seasoned negro and part of them are to be £50 new negroes. I leave you to judge of what the troop is to be composed! You cannot buy any negroes for £70 worth having and new children in the stores are 50 sterling each.'

Barbuda plays a large role in this first collection. Even tourist literature of the 1980s cannot make much of this small, bleak island twenty-five miles from Antigua. It had little agricultural value and, it is claimed, the Codringtons acquired it for a singular, and somewhat reprehensible, purpose. The present government of Antigua sums up that purpose unequivocally: 'They [the Codringtons] acquired Barbuda on 9 January, 1685 and contained control over it for a century and a half, using the island as a breeding ground for slaves for their own, and other plantations. . . . In a real sense, therefore, many Antiguans are direct descendants of Barbudans.'

In the controversy over the disposal of the main collection of papers in 1980, this view of history was vigorously attacked. Dr R. C. Simmons, of Birmingham's School of History, is emphatic that 'Barbuda was not a battery farm for the rearing of slaves. This myth has been widely asserted but is not supported by evidence.' David Lowenthal and Colin Clark, in a letter to *The Observer*, supported this statement: 'The very papers just sold show conclusively that there was never a deliberate programme of slave-breeding in Barbuda, nor did the Codringtons ever contemplate this as a possibility.' In the calendar published by Robson Lowe in 1951, however, there is a letter dated 18 January 1794 from a Joseph Walrond, who later became Christopher Codrington's brother-in-law, in which Walrond makes the suggestion that Barbuda should be used as a negro nursery, and discourses on the benefits of feeding the slaves there with pilchards and pork when corn is not in supply. And Dennis Reynolds, the estate manager of Barbuda, reports on the spread of venereal disease on the island 'affecting the breeding powers of the negroes'. Codrington employees evidently strongly disliked Barbuda: more than one manager is criticized for leaving his post for long periods to enjoy the more pleasant atmosphere of Antigua.

The letters are vital for the light they shed on the move towards emancipation. Hindsight has produced a scenario for this rather like the 1945 liberation of Europe, with delighted slaves throwing off their shackles. The letters display a rather different picture.

First there is incomprehension, then gloom among the estate owners and agents. A Bristol shipper writes to Sir William in 1789: 'The pamphlets you sent me are indeed replete with Ignorance and Falsehood. I at first laughed at the attempts of the Manchester fanatics but now find it a serious business, taken up by Mr Wilberforce and others. . . . They do not require any modification of the Slave trade but a total abolition.'

Three years later there is the fear that the 'Abolishers of Slaves' will bring down the price of West Indies goods. The wind of freedom stirs up alarm and fear throughout the West Indies. In 1812 Langford Hodge is writing: 'The insurrections in Barbados will probably spread. Mr Wilberforce and his adherents have created a volcano. I believe these calamities will be to them sources of Real pleasure.' The Amelioration Act preceding outright abolition creates difficulties: 'You are now bound to give equal to 9 pints of grain a week to each negroe. . . . Each male is to have a pair of trowsers, each female one petticoat twice a year.'

Then, in a remarkable series of letters written between 1829 and 1834, R. Jarrit, the estate manager at Betty's Hope, chronicles the changing relationship between erstwhile slave and whites. It records the first of those complaints against the 'uppity nigra' which are to be a constant both in the islands and on the North American mainland. The Coloured editor of the *Weekly Register* has calumniated Jarrit's family. Jarrit horsewhips him soundly, but complains: 'The Magistracy of St John's is all a farce: the Coloured People commit excess with impunity. It is in vain to make any complaint against the Coloured People. Mulattos there are none now. They are all Coloured gentlemen and Coloured ladies. It is a misfortune here to have a white complexion.' He waxes heavily satirical over the minimum provisions that the Act lays down for emancipated slaves. 'The negroes are to have a double allowance, I am told, work only nine hours, the women to be found in Stockings, Bonnets, Shoes, Kettles, Pots etc and if living Six Miles from Church to be found a conveyance and many other things of the greatest absurdity. . . .'

But there is, too, the other side of the coin – the slaves who do not want to be 'freed' and tossed out on to an open market to fend for themselves. In 1834 John Winter the manager at Barbuda, writes: 'I read your letter to them but I don't think it made any impression on their minds, they run away with an idea that their usual comforts will still be allowed them when free, as they are now. They say they want their freedom – but the older ones say they do not, that their master had all their work when they were able and he must feed them now they are old. . . .'

The slaves of Antigua and Barbuda were freed in 1834 but it had little effect upon the colony. The only work available was on the sugar plantations and these remained firmly in the grasp of the great planters. The wealth of the Codringtons was unaffected. The endless hogsheads of sugar continued to be trundled down to the stone quays at St John's, loaded, taken across 4,000 miles of sea to Europe, there to be turned into ball gowns and banquets, Tuscan columns and Grand Tours and bibelots. During the reign of the Sir Christopher who died in 1864, and his wife Georgina, Dodington

Hall achieved its apogee of splendour, famous throughout Europe for the prodigality of its hospitality. So the dual life went on, the whispering fields of waving canes on the Caribbean islands feeding the splendours of the Shropshire mansion throughout the high noon of Victorian England and the long sunset of Edward.

But then, in World War I, there came a revolution, a quiet, utterly devastating revolution in the form of an ugly root – sugar beet. The Dutch had developed it, for it grows best on heavy, low-lying land, and a Britain besieged by hostile submarines gratefully adopted it, releasing shipping space for food that could not be produced at home. Cane sugar became a luxury – and one, moreover, that could be more cheaply produced in other tropical countries with better water supplies. The Caribbean sugar industry began its long plunge towards insolvency. The planters sold up and left, the speculators put their money elsewhere: in 1971, in a desperate attempt to shore up the island's only industry, the government acquired the remaining sugar estates. And in 1980 – on the brink of gaining independence – that government launched a blistering attack on 'the failure of the British Colonial Government to pay attention to the need for a diversified economy.' The island had been run by and for the great sugar planters, it was claimed, whose sole interest lay in the production of sugar. This creation of a single industry economy not only totally eroded the very basis of the island's economy, but severely hampered education. 'The local legislature, which was predominantly represented by the sugar plantocrats, assumed responsibility for primary education mainly to provide a large reservoir of cheap labour. Its sole aim was to keep the labour force tied to colonial sugar.' In other words, the black peoples of Barbuda and Antigua had been doubly penalized in an increasingly complex world – once by being wrenched away from their roots and once by being denied the means of access to those roots via education.

Meanwhile, 4,000 miles away in Dodington Park, Shropshire, the papers gathered dust, maturing like a fine wine, their value and significance changing unknown to their owners in response to the deep-running changes in the outside world. After the 1951 sale of letters the bulk of the collection was moved to the Public Record Office in Gloucester. There were some 8,000 items occupying thirty feet of shelving, incorporating letters and maps, deeds, sales records, all carefully catalogued by the county archivists. As Antigua moved slowly towards independence, discussions began about the future of a collection which, though legally belonging to an English family in Shropshire, contained the manes of a multi-racial society on the other side of the world. It was tentatively agreed that the collection would remain in public care in Gloucester until such time as the new nation could build a proper museum and record office in St John's. Then the current head of the family, Sir Simon Codrington, instructed the international firm of auctioneers, Sotheby's, to put the papers on the market. It was generally believed that their value lay between £30,000 and £40,000 and the Antiguan government made a private offer on this basis. It was refused: the papers would be sold to the highest bidder.

Bitterly, an Antiguan spokesman remarked: 'The Codringtons made their wealth from Antigua for 200 years. What these papers should be worth to them is 200 fat pigs – the price for which they got Barbuda. We find it difficult to understand that, having paid for their home off the backs of our ancestors, they now want us to pay again so that they can continue to live there.'

There was an element of truth in the bitter remark. Dodington Park was built by Wyatt in 1796 at a cost of £120,000: in 1980 repairs to its roof alone cost more than a quarter that sum. House and owner faced the problem that faced the majority of 'stately homes' and their owners in the second half of the twentieth century. With their traditional sources of income heavily taxed or non-existent, who was to pay for their upkeep? And how? Dodington Park entered the 'stately home trade', attracting about 150,000 visitors annually. But, 'One isn't well off, you know', Sir Simon Codrington commented. 'One is really only the caretaker for the heritage of England. I'm not a mean old stick, but I am afraid that what I consider personal family documents have got to be sold for various reasons, including keeping the stately home going.'

Suddenly, what was an arcane controversy – of interest, one might reasonably have supposed, only to a handful of specialists – became a cause célèbre in the popular as well as the quality press. In part, this was undoubtedly because the story possessed three of the four ingredients which Somerset Maugham described as being essential to any good story – sex, snobbery and mystery, religion alone being absent. Much play was made with the protagonist's status (in the words of the *New Standard*, 'much-married, ex-Etonian stately home owner Sir Simon Codrington, 57') and the supposed fact that the Codrington fortune had been made out of running a species of human stud farm. And the element of mystery was to enter when the identity of the final purchaser of the papers was kept a secret.

But, in the main, the sense of indignation expressed in the correspondence and editorial columns of most of the national papers, as well as the local West Country journals, undoubtedly rose from the sense of contrast between the owner of a stately home, even one with financial difficulties, and the extreme and abject poverty of the thousand-odd residents of Barbuda. For even in the quality press it was the story of Barbuda, the 'stud farm', which took the lead. As it happened, a small section of the tiny population wanted to break away from Antigua, a *reductio ad absurdum* of the whole independence movement that caused no little embarrassment to the new government of Antigua with its population of 77,000. In a letter to *The Times* Adrian Ray, a lecturer in geography who had taught on Barbuda, emphasized 'the cultural and material poverty of these people whose history is even more sad than most of those whose origins lie in the slave trade'. He touched on the point that was to be developed in depth both by individual writers and editorially by most of the papers, the Barbudans' natural right to the knowledge of their origins. 'It is galling that Sir Simon Codrington, whose ancestors placed people on Barbuda to be bred in much the same way as farm animals today, sees fit to make more money out of these very slaves, who made fortunes for traders and plantation owners, rather than give to their descendants the few clues to their origins which exist today.' The idea of auctioning the papers, echoing the slave auctions of the past, was distasteful to many. 'Even in the bad old days, slaves who had acquired enough money to buy their freedom were allowed to do so without having to outbid others at auction', commented Professor David Lowenthal. Colin Tennant, owner of the nearby island of Mustique, was caustic: 'The [Codrington] family of course have centuries of experience of selling their chattels at public auction.'

One of the few voices raised in defence of the Codrington proposal was that of Robson Lowe, the philatelist. He pointed out that, when the first batch of correspondence had been discovered at Dodington Park, he had been invited to calendar the material before it was dispersed. The material had, in any case, been microfilmed and copies deposited in three American universities which were particularly interested in Antigua and the slave trade. Furthermore, 'Before the publication of the volume [of calendared material] the archive was offered to the authorities in Antigua from whom no reply was received. The book was advertised in the Antiguan press, which resulted in the sale of three copies. So much for the local interest in Antigua's history.'

This seemed a particularly valid point in the context of the controversy and I raised it with Dr Claudius Thomas, High Commissioner for the East Caribbean Commission. He replied, with some vigour, that Antigua was a

British colony in 1951, 'and the reaction then may be thought of in that light. In December 1980, Antigua was on the verge of independence and the reaction should be seen in that light. In December 1980, by public collection from the people of Antigua, about £40,000 was donated in an attempt to buy the papers.' Relative to the population of Antigua, it is as though the British public had raised, by public collection, £30 million to buy back the Magna Carta.

At the auction of the papers in London in December 1980 there were only two bidders. Most potential buyers had followed Colin Tennant's suggestion and, out of sympathy for Antigua, refrained from entering the auction. The two bidders, therefore, were a representative of the Antiguan government and an agent acting for an unknown principal. The papers fetched an astonishing £106,000, more than three times the estimated maximum: ironically, it was the Antiguan representative bidding against the agent who trebled the value of the papers for the Codrington estate. After the auction, the Antiguan representative expressed bitter disappointment. 'We think the buyer has paid too much. Whatever price we had offered, I am sure he would have gone higher. It has nothing to do with the value of the papers.'

Who was the person whom the press promptly dubbed the 'Mystery Man'? His agent would say nothing more than that he was 'a man of good will towards Antigua and the West Indies' and that it was by no means unlikely that, in due course, the papers might fetch up in Antigua.

10
Whose Heritage?

'You are stealing that poor girl's face.'

American matriarch to tourist
photographers

'We are in some ways fortunate that so much was
preserved overseas.'

D. R. SIMMONS, Auckland Museum,
New Zealand on the dispersal of Maori
artifacts

There is only one train a day from Puno down to Cusco in the high Andes and, as ever, it was intolerably crowded. Even the first-class compartment was packed, while the second-class was a solid mass of humanity. The train presented a remarkable variety of casual dangers: a broken window with jagged shards, a large hole in the floor in which a child became trapped, a broken lock on one of the doors. Nevertheless, there was a constant movement of Indian women selling food, ranging from bread to huge chunks of roast pork, each wearing a brightly coloured shawl in which as often as not a child was wrapped up along with vegetables, each carrying a bundle of wares and achieving miracles of balance clambering in and out of doors – and windows – as the train racketed along.

At each wayside halt, the train was surrounded by more saleswomen and the tourists poured out from their first-class compartment, intent on recording the 'quaint, primitive scene' on film. At one of these halts a pretty young girl, wearing a brilliant traditional skirt and top hat, and with a child at her breast and offering little cakes with her free hand, was pounced upon by a German with an enormous camera. Others immediately joined him and for three or four minutes the bewildered girl was surrounded by glittering electronic equipment thrust into her face. Satisfied, the photographers withdrew. Timidly, she came forward to offer her wares, but the tourists waved her irritably aside, even though their monopoly of her had cost her the few precious minutes of the halt. At that an American matriarch, somebody's formidable grandmother in her late sixties, who had been watching the scene, thrust her head out of the window and cried, 'You are stealing that poor girl's face. You've taken up her time. Give her something.'

It is a far cry from Lord Elgin's marbles to a Peruvian Indian girl, from the removal of several hundred tons of stone to the chemical recording of a human image. But as the tide of mass tourism rises ever higher, penetrating into ever more remote areas, and as once primitive societies explode into technology, bringing twentieth-century man in contact with, perhaps, Stone Age man, so the concept of *elginisme* has undergone a subtle but very real change, with ancient customs prostituted for entertainment. The rain dance of the Navajos; the *haka* of the Maori; the *aloha* of Hawaii; the flamencos of Andalusia – all have undergone the transformation in little over a generation. In February 1981 the UNESCO organization known as the World Intellectual Property Organization set up a working group to study the possibilities of extending protection to certain aspects of folklore. WIPO is the body which administers such legal affairs as international protection of copyright, trade marks, patents and the like. Would it be possible to extend this protection into the intangible field of folk customs? WIPO thought it would and put forward the recommendation that there should be, in principle, protection 'against illicit exploitation and other prejudicial actions in expressions of folklore including verbal expressions, such as folk tales: musical expressions such as folk songs: expressions by action such as folk dances'. On the face of it, such protection seems unlikely. 'It's preposterous', a morris dancer exploded. 'Is a WIPO inspector going to stand in the High Street, taking notes, fining me every time I inadvertently use somebody else's steps?'

It is impossible not to feel sympathy with the indignant morris dancer, but some such sentiments were probably expressed when the concept of literary or musical copyright was first advanced. And as the twentieth century's hunger for the 'real', the 'traditional', the 'antique' grows ever more ravenous, so some such protection will become essential. And the first beneficiaries in this field might well be the 'Red Indians' of North America.

Until the twentieth century, the fate of aboriginals in countries taken over by Caucasians was extermination or subjection. Currently, the chief characteristic of aboriginals forced to share their ancient home with dominant whites is a dawning self-awareness, a determination to preserve and enhance identity and, as an inescapable corollary, an equally strong determination to obtain the return of those treasures which their self-imposed neighbours have acquired.

The Amerindian, who was first dispossessed and then traduced, is becoming an expert in this. At least three generations of whites have grown up regarding the red man as either monster or clown, his sole contribution to the common culture to be wiped out in Western films. But the same impulse which led to the break-up of the European empires and the emergence of sovereign states from among the once subject peoples led to the assertion of a separate identity among North American Indians. Some of the tribes had degenerated beyond hope of re-constitution but some, like the Zunis of Arizona, had somehow maintained a sense of nationhood against all odds. And, in a battle to obtain a vital religious object, the Zunis posed a deep and embarrassing question: what happens when a religious symbol is turned into a museum exhibit?

The Zunis first came into the ken of the white man through the white man's apparently insatiable lust for gold. In the late sixteenth century there came, to the Spanish viceroy of Mexico, tales of immense treasure somewhere in the north where lay that vast gash in the earth known as the Grand Canyon. The 'Seven Cities of Cibola' became part of the mythology of the Conquistadores, seven great cities each ruled by a king, where gold was as common as iron, where turquoises and silver were used as building materials, seven fabulous cities beyond the Arizona desert. The viceroy commissioned a remarkable priest, Fray Marcos, to find this eldorado. Fray Marcos obediently travelled northward, returning with stories of a brilliant civilization rich indeed in gold and silver and turquoises, so rich as to rival even famed Peru.

It would seem that Fray Marcos was spiritually related to Baron Munchausen. Subsequent opinion is that he never went further north than the Gula River but based his reports on those of an equally fanciful traveller. But the viceroy was impressed and a strong expedition was sent northward to take over this civilization in the name of the king of Spain. They found no cities of gold, no avalanches of turquoises but, instead, a highly developed and remarkably pugnacious people living in substantial, but certainly not rich, towns. Battered, beaten, they returned to Mexico with the news that Fray Marcos was, at best, a romancer.

In due course the white man did indeed take over the land and, in due course, after the savagery of the Spaniards came the far more destructive savagery of the Anglo-Saxons. In Africa and Asia there had been a certain dignity in the conflict between invader and invaded. In West Africa Sir Garnet Wolseley had regarded himself as a soldier fighting soldiers: in West America the newcomers regarded themselves as exterminators of vermin. A Californian newspaper, published in the late nineteenth century, described the Indians of west and south as 'a set of miserable, dirty, lousy, blanketed, thieving, lying, sneaking, murdering, graceless, faithless, gut-eating skunks as the Lord ever permitted to infest the earth and whose immediate and final extermination all men should pray for'. It was common practice in California to get up hunting parties to exterminate entire groups.

But gradually there began a counter-movement, originating largely among scholars, who slowly realized that under their very feet was a mystery as profound, a study as fascinating as any to be found in the most exotic parts of the world: who were these red-skinned people with whom they were sharing a continent? Among them was a flamboyant young man, Frank Cushing, an ethnological assistant who was just twenty-two years old when he made his home among the Zuni. Cushing could perhaps be described as a Belzoni-with-a-conscience. He had the same inexhaustible energy, the same boundless curiosity – and the same gift with words and paintbrush. Although more than once threatened with death, he succeeded in witnessing some of the most secret rites among the Zuni, passing on that information to a wider world through two books, one an academic report, the other a headlong, effervescent story of adventure and derring-do, illustrated with charming watercolours. *My Adventures among the Zuni* brought home to thousands of Americans that the Amerindian was not a spoiled or undeveloped Caucasian but a human being on a parallel course.

In the early years of this century, the despised 'Red Indian' came into his own. Or, to be exact, his artifacts did: many a poor family scratching a living found that treasure hunting for Indian artifacts was a very profitable sideline. Just as in Africa, the curio-hunter followed hard on the heels of the academic and, as the trade became profitable, was transformed into the respectability of the antique dealer. The museums began to fill up.

In October 1978 an auction sale under way in New York was abruptly halted by Federal officials. The object they seized was by no means impressive: it has, indeed, been described as looking like a weatherworn fence post. But it was, according to the Native American Rights Fund, a religious object – that is 'an object which was created for a specific ritual of spiritual progress', and it was described in the auction catalogue as a Zuni war god.

The strange Zuni war gods, deliberately abandoned and depicted here in Frank Cushing's Zuni Folk Tales, *1901.*

According to Cushing, the war gods of Zuni played an unusual role, both in the way in which they were treated and in their function. They would appear to act as a species of supernatural lightning conductor, attracting and dissipating forces of evil. Unlike most religious objects, which are carefully protected and preserved, the function of the Zuni war god was to fall to pieces. Each year they are carved and placed in shrines in remote areas and there allowed to rot.

Such was the religious belief in the nineteenth century. But to the surprise and embarrassment of a large number of museum officials and fine art auctioneers, a Stone Age faith seems to be flourishing healthily in twentieth-century America, a fact tacitly recognized by the Native American Rights Fund. 'For many tribes, the free exercise of their religion has been further complicated by the fact that many religious artifacts have been lost to museums, private collectors or foreign countries. Native religious leaders complain that they are unable to perform religious ceremonies without the artifacts.'

The Zuni war gods, placed in unsupervised shrines far from habitations, were particularly vulnerable to the collecting mania. Their appearance, too, was such that any uninformed person would quite innocently assume them to be discarded objects. These two factors led the tribal leaders to mount their campaign for the protection of the images and, launched by one of the few Indian tribes to maintain a strong sense of identity, that campaign was successful. Federal authorities held the impounded carving until an agreement was reached between the 'owner' – a collector who had acquired it in good faith – and the tribe.

The Zunis then turned their attention to the state museum at Denver which held one of the carvings. The museum's director put forward an ingenious argument based on the fact that the war gods belonged to the tribe and not to an individual. Denver Art Museum, too, belonged to the 'tribe' – the state as a whole – of whom the Zunis formed a part. The Zunis declined to accept the sophisticated reasoning and again won their point. With a lively awareness of the effect of establishing a precedent in a museum which held some 15,000 Amerindian objects, the museum's director refused to publish details of the negotiations between the museum and the tribe. The carving was quietly removed from public display and a press announcement issued recognizing, for what must be the first occasion in museum history, the distinction between art object and religious symbol. 'The board of trustees has been advised by qualified anthropologists and its own staff that in the Zuni religion, as stated by the Zuni leaders, it is true that the war god is a deity and a present, animated object of worship rather than a symbol or art object.' Uneasily one wonders what might be the effect upon the art collections of the world if a Christian were to obtain a similar ruling regarding the prevalence of Christian icons, the Cross in particular, on public but secular display.

As more and more once subject peoples achieve independence and look for an identity upon the international stage, so the controversies continue and increase. In the spring of 1982 the British Museum came under attack from three different countries. Sri Lanka, which has rivalled Nigeria in agitating for return of national treasures, presented an impressive 'shopping list' of 35 items whose return was demanded in order to build up a museum of cultural heritage in Colombo. Greece brought up the hoary issue of the Elgin Marbles. The leader of the attack on this occasion was the glamorous figure of Melina Mercouri, ex-actress and now Minister of Culture – finding support, too, in the British House of Lords in the person of the former Labour Arts Minister, Lord Jenkins: 'Do not adopt an indefensible policy of "what we have, we hold"', he adjured a silent British Museum. Egypt joined in with a demand for the return of an 18-inch-long piece of battered stone, part of the beard of the Sphinx, which a Genoese sea-captain – Giovanni Caviglia – had presented in 1817 'as a testimony to his attachment to the British Nation'.

On the other side of the world the divided nations of South America remembered their common heritage and formed the Andean Cultural

Patrimony. Transcending political differences and emphasizing their common Andean patrimony, the plan was designed as much to educate the differing Latin-American peoples to recognize and so protect their heritage, as to fight off the greedy cultural entrepreneurs from the 'developed' world. The project was launched in 1977 under the auspices of UNESCO. In 1979 UNESCO itself launched what must be the most clumsily named committee in the history of bureaucracy – 'The Inter-governmental Committee for the promoting of the Return of Cultural Property or its restitution in case of Illicit Appropriation'. The verbosity of the title is testimony to its creators' anxiety to offend nobody. The United Kingdom politely declined to become a member, giving as a reason 'the risk that full membership would possibly be an embarrassment under certain circumstances'.

The Committee's meetings continued ponderously but seem to have little direct effect, except occasionally pouring more oil on troubled flames. Nevertheless, the international atmosphere is undoubtedly changing. Not all ex-colonial powers grimly hang on to what they have at all costs. Outstanding among positive approaches is the five-year plan of co-operation established between the Netherlands government and its one-time colony of Indonesia. The Dutch have already returned archives going back to the sixteenth century to the current Indonesian government (or, rather, 'donated', for their legal right to this material is as clear-cut as the legal right of the Codringtons to the Antiguan papers). The two countries set up a joint committee whose recommendations on 'cultural co-operation' are a model of their kind. They recognized that Indonesian cultural objects had been scattered throughout the civilized world and drew up plans to make a master inventory. They then tackled the thorny question of the definition of objects of 'historical-emotional value'. The first stage was to be the transference 'of state-owned objects which are directly linked with persons of major historical and cultural importance or with crucial historical events in Indonesia. The transfer should be executed as early as possible.' And regarding objects in private hands, the Dutch government promised to do all that it could to establish the necessary contacts.

The sane and civilized attitude of the Dutch authorities is matched by the attitude of a once-subject people on the other side of the globe, the Maori of New Zealand. Between March and October 1978 Dr D. R. Simmons, Assistant Director of the Auckland Institute, took part in a remarkable odyssey, visiting 69 museums in 12 countries, including Russia, in search of Maori antiques. These are the objects which have been disappearing from

New Zealand ever since Captain Cook began bargain hunting and now have achieved additional significance in yet another ex-colonial society becoming aware of its non-European heritage. The sequence of contact between Europeans and Maoris paralleled in many ways the contact between Europeans and Amerindians – initial mutual respect, followed by conflict which produced contempt on the part of the white victor and a sullen resentment on the part of the brown loser. But in New Zealand Europeans seem to have had a great sense of responsibility, and Maoris a greater degree of resilience than their counterparts in the New World. Admittedly, after the Maori wars, 'Parliament did much that seemed better designed to exterminate the Maori than to revive him', W. H. Oliver noted in his history of New Zealand. 'But on the credit side of the balance may be placed an act of 1867 placing four elected Maori representatives in the House.' Revival of Maori self-respect, re-assessment of Maori culture came from within, stimulated by members – some of mixed blood – of the group known as the Young Maori Party, formed in the late nineteenth century.

But whatever may have been the European opinion of Maori morality and intelligence, from the beginning Europeans were fascinated by Maori artifacts. On each of Captain Cook's three voyages between 1769 and 1777 he, or officers of his ships, collected material either to be sold or presented to museums on return to England. An example of the dispersals which followed is the sale held by a dealer called Humphries in 1782. Maori objects from this one sale went to museums in Gottingen, Vienna, Florence, Berlin – and Exeter. Weber, the Swiss artist who accompanied Cook, presented a rich collection to his native city of Berne. After Cook, other European explorers took their toll: the Frenchmen Duperry in 1824 and D'Urville in 1826 gave their collections to the Naval Hospital at Rochefort, while the Russian explorer Bellinghausen donated his to St Petersburg. The collecting mania of the ordinary sailor also contributed to dispersal. In Berlin David Simmons found the earliest collected house carving from New Zealand. 'It had been cut into many pieces to fit into a sailor's kitbag.'

The object of Dr Simmons's eight-month tour of European museums was to record as many collections as possible and thus fill in the gaps that existed in New Zealand regarding the country's own past. And in addition to this academic objective was the provision of a cultural stimulus for New Zealand's contemporary artists by providing for them models taken from long-vanished tribal styles.

David Simmons tracked down and recorded some 5,000 Maori artifacts. He made some surprising discoveries. At the Hunterian Museum in

Glasgow, material was produced from a cupboard which, although catalogued, had never been placed on exhibition since Cook gave it to his friend William Hunter. It included eight cloaks decorated with dogskin. 'The dog hair which is usually grey or absent in most known cloaks was in these cloaks fresh and new, rich reddy brown and white.' Most of the Maori artifacts had been well looked after – but Dr Simmons did find two museums in France where the precious artifacts had been bundled on one side on the outbreak of World War II and ignored ever since. In Florence, he made a remarkable discovery: a collection of rare canoe carvings. They were obtained by an Italian artist called Biondi in 1860 – and 1860 marked the point when the prestige symbol of a chief changed from being a well-carved canoe to a well-carved house. 'The canoes were no longer of any social use and were sold to whoever would pay for them. If New Zealand museums had been active at that time they could have collected many canoe carvings. We are in some ways fortunate that so much was preserved overseas.'

I asked David Simmons about the Maori reaction to the vexed question of restitution or return. These artifacts had certainly not been looted in the conventional sense, but equally certainly they represented as vital a link in the chain of New Zealand history as the Parthenon sculptures do in Greek history, or the Benin bronzes in Nigerian. 'I did raise the question of repatriation with the New Zealand Maori Council before I left and their reply was: while they would very much like to see their treasures back in New Zealand, they also felt it was important that other people should know about the Maori.' The sane, essentially civilized reply gives a new perspective to an old problem. Or, rather, restores an older, more attractive perspective than the current legalistic squabble about who owns what of mankind's heritage.

Bibliography

General

Judith Grant, *A Pillage of Art*, 1966, traces the looting of Greek statuary from Sulla (81 BC) to James Woodhouse (1865); Karl Meyer, *The Plundered Past*, 1974, homes in on the illegal, and quasi-legal, acquisition of art objects in the contemporary art world; Hugh Trevor-Roper, *The Plunder of the Arts in the 17th Century*, 1970, argues that Hitler and Napoleon were failed looters and that 'to find an effective dislocation of art on a comparable scale' we must go back to the Thirty Years' War; Francis Henry Taylor, *The Taste of Angels*, 1948, surveys the collecting mania from Imperial Rome to World War II.

Chapter I *Classical Landscape without Figures*

William St Clair's *Lord Elgin and the Marbles*, 1967, gives the general background. Adolf Michaelis, *Ancient Marbles in England*, 1882, fairly summarizes official memoranda. The *Classical Journal*, September 1811, carries a 'Notice of Memorandum on the Subject of Earl of Elgin's Pursuits in Greece' and B.R. Haydon contributes a 'Judgement of Connoisseurs upon Works of Art compared with that of Professional Men in reference more particularly to the Elgin Marbles' to *The Examiner*, 1816. The Greek government published a brief summary of the affair in their information series *Greece*, No 56, 28 January 1977. Cockerell's book was edited by his son Samuel Pepys Cockerell and published under the title of *Travels in Southern Europe and the Levant – the Journal of C.R. Cockerell*, 1908.

Chapter II *The Plundering of Egypt*

Giovanni Belzoni's *Narrative of the Operations and Recent discoveries within the Pyramids, Temples, Tombs and Excavations in Egypt*, 1820, is his own best monument. But so bizarre a character has attracted a number of writers. Stanley Mayes's *The Great Belzoni*, 1961, is not only a full biography but also carries an appendix of Belzoni's discoveries now in the British Museum. Brian Fagan's *The Rape of the Nile*, 1977, distils from the enormous mass of Egyptiana a highly readable and damning indictment of the depredations of 'tomb robbers, tourists and archaeologists' in Egypt. Arnold Brackman's *Search for the Gold of Tutankhamun*, 1978, is a popular but authoritative account of the world-wide interest created by the discovery of the tomb. Thomas Hoving's *Tutankhamun: the Untold Story*, 1979, is an account of the illicit activities of the tomb's discoverers. Gert von Paczensky's detective work appeared as an article 'Teilt Nofrotete!' in *Die Zeit* 24 April 1978. *Who was Who in Egyptology*, 1972, by Warren Dawson and Eric P. Uphill is an invaluable account of the explorers and archaeologists of Egypt. Among earlier accounts of travels and discoveries in Egypt are: Wallis Budge, *By Nile and Tigris*, 1920: John Burckhardt, *Travels in Nubia*, 1819, and the seminal *Travels in Upper and Lower Egypt*, by Baron Vivant Denon, 1807.

Chapter III *The Gold of Ashanti*

A comprehensive account of the Ashanti Wars is Alan Lloyd's *The Drums of Kumasi*, 1964.

Among those who took part in the campaign and left accounts are: H. Brackenbury, *The Ashantee War*, 1874; C.H. Armitage, *The Ashanti Campaign of 1900*, 1901 (contains an account of the search for the Golden Stool); H. M. Stanley, *Coomassie and Magdala*, 1874: Sir Garnet Wolseley, *The Story of a Soldier's Life*, 1903. On the centenary of Wolseley's campaign the Ghanaian government published a pamphlet, *The Call for the Return of the Asante Regalia*, 1974. M. D. McLeod's *The Asante*, 1981, was published as an introduction to the Museum of Mankind's exhibition. William Fagg's article 'Ashanti Gold' appeared in *The Connoisseur*, January 1974, and he kindly loaned the text of an unpublished lecture 'Africa and the Temple of the Muses'.

Chapter IV *The Stone of Scone*

Holinshed's *Historie of Scotland* gives an account of its supposed Greek origins, while Cyril Davenport's *The English Regalia*, 1897, provides an authoritative survey of its legendary history. Most of the material for this chapter, however, was derived from newspaper stories (of which Douglas Eadie's 'Hamilton's Heist' in *The Guardian* provided an excellent digest) and personal contacts.

Chapter V *The Crown of St Stephen*

For the medieval history of the crown see Ludwig Pastor, *The History of the Popes from the Close of the Middle Ages*, Vol 1, 1900, and Ferdinand Gregorovius, *History of the City of Rome in the Middle Ages*, Vol III, 1903. Much of the material was supplied by the Hungarian Embassy in London, but based upon verbatim transcripts of US Government cables, UPI reports and cuttings from US newspapers. Anthony Mockler's article 'Saint Stephen's Crown' in the *Spectator*, 14 January 1978, and a report by Nicolas Adam, 'Who holds the Crown?', in the *Observer* Magazine, 5 November 1972, provide English viewpoints.

Chapter VI *Napoleon Bonaparte*

Dorothy Quynn's disquisition 'The Art Confiscations of the Napoleonic Wars' in the *American Historical Review*, Vol I, No 3, 1945, is a densely worked scholarly article with a wealth of source indications. Francis Taylor's *Taste of Angels*, 1948, carries a lengthy transcript of Robertson's journal. W. Buchanan, *Memoirs of Painting*, 1824, describes a number of collections built up from the loot. The Historical Manuscripts Commission's *Report on the Manuscripts of Earl Bathurst, preserved at Cirencester Park*, 1923, includes Hamilton's correspondence. For Lord Liverpool's letters see Charles D. Yonge, *The Life and Administration of Robert Banks, Second Earl of Liverpool*, 1868. For the French viewpoint see Léon de Lanzac de Laborie, *Paris sous Napoleon*, VIII: *Spectacles et musées*, 1913; Charles Saunier, *Les conquêtes artistiques de la Révolution et de l'empire*, 1902 (which contains, among much else, Quatremere de Quincy's *Lettres au général Miranda . . .*, 1796); Eugene Muntz, 'Les annexions d'art ou de bibliothèques et leur rôle dans les relations internationales', in *Revue d'histoire diplomatique*, Vol IX, 1896. Guido Perocco's *The Horses of San Marco* (trans. by John and Valerie Wilton-Ely), 1979, is an exhaustive technical and historical study made when the Horses were taken down for restoration. John Julius Norwich's *Venice: the Greatness and the Fall*, 1981, gives a vivid account of the last days of the Republic. Mario dell' Arco's *Pasquino e le Pasquinate*, 1957, contains a rich selection of the epigrams of Rome's 'talking statue'.

Chapter VII *Adolf Hitler*

For Hitler's personal motivation see Albert Speer, *Spandau: the Secret Diaries* (trans. by Richard and Clara Winston), 1976, as well as his *Inside the Third Reich* (trans. by the same), 1971, and Joachim Fest's *Hitler*, 1974. Charles de Jaeger's *The Linz File*, 1981, describes Linz from his personal knowledge; James P. O'Donnell's *The Berlin Bunker*, 1981, is a brilliant re-creation of the last days, including valuable interviews. Goering's complex character is well analysed in *Hermann Goering* by Roger Manvell and Heinrich Fraenkel, 1962, while *Goering* by Willi Frischauer, 1951, is an effective journalist's-eye view. Both books deal with Goering's compulsive acquisition of art.

Among the few books which describe the actual process of looting are: *The Jackdaw of Linz* by David Roxan and Ken Wanstall, 1964, an invaluable survey based on ALIU *Consolidated Interrogation Report* No 4; de Jaeger's *The Linz File*; Jean Cassou, *Le pillage par les Allemands des oeuvres d'art appartenant a des Juifs en France*, 1947; Thomas Carr Howe's *Salt Mines and Castles*, 1946, and George Mihan's *Looted Treasure: Germany's Raid on Art* (no date, but probably 1942 – the pseudonymous author was an Eastern European refugee in England). The Art Looting Investigation Unit's Reports have now been declassified. An index has been prepared by the National Archives (US) Diplomatic Records Branch under the title of *Records of the American Commission for Protection and Salvage of Artistic and Historic Monuments*. An official British account is Lt-Col Sir Leonard Wooley's *A Record of the Work done by the Military Authorities for the Protection of the Treasures of Art and History in War Areas*, 1947.

The account of the 'treasure hunt' has been pieced together from personal investigation and from newspaper reports spread over the past 30 years. These latter include: Major Edward Adams, 'Looted Art Treasures go back to France' in *The Quartermaster*, September/October 1946; John Hughes, '1,800 Tons of Loot' in *The Soldier*, Vol 4, No 3, 1948; 'Nazi Loot Pops up in Pasadena' in *Life*, 25 January 1963; Conrad Allen, 'In Search of Italy's Lost Art Treasures', in *Sunday Telegraph*, May 1960; Colin Simpson and *Insight* team, 'Goering's Venus Emerges from Major Mariette's Treasure Trove', in *Sunday Times*, 1973; *Time* Magazine, 'A Quiet Man who Collected Art', 29 November 1976, and 'Nabbing the Nazi Art Collector', 20 December 1976.

CHAPTER VIII *City of Blood*

H. Ling Roth's *Great Benin: its Customs, Art and Horrors*, 1903, provides an excellent point of departure for the study of the city. Commander R. H. Bacon's *Benin, City of Blood*, 1897, is a bluff, no-nonsense eyewitness account by a member of the Punitive Expedition. Alan F. C. Ryder's *Benin and the Europeans*, 1969, is a scholarly history of the Benin empire seen through European eyes. Sir Richard Burton's contribution to the 1865 edition of *Fraser's Magazine*, 'My Wanderings in West Africa, Pt II: The Renowned City of Benin', set the tone for many subsequent accounts. *Black Mother: Africa and the Atlantic Slave Trade*, 1980, by Basil Davidson puts Benin in the larger context. For the works of art see Philip Dark, *An Introduction to Benin Art and Technology*, 1973. The *Catalogue of Works of Art from Benin, the property of a European private collector* put out by the auctioneers Sotheby Park Bernet Ltd (16 June 1980) not only contains excellent descriptions and photographs but also prices realized. Ugbomah's film *The Mask* was reviewed in *West Africa*, 11 August 1980, under the title '*The Mask* is a very rough film'; *The Guardian* of 8 February 1977 carries an account of Festac by Antonio de Figueiredo, 'America courts black Africa'; Alma Robison's attack on European acquisitiveness, 'Art objects in foreign hands', is in *Africa*, July 1976.

CHAPTER IX *The Corporate Memory*

The Codrington Correspondence, 1951, by Robson Lowe is an indispensable calendar of the papers sold in 1951. *The West Indies*

Enslaved and Free, 1883, by W. Moister is a sympathetic but observant account of the conditions of slaves by an English missionary in the Caribbean. In December 1980 the Government of Antigua published a number of papers of which 'British Sugar Colonialism' condemned British overseas politics. Basil Davidson's *Black Mother* is again very relevant to this chapter. The rest of the story was built up from personal investigation and newspaper cuttings, among the latter being *The Times*, 'An Auction of Antiguan Papers' (editorial) and readers' letters, 13 December 1980, and Peter Deeley 'New Riches from a Slave-owning Past', *The Observer*, 14 December 1980.

CHAPTER X *Whose Heritage?*

The Golden Hordes, 1975, by Louis Turner and John Ash presents a scarifying picture of the impact of mass tourism on unsophisticated peoples. Frank H. Cushing's *My Adventures in Zuni* has recently (1970) been reprinted. For an account of the war god controversy see Anne Sutton Canfield's article 'Ahayu:da – Art or Icon' in *Native Arts West*, July 1980. The Proyecto Regional de Patrimonio Cultural Andino has published a number of studies of which the *Inventario y Catalogacion* and *Salvemos los nuestro* are particularly relevant. Among memoranda of Dutch-Indonesian co-operation the Netherlands government has issued: *Joint Recommendations by the Dutch and Indonesian Team of Experts . . .*, 1975, *Report of the Work Programme . . .*, 1977, and *Report of the Discussion on a Draft of a Five-year Plan . . .*, 1978. The New Zealand section was based on reports kindly supplied by Dr Simmons, while for background information see W. H. Oliver, *The Story of New Zealand*, 1960.

List of Illustrations

Index